COMMUNICATION, LANGUAGE, AND MEANING

Psychological Perspectives

EDITED BY

George A. Miller

Basic Books, Inc., PUBLISHERS

NEW YORK

Acknowledgments: A version of the chapter by Peter Marler was published in *American Scientist* in 1970; certain passages in the chapter by Roger Brown are also included in *A First Language: The Early Stages* (Cambridge, Mass.: Harvard University Press, 1973). We are grateful to these publishers for permission to reprint this material.

THE AUTHORS

STUART A. ALTMANN is Professor of Biology and Anatomy at the University of Chicago, where he studies animal behavior with a special interest in primate communication.

ROBERT FREED BALES is Professor of Social Psychology at Harvard, where he received his Ph.D. in sociology in 1945. He is well known for his studies of interactions between members of small task-oriented groups.

URSULA BELLUGI is a researcher in psycholinguistics at the Salk Institute for Biological Studies.

THOMAS G. BEVER is Professor of Psychology and Linguistics at Columbia. He received his Ph.D. in linguistics from the Massachusetts Institute of Technology. His research investigates the psychological foundations of linguistic communication, with special interest in child language.

ROGER BROWN is Professor of Social Psychology at Harvard. He received his Ph.D. from the University of Michigan in 1952. He has written broadly in social psychology, but with a central interest in language and linguistic development.

JEANNE CHALL is Professor of Education at Harvard's Graduate School of Education. She received her Ph.D. from Ohio State University in 1952. Her reviews of research on learning to read have been widely influential.

EDWARD E. DAVID, JR. served as Science Advisor to President Nixon from 1970 to 1973. He received his Sc.D. from the Massachusetts Institute of Technology in 1950 in electrical engineering, and worked on acoustic aspects of speech and hearing at the Bell Telephone Laboratories.

JOSHUA A. FISHMAN is Distinguished University Research Professor in the Social Sciences at Yeshiva University. He received his Ph.D. from Columbia in 1953. He is the author of numerous articles and books on the sociological aspects of language.

NORMAN GESCHWIND is the James Jackson Professor of Neurology at the Harvard Medical School, where he received his M.D. in 1951. His research explores the anatomical bases

v

of the higher functions of the nervous system in animals and man.

JANELLEN HUTTENLOCHER is Professor at Columbia Teachers College, where she studies cognitive and developmental psychology. She received her Ph.D. from Harvard in 1960.

JAMES J. JENKINS is Professor of Psychology and Director of the Center for Research in Human Learning at the University of Minnesota, where he received his Ph.D. in 1950.

JERROLD J. KATZ is Professor in the Philosophy Department at the Massachusetts Institute of Technology. He received his Ph.D. in philosophy at Princeton. He is best known for his efforts to base the theory of semantics on foundations provided by modern linguistic theories of transformational grammar.

SAMUEL JAY KEYSER is Chairman of the Department of Linguistics at the University of Massachusetts and editor of the journal *Linguistic Inquiry*.

EDWARD S. KLIMA is Professor of Linguistics at the University of California, San Diego.

PAUL A. KOLERS is Professor of Psychology at the University of Toronto. He received his Ph.D. in 1957 from New York University. His interests in the cognitive processes range from vision to bilingualism.

ERIC H. LENNEBERG is Professor of Psychology and Neurobiology at Cornell. He received his Ph.D. from Harvard in 1956. His research combines psychological, biological, and medical approaches to the study of speech and language.

ALVIN M. LIBERMAN is Professor of Psychology at the University of Connecticut, a member of the research staff of the Haskins Laboratory, and an Adjunct Professor of Linguistics at Yale, where he received his Ph.D. in 1942.

J. C. R. LICKLIDER is Professor at the Massachusetts Institute of Technology. He received his Ph.D. in psychology from the University of Rochester in 1942. His research interests center on the problems of interaction and communication between men and computers.

WILLIAM J. McGUIRE is Professor of Psychology and Chairman of the Department of Psychology at Yale, where he received his Ph.D. in 1954. His major research interests are selective perception, attitude change, and cognitive structure.

BRENDAN MAHER is Professor of Psychology at Harvard. He received his Ph.D. in 1954 from Ohio State University. His experimental studies of psychopathology are well known.

PETER MARLER is Professor at The Rockefeller University. He holds Ph.D. degrees in botany from the University of London and in animal behavior from Cambridge University. His research ranges broadly over the subject of mechanisms underlying animal behavior.

GEORGE A. MILLER is Professor at The Rockefeller University. He received his Ph.D. from Harvard in 1946, and is the author of numerous papers and books on the psychology of language and communication.

PAUL M. POSTAL is a member of the staff of IBM's Thomas J. Watson Research Center. He is well known in linguistics for his contributions to the theory of transformational grammar.

HERBERT RUBENSTEIN is Professor of Linguistics and Psychology at Lehigh University. He received his Ph.D. from Columbia in 1949. His current research interest is the structure and functioning of the internal lexicon.

WILBUR SCHRAMM is Janet M. Peck Professor of International Communication and Director of the Institute for Communication Research at Stanford. He received his Ph.D. from the University of Iowa in 1932.

PREFACE

Popular attitudes toward communication and language run the gamut from extravagantly positive—"It is language that makes us human"—to suspiciously negative—"Language falsifies experience." We praise it one day for making possible human understanding and damn it the next for our even more human misunderstandings. We dislike signs that clutter our landscape, but complain bitterly when some directional sign is not provided. We insist on freedom of speech and object when the wrong people exploit it. We know that full information is indispensable for a free economy, but mistrust everything an advertiser says. We believe in universal literacy, but find reading a bore. So the contradictory catalogue runs.

Like it or not, however, there is no escaping it. Language in spoken or written form fills our days and minds. We rely on it for a thousand purposes, from Absolution to Zoography. Even in the simplest human societies, linguistic competence is the price of admission. In our own modern society, no hermit, no fugitive, can escape the range of our communication technology. From writing to printing to telegraphy to radio to television the pace of that technology has steadily accelerated.

Wise men knew their importance long ago, but only in the twentieth century have we begun to subject communication and language to the kind of scholarly and scientific analysis their importance merits. Today the study of communication and language flourishes as never before. Technological innovations and the emergence of vast new communication industries provided the economic and social background for this development, and almost every field of intellectual endeavor has, directly or indirectly, contributed to it. Psychologists, linguists, philosophers, engineers, physicians, teachers, acousticians, anthropologists, sociologists, mathematicians—the list of disciplines that have brought their concepts and methods to bear on communication and language is too long to record.

Because communication and language are so ubiquitous and have been studied from so many points of view for so many di-

ix

verse purposes, no one person could be competent to survey any substantial part of this work and to report on it in authoritative terms. The they-don't-speak-our-language syndrome becomes acute for anyone who would talk about language in ways that might transcend the boundaries of his own professional training. God created in Babel the first proliferation of languages; now man has compounded the problem by his own invention of languages for talking about languages. This metababel has caused its own communication problems for students of communication.

In view of the obvious importance of this subject for every aspect of our personal and social lives, this situation is particularly unfortunate for interested laymen or beginning students who have sensed that something exciting is going on here and who would like to have a simple, trustworthy introduction—a guide to orient them in their own explorations of this important area. Some authors have tried to provide such introductions, but many experts would have to collaborate to achieve a well-balanced survey. Unfortunately, it is seldom easy to persuade many experts to take time from their own technical studies to write in simple terms for the larger audience.

The existence of the present book, however, is proof that on certain rare occasions such a group can be assembled for collaborative exposition. The present opportunity arose when the Voice of America asked me to design and edit a Forum Lecture Series on "Psychology and Communication." With this excuse, and with the active support of Max Grossman at VOA, I was able to persuade the group of authors whose chapters appear here to prepare and record thirty-minute talks on their specialities for broadcast outside the continental limits of the United States.

On reading over these lectures after the original job was done, it became obvious that something worthy of further attention had been achieved. So, with the permission of the contributors—only one declined to have his talk included—their manuscripts were edited to remove any radio "vocalisms" and impose a little more uniformity in style, suggestions for further reading were appended, and the collection was submitted for publication as a book. The result you now have in hand.

I must take this opportunity to express my deep gratitude to the authors, not only for their willingness to prepare the original lectures—no small task, for the more you know about a subject the harder it is to talk simply and plainly about it—but also for their patience and good humor through my slow and sometimes presumptuous efforts to edit their work. I can only hope that the results will please them, and that they will share with me the opinion that our joint efforts have produced an intelligible book for the general reader on one of the most active and exciting fields of scholarship in America today.

GEORGE A. MILLER

Princeton, New Jersey
January 1973

CONTENTS

COMMUNICATION, LANGUAGE, AND MEANING

1 PSYCHOLOGY AND COMMUNICATION

George A. Miller

There is an old and not very funny story about stepping on a dog's tail. If the dog barks, you can call it an accident, but if you step on his tail in New York and he barks in London, you have to call it communication.

Certainly there are many different kinds of communication and, for all I know, stepping on a dog's tail may be one of them, although I hope not. The point of the story, if it has any point at all, is that "communication" is a very abstract word. It can be accomplished by an endless variety of means. If we try to say in the most general terms what all the different kinds of communication have in common, it comes down to something like this: *Communication occurs when events in one place or at one time are closely related to events in another place or at another time.* For example, the vocal sounds made when one speaks into a radio microphone are closely related to the vocal sounds produced wherever and whenever an audience happens to hear them. Any physical process that has this capacity to span space and time can be used as a communication system. Human speech, which provides a way for events in the nervous system of the speaker to affect events in the nervous system of another, is one kind of communication, but it is only one of many different ways the abstract concept of communication can be realized in a practical form.

It is in this very abstract sense that we can talk about communication between machines, or the communication of diseases, or the hereditary communication of traits from parents to their offspring. However, this discussion is about the kinds of communication that go on between animals in general, and between human beings in particular.

The word "psychology" also covers a great variety of things, but most psychologists would accept a rather abstract definition along the following lines: *Psychology is the science that attempts to describe, predict, and control mental and behavioral events.*

This definition hides a certain amount of disagreement among those who call themselves psychologists. Some would argue that they are interested only in *behavior,* and others would reply that you cannot ignore *mental events.* And some psychologists would say that they only want to *describe* what people do, whereas others believe their major responsibility is to *predict* what people are going to do, and still others argue that the real test of psychology as a science is the ability to *control* what people do. Rather than try to settle all these arguments, therefore, all points of view are included in the definition.

Before putting these definitions of communication and psychology together, let us consider the possible use of psychological science to *control* mental and behavioral events. Many people become very upset when they hear that psychologists are trying to control them. People don't want to be controlled. They don't want to be "brainwashed." They want to be free to think and do whatever seems right to them. They are worried that these scientists are developing in their laboratories some new and monstrous technology that will reduce human beings to mechanical robots. So the whole question of control as a scientific objective is clouded by moral and political overtones.

Do we in fact have techniques that enable us to control people? The answer is "yes." There presently exists a behavioral procedure that can exert powerful control over people's thoughts and actions. This technique of control can cause you to do things you would never think of doing otherwise. It can change opinions and beliefs. It can be used to deceive you. It can make you happy or sad. It can put new ideas into your head. It can make you want things you don't have. You can even use it to control yourself. It is an enormously powerful tool with a universal range of application.

The behavioral technique that I have in mind was not invented by psychologists. This particular technique of control has existed at least as long as human beings have. Far from thinking of it as an evil or threatening thing, most people regard this particular kind of control as one of the greatest triumphs of the human mind, indeed, as the very thing that raises man above all the other animals.

The technique of control that I am talking about, of course, is human language. Language is by all odds the most subtle and powerful technique we have for controlling other people. Nothing that psychologists can invent in their laboratories is likely to be nearly as influential in controlling people as is this familiar tool we call language. The point very simply is that it is not necessary to think of all techniques of control as essentially evil or immoral. Some are absolutely essential for the existence of civilization as we know it.

Let me now put the definitions of psychology and communication together. Communication is a process that occurs when different events are closely related. The *psychology* of communication, therefore, must be concerned with relations between different mental or behavioral events. In the most common and familiar case, what a speaker says is one set of events, and what his listener understands is the other set; if these are closely related, we say that communication is occurring. But the psychology of communication is not limited to talking or listening. Other kinds of events, intentional or unintentional, can also serve the purposes of communication.

In its broadest form, therefore, the psychological study of communication includes not only the study of spoken communication between people, but also the many kinds of unspoken communication that go on constantly when people interact. And it even includes the kind of communication that goes on between animals. A complete survey of this subject would have to include all these kinds of communication. As a practical matter, however, spoken communication between people is the most interesting kind of communication, and probably the most important.

Interest in the nature of speech and language is a very general characteristic of twentieth-century thought. This century has seen the emergence of descriptive linguistics as one of the most rigorous and analytical of all the social sciences, but interest in language has not been confined to linguists alone. Anyone who tries to understand the intricacies of human thought finds it necessary to understand first the intricacies of the symbolic systems through which human thought makes itself manifest. Thus logicians, philosophers, and psychologists must share the linguist's concern with language.

Moreover, in parallel with this broad study of language has run an amazing revolution in our technology of communication. In this century the telegraph, telephone, phonograph, radio, television, and communication satellite have accustomed us to instantaneous communication from the most distant corners of the world.

These two developments—the scholarly study of language and the creation of a vast technology of communication—seem to have begun as independent manifestations of the spirit of our times. But with the emergence of digital computers as language-processing systems, the world of the academy and the world of technology have at last joined forces in their attempts to understand the nature of language and communication. Indeed, in order to communicate with our computers, a whole new class of artificial languages had to be invented. Each decade seems to bring some new advance, to open some new possibilities.

Psychologists who are interested in language and communication, therefore, feel themselves to be part of a much larger army of workers contributing to the purification of ideas that rank among the great triumphs of the modern mind. This feeling of identification lends an excitement to the field that is often difficult for outsiders to comprehend. It means that the zoologist who records the grunts and gestures of the great apes, or the psychologist who analyzes the almost unintelligible utterances of young children, or the neurologist who stimulates the centers in the brain that control speech, or the engineer who designs telephone circuits to transmit the human voice more efficiently, or the grammarian who states rules for forming grammatical sentences, or the logician who analyzes the way we should use words like "some," "all," and "none," or the philosopher who tries to untangle linguistic sources of philosophical confusion, or the sociologist who measures the social effects of mass media of communication—all these workers and many others can see themselves as participating in and contributing to one of the great intellectual adventures of the twentieth century. Seen in isolation, any one of these studies might seem uninteresting, even pointless. Considered together, however, they point to a concern for language and communication as one of the principal preoccupations of our time.

The central object of all this interest and excitement, of course, is human language. There seem to be at least two different ways to define what a language is. According to one definition, a language is a socially shared means for expressing ideas. This might be called a *functional* definition, because it is stated in terms of the function that a language serves. Another definition says that a language is all the conceivable sentences that could be generated according to the rules of its grammar. This might be called a *formal* definition, because it is stated in terms of the forms of all the sentences that can be generated by the grammatical rules. The formal definition tells you how to decide whether or not a particular utterance is a sentence in the language; the functional definition tells you what the sentence is used for. Both definitions reflect important aspects of language.

According to the formal definition, a language is defined by its grammar. So that moves the problem one step deeper. What is a grammar? A sentence is a string of sounds that has a meaning to the people who know the language. The basic problem, therefore, is to understand how the sounds and the meanings are related. A grammar is a set of rules that describes how the realm of sound is related to the realm of meaning.

Considered abstractly, a grammatical sentence is a highly complex and structured thing, and it faces in two directions. On the one hand it must have a semantic interpretation, a meaning, and on the other hand it must have a phonological realization, a pronunciation, an acoustic shape. The formal problem for the grammarian, therefore, is to describe this abstract concept in such a way that both its sound and its meaning are explained.

Anyone who speaks a language, of course, must know how its sounds and its meanings are related. That is to say, he must know the grammar of his language. When we say this, however, we do not mean that he could explain the grammar to someone else; we say he knows it because he uses the language appropriately. His knowledge of grammar is implicit. Only when he studies grammar in school does he begin to make this grammatical knowledge explicit and communicable to others. One of the fascinating problems for a psychologist interested in human communication is to explain exactly what it is that a person knows implicitly when he knows a grammar, and how this information is organized and stored in his memory.

In order to be able to use a language effectively, of course, a person must know much more than its grammar. We could consider that this knowledge is organized on five distinguishable levels. On the first level he must have *phonological* information about the sounds of his language. On the second level he must have *syntactic* information about the formation of sentences. On the third level he must have *lexical* information about the meanings of words and combinations of words. On the fourth level he must have *conceptual* knowledge of the world he lives in and talks about. And on the fifth level he probably has to have some system of *beliefs* in order to evaluate what he hears.

Grammar, of course, deals with only the first three of these levels—phonology, syntax, and lexicon—and with the relations between them. A psychologist interested in language, however, must also remember that a person's concepts and beliefs play an essential role in his use and understanding of linguistic messages.

For example, suppose someone were to say, *Mary and John saw the mountains while they were flying to California.* If we consider this sentence simply from a grammatical point of view, it is ambiguous. It has at least two meanings: It could be paraphrased, *While Mary and John were flying to California they saw the mountains;* or it could be paraphrased, *While the mountains were flying to California Mary and John saw them.* There is nothing that we know about phonology or syntax or the meanings of the words involved that will help us decide between these two meanings.

But that is ridiculous! Everyone knows that mountains do not fly. Anyone would know immediately that the sentence *Mary and John saw the mountains while they were flying to California* means that Mary and John were flying, not the mountains.

8

But how do we know this? Is it part of the lexical meaning of the word *mountain*? Certainly not. You can look up the meaning of *mountain* in any dictionary you like, and it will not tell you that mountains do not fly. Such knowledge is part of one's conceptual information about the world one lives in, not part of one's lexical knowledge about the meanings of words. So in order to understand how people understand language, we must recognize that they use their general conceptual information as well as their specific lexical information.

But suppose, just for the sake of argument, that we were wrong. Suppose that in the subsequent conversation it turned out that the speaker really did intend to say that the mountains were flying to California when Mary and John saw them. What would we say to that? I don't know what you would say, but my response would be, "I don't believe you." In the final analysis, I would appeal to my system of beliefs in order to evaluate what the speaker was saying. So beliefs, too, must play a role in linguistic communication.

Our conceptual knowledge and our system of beliefs are not really part of our linguistic knowledge, but they play a very important role in the way we understand language in actual use. This brings us back to the other definition of language, the functional definition, which says that language is used to express ideas. When we use conceptual information or our beliefs to interpret a sentence, we are going beyond the linguistic form of the sentence and are evaluating it and interpreting it in terms of the plausibility of the ideas it expresses, and in terms of the way it is being used in the social situation in which it occurs.

Lest you think that concepts and beliefs are relatively unimportant in the way we use language, here is another example. Suppose I tell you, completely out of context, that *John drinks wine*. How would you understand this sentence? Suppose you know who John is, you know what wine is, and you understand what it means to drink wine. Suppose you know all these words, and you understand the grammatical structure of the sentence perfectly well. You still would not be certain what I meant. You would not know why I said such a thing to you. You would not understand my intentions. When I say *John drinks wine* I might be doing any of several things. I might be warning you. I might be informing you. I might be making a prediction. I might be making a promise, or an accusation, or a joke. I might be telling a lie, or asking permission, or expressing criticism. I might be doing any one of a number of different things, and unless you knew which one I intended to do, you would not really understand the meaning of my speech act.

Most of our misunderstandings of other people are not due to any inability to hear them, or to parse their sentence, or to understand their words, although such problems do occur. Our major source of difficulty in communication is that we so often fail to understand the speaker's intentions.

Because such failures are so common, most languages have special verbs that a speaker can use to make his intentions clear. For example, if I say *Let me warn you that John drinks wine*, it would mean something entirely different from saying *Let me assure you that John drinks wine*. *Warn* and *assure* are intentional verbs. In many situations, of course, these special verbs of intention are unnecessary, because the social context makes it perfectly clear what the speaker's intentions must be. But sometimes, when they are omitted, confusion and misunderstanding can result.

I said earlier that human language is the most effective means of communication that we know about. It has an almost magical power to affect the minds and the actions of those who use it. Nevertheless, it is not a perfect instrument, and we often encounter examples, like those I have just described, where ambiguity intrudes and misunderstanding results. The question arises, therefore, whether anything could be done to make language even more effective than it already is.

What are some of its inadequacies? One trouble with spoken language is that it is transient, but the invention of writing corrected that. Another is that it can reach only a limited number of people, but the invention of printing corrected that. Writing and printing are slow, of course, but radio and television corrected that. The modern development of communication technology has greatly extended the usefulness of human language as a means of communication.

But what about its adequacy for expressing ideas? Here again we find that many inadequacies have been corrected. It is difficult to carry out a complicated line of reasoning in ordinary language, but we have invented the artificial language of logic to correct that trouble. Ordinary language is a poor tool for expressing quantitative relations, but we have invented mathematics to correct that. And ordinary language is not an efficient way to give instructions to computing machines, so we have invented many new languages for that purpose. All of these artificial languages can be seen as extensions of natural language, which enable us to be more explicit and more precise and to eliminate ambiguity.

Ordinary language does not have words for many of the new things and new ideas that modern science and technology have created, but new words are invented for them. Today the vocabulary of English is growing at an extremely rapid rate as new scientific and technical terms are being defined. At an earlier period, around the time of Shakespeare, the English vocabulary grew very rapidly because many words were added to describe feelings and emotional states. And somewhere in its evolution the special verbs that mark a speaker's intentions were added. Thus, many inadequacies and ambiguities of language have been corrected by the simple device of inventing new words.

We see, therefore, that the power of language has been growing steadily for hundreds of years. It is not likely to stop growing now. It is instructive to try to imagine how language might be further strengthened in the years to come.

We can expect technology to continue, of course. Someday our telephones will have television screens, too, and computers will play an increasingly important role in facilitating the flow of information between people. We can also expect more artificial languages designed to express the increasingly complicated ideas of science and mathematics. And we can certainly expect that a steady flow of new words will be added to the language. All that simply continues what has already begun. But are there other inadequacies of language?

One serious inadequacy, of course, is that people speak so many different languages that many people are unable to understand one another. Such a problem could be corrected if, in addition to his native language, everyone also learned a world language. This has long been a dream of civilized men, and many suggestions have been proposed to achieve it. So far none of these suggestions has won worldwide acceptance, but the need to overcome this inadequacy of language is so obvious that the problem will eventually be solved.

Some people feel that a major weakness of language is its inability to capture the more elusive aspects of human consciousness. They wish that language could express mystical insights. This complaint that language is too rational to express some of the finest visions of the human mind is increasingly heard from those who have experimented with drugs and have experienced the unusual states of consciousness that are possible. They want some way to talk about that experience, and ordinary language seems inadequate. It is an intriguing idea, but I am not very optimistic that this inadequacy of language can ever be overcome. A mystic, by definition, is a man who has seen some truth that cannot be communicated to others. Making such visions communicable would destroy their mystical character. In the private realms where one person's experience can never be compared with another's, the socially shared conventions of language can have little value. Communication about these private psychological experiences can only be carried by analogy, by metaphor, by poetry. Probably poetry should be counted among the ways we have extended the power of ordinary language.

Perhaps someday we will communicate with an advanced civilization in outer space, and they will tell us about even better ways to communicate. For the present, however, human language provides the best communication we have. It has made possible whatever civilization we have so far managed to achieve.

2 PSYCHOLOGY AND THE THEORY OF LANGUAGE (structuralist)

Samuel Jay Keyser

A friend of mine likes to start the first lecture of his introductory course in linguistics by demonstrating a talking doll. When you pull a string in its back, the doll says things like, "Hello. My name is Sandy," or "I want to play. Don't you?" Whenever you pull the string, the doll begins a new sentence; it never starts in the middle, even if you only pull the string out part way. There is no strict sequence of sentences. Their number is very small, perhaps ten or so, and the order in which they are heard is random.

Suppose we ask the question: How is the doll able to talk? From the brief description just given, it would not be easy to answer this question. Several possible answers might come to mind and it is very possible that the one crucial clue to help us choose between answers will never occur.

The talking doll problem is very much like the talking human problem. Linguists and psychologists try to figure out how people talk. They must do so without looking inside. For one thing, if they could look inside the human brain safely, it is not clear what they could learn by looking. Instead, researchers listen to what people do when they speak and try to make intelligent guesses about the inside organization on the basis of what [theory] happens on the outside. [what I tried to do (1 thing)]

My friend considers the talking doll to be a practical demonstration that determining how people speak is impossible since the problem cannot be solved even for a doll.

Yet linguists and psychologists think that there might be a solution to the problem of what people do when they speak and

13

listen because there are many universal statements true of every language in the world. It is the business of the theoretical linguist to find these universals by observing language. The psychologist then asks: If there are certain things that all languages have in common, might not these things be outside reflections of the structure and operation inside the human brain?

The importance of linguistic universals for insight into the structure and operation of the human brain depends crucially on the universals themselves. If they are trivial, very little can be learned from them. And there are, of course, many such trivial linguistic universals. For example, in no language is it the case that all sentences with an even number of words are grammatical while all sentences with an odd number of words are not. Or, to take another example, there are no languages in which a question is formed from a declarative sentence by saying the declarative form backwards. Such universals are true, but they are also silly and very little can be learned from them.

There are, moreover, universals that are perfectly true and not silly, but are also not very interesting. For example, no language in the world contains simple words longer than, say, fifteen syllables. This does not include words that are made up of other words, such as the compound noun *airplane pilot briefing room weather kit briefcase key ring container rack holder*. This word, made up for the occasion, contains twenty syllables; but the simple words that it contains are only one, two, or three syllables long. And this is true of simple words in every language in the world. They are not very long. The reason is not hard to imagine—simple words must be easy to remember as well as easy to say.

There are, however, more interesting universals. They are more interesting because they are unexpected and because their significance is not as obvious as the limitation on the length of simple words. One unexpected and therefore interesting universal can be illustrated with a children's secret language called *pig latin*. The most obvious characteristic of the language is that it is produced by manipulating regular speech in a systematic way. In other words children who speak pig latin have learned a rule. The rule is straightforward. Select any word in the

English language and put the first sound of the word at the end and add the sound *ay* (as in *hay*). For example, the word *pig* is pronounced *igpay*. The word *latin, atinlay*. The phrase *pig latin* is *igpay atinlay*. And the sentence *pig latin is fun, igpay atinlay isay unfay*. As you can see, when it is spoken rapidly by fluent speakers, it does indeed become a secret language.

Now there is another rule in English which all speakers know: the plural rule. This rule tells what the regular plural of words will be. It says, for example, that the plural of the word *pig* is made by adding a *z* sound as in *zebra* to produce the plural *pigs,* or that the plural of *book* is *books,* that is, with an *s* sound added. What are the plurals of these two words in pig latin? The plural of *pigs* is *igzpay* and the plural of *books* is *ooksbay*. What is interesting about these plurals is that they can only be accounted for if we suppose the plural rule and the pig latin rule are applied in a fixed order.

To see that, let us start with the simple word *book*. To form the plural, apply the regular plural rule which tells us to add an *s* and pronounce it as *books*. Then we apply the pig latin rule by moving the first sound, in this case *b,* to the end of the word and adding *ay*. This gives us *ooksbay,* which is the correct pig latin plural. Suppose we applied the rules in the other order. We would start out with *book* and apply the pig latin rule—move *b* to the end of the word and add *ay*—to get *ookbay*. Now, however, the plural ending of words that end in *ay* in English is a *z* sound. Moreover, the plural is always attached to the very end of a word in English. So, given a word like *ookbay,* the plural rule would determine that its plural form is *ookbayz,* with a *z* sound at the very end. This is not the correct plural pronunciation in pig latin, however. We could always complicate the plural rule so that things would work out right. But if we simply allow the rules to be ordered—first regular plural rule, then pig latin rule—it is not necessary to complicate the plural rule.

What effect does rule ordering have on other rules? We mentioned above that the regular plural rule in English tells how the plurals are normally sounded in English. There are three different ways in which the plural is sounded in English:

z as in *pigs*, *s* as in *books* and, finally, *iz* as in *wishes*. Those who were taught English as a second language might have been taught the plural rule of English in something like the following form:

1. If the word ends in s, z, ch, dg, sh, or zh, then pronounce the plural as *iz*. Examples are *kisses, mazes, churches, judges, bushes, garages.*
2. If the word ends in p, t, k, f, or th, then pronounce the plural as *s*. Examples are *caps, hats, books, cuffs,* and *baths.*
3. If the word ends in b, d, g, m, n, l, r, or a vowel then pronounce the plural as *z*. Examples are *cubs, lids, pigs, hams, guns, girls, wars,* and, for words ending in a vowel sound, *eyes, cows, seas,* and so forth.

The sounds listed in each rule all have something in common. For example, the sounds *s, z, ch, dg, sh,* and *zh* are all hissing and hushing kinds of sounds. They are made by pushing air through a narrow slit between the tongue and the upper teeth and the overall effect is a very noisy rush of sound. We call these sounds by the name of the quality they seem to have in common. Thus, we can replace the first rule by a new rule that does exactly the same thing:

New rule 1. If a word ends in a hissing or hushing sort of sound, the plural is pronounced *iz*.

The sounds in the second rule also have something in common. Thus, *p, t, k, f,* and *th* are all voiceless sounds. There is a very easy way to tell whether a sound is voiceless or not. Take your thumb and forefinger and place them very gently on your Adam's apple, the little knot on your neck which moves up and down when you swallow. Now say the sound *b* as in *book.* You will feel a gentle vibration in your fingertips. This indicates that the sound you are making is voiced. The vibration is the vocal cords vibrating as the air passes through them. Now with your fingers still on your Adam's apple, say the sound *p* as in *pig.* There is no vibration. This indicates that the vocal cords are not vibrating. Sounds that do not vibrate the vocal cords are voiceless and sounds that do vibrate the vocal cords are voiced. The sounds in the second rule of the plural rule are all voiceless. These sounds are *p, t, k, f,* and *th.* And if you will pronounce them all with your fingers over your Adam's apple, you will see that no vibration occurs. We can then state the second plural rule in a different way:

New rule 2. If a word ends in a voiceless sound that is not a hissing or hushing sound, the plural is pronounced *s*.

Finally, the sounds in the third part of the plural rule all have something in common also. They are all voiced sounds. So we may state the third plural rule as follows:

New rule 3. If a word ends in voiced sound that is not a hissing or hushing sound, the plural is pronounced *z*.

These three rules are all unordered with respect to one another. That is, take any word in the English language that takes a regular plural and you may apply the above rules in any order you please and you will end up with the correct plural. There is, however, a certain amount of repetition in the above rules. The term hissing and hushing appears three different times; once in each subrule. Indeed, it is this repetition that allows the rules to be applied in any order.

Remember that rules have to be ordered in at least some cases. The pig latin rule must follow the operation of the plural rule, for example. What would happen to the new plural rule if we were to impose an order on it even though, as we have already seen, it is not required in order to get the right ending with the right word. The plural rule with its three subparts ordered would look like this:

Ordered plural rule:
Pronounce the plural as:
a. *iz* if a word ends in a hissing or hushing sound.
b. *s* if a word ends in a voiceless sound.
c. *z*.

To see how this rule works, let us figure out the plural of a word like *pig*. Since the subparts of the rule are ordered, we must apply each subpart as we come to it in the given order. We take the word *pig* and apply subpart a, which says that the plural is pronounced *iz* if the word ends in a hissing or hushing sound. *Pig* ends with *g* which is not a hissing and hushing sound so the first subpart does not apply. We take the second subpart,

17

which says to pronounce the plural as *s* if it ends in a voiceless sound. However, *pig* does not end in a voiceless sound so this subpart does not apply. We take the last subpart. All it says is to pronounce the plural as *z*. In other words, if a word does not apply to either of the earlier subparts, then its plural must be *z*. And we see that that is exactly right for *pig*.

Unless you go through the rule in this order, you will get a wrong plural. Take the word *church,* for example. Its last sound is hissing and hushing, but if you were to go to the last part of the plural rule first, you would get the incorrect plural *churchz,* instead of the correct *churchiz.*

The differences between the unordered and ordered plural rule are striking. For one thing, the ordered plural rule mentions the term hissing and hushing only once, but the unordered rule has to mention it three times. The unordered plural rule has to mention the term voiceless and the term voiced, but the ordered plural rule only has to mention the term voiceless. Pig latin made us suppose that certain rules are ordered and now we find that when we extend order to rules that do not need to be ordered, a simpler rule results.

In fact, the simplicity is even greater than we have managed to show so far. There are certain other parts of English that bear a striking resemblance to the plural rule. For example, there are three different ways of pronouncing the regular third person singular present tense ending of verbs in English, namely, *iz, s,* or *z*; and the way these three sounds are arranged is identical with the way the plural rule works. For example, in the sentence *John hitches rides all over Europe,* the verb *hitch* ends in a hissing and hushing sound and the third person is pronounced *iz*. If a verb ends in a voiceless sound, it takes *s* as a third person singular ending—for example, *John hikes all over Europe.* Finally, if a verb ends in a voiced sound, it takes *z* as a third person singular ending. Thus, we would say *John rides all over Europe.*

Now how shall we include the rule that tells how the third person singular form of verbs in the present tense is to be pronounced in English? We have already seen that it is best to use ordered rules since the result is simpler and since we need ordered rules anyway. Suppose we state the rule for the third person singular present tense ending like this:

Third person present tense ending rule:
Pronounce the third person singular present tense as:
a. *iz* if a word ends in a hissing or hushing sound.
b. *s* if a word ends in a voiceless sound.
c. *z*.

Now this rule is virtually identical to the plural rule. To have both rules in the grammar is like having the term hissing and hushing appear three times in the unordered plural rule. There is an obvious repetition and it would be interesting to see if we can eliminate it.

Suppose we order the plural rule and the third person singular ending rule so that they stand right next to one another. If we do this, then we can merge the two rules into a single rule that expresses their similarities as well as their differences. We replace the partially identical rules with this single rule:

Pronounce the plural and the third person singular present tense ending as:
a. *iz* if the word ends in a hissing or hushing sound.
b. *s* if the word ends in a voiceless sound.
c. *z*.

We do not have to order these two rules next to each other, but if we do we can simplify the rules greatly by abbreviating them in the fashion just indicated. This is desirable because there is another rule in English that works just like the plural/third person rule. The possessive ending in English is pronounced in three different ways: *iz, s,* or *z,* depending upon whether the word to which it is attached ends in a hissing and hushing sound, a voiceless sound, or a voiced sound. For example, one says *the judge's decision, the book's cover, the pig's bladder.* But rather than repeat the plural/third person rule all over again for the possessive, we merge the possessive rule with the plural/third person rule so that they all form a single rule; namely,

Pronounce the plural, the third person singular present tense ending of verbs, and the possessive ending as:

    a. *iz* if the word ends in a hissing and hushing sound.
    b. *s* if the word ends in a voiceless sound.
    c. *z*.

Rule ordering has allowed us to see that the way the plural, the third person singular, and the possessive forms are pronounced is actually the same. This is demonstrated by the fact that they all obey the same rule.

All of the examples of ordering have been drawn from the sounds of English, but it is possible to make the same point about rule ordering using syntactic examples.

We said earlier that unexpected universals raise the question of their psychological meaning. In trying to find out something about the operation and the structure of the human brain without looking inside, we have discovered that human language requires ordered rules, and that ordering lets us state rules that are simpler than unordered rules, and that it lets us relate rules that are partially identical.

At this point the linguist turns to the psychologist (who is often the selfsame person) and asks what this could possibly mean about the structure and operation of the mind. Both are convinced that it must mean something, for otherwise it would be an incredible coincidence that all languages order rules and that ordered rules result in simpler grammars. Unfortunately, at this stage of research there is only speculation. This should not be surprising because the linguist and the psychologist are asking the most difficult of all possible questions; namely, how people work. Speculation is worthwhile though, even if only to let everyone else know how little we know.

A grammar that orders rules allows certain generalizations to be made that cannot otherwise be reflected in a grammar. This happened when the plural rule merged with the third person singular and the possessive rules. We also saw that grammars that order rules are more concise than grammars that do not (concise is used in the technical sense that it enables one to state simpler rules). Linguists have made conciseness a formal requirement that grammars must meet. In other words, if there are two grammars, and one is more concise than the other, the more concise grammar is better. There is another way of looking at the conciseness requirement, however. If there is a grammar that is not as simple as it might be but, by means of rule ordering, it could be made simpler, then the conciseness requirement demands that it be changed so that it becomes more concise.

What might the conciseness requirement say about the mental operation of human beings? It is barely conceivable that the conciseness requirement reflects a strategy that speakers unconsciously use when they are in the process of learning how to speak. Put in its crudest form, speakers, while learning how to speak, will make successive changes in their rules according to the conciseness requirement since to do so increases the generality of their rules. And this is an obvious advantage in learning a language since it implies that rules put together in accordance with a strategy that increases generality are more apt to cover cases that go beyond the immediate facts that they were made for. This is a sensible strategy for the child who is learning language. It means that he will learn more about his language than is simply contained in the immediate set of facts confronting him. To put this into the form of a slogan, it is possible, with the correct learning strategy, to go farther on less.

We can see how this might work in the few examples we have already discussed. The plural rule must precede the pig latin rule or else we will get the wrong results. The conciseness requirement demands that the third person singular and the possessive rules be merged with the plural rule. But now notice that these rules make a prediction that goes beyond the facts for which the rules were originally made. The rules predict what the pig latin forms must be for the third person singular forms of verbs and for the possessive forms of nouns. The rules predict, for example, that the third person singular form *hitches* as in *John hitches rides* must be *itcheshay* and not *itchhayz*. The rules also predict that the form of the possessive noun *John's* must be *ohn'zjay* and not *ohnjayz*. And, indeed, both of these predictions turn out to be correct. This simple example shows how rules, based on the conciseness requirement, can make predictions that go beyond the facts at hand. A learning strategy that makes such predictions possible seems like an eminently sensible sort of strategy for human beings to adopt, not only when they are learning their first language, but perhaps when they are learning other things as well.

All this is merely speculation. But one thing is clear. Linguistic universals, as hard as they are to come by, are not by themselves very satisfactory answers for linguists. For one is immediately led to ask why they take the shape they do and not some other shape. And here the answer seems almost unavoidable that they take the shape that they do because the human mind is the way it is. It is for this reason that psychology and the theory of language are indistinguishable.

3 THE REALM OF SYNTAX

Paul M. Postal

We all have a certain familiarity with the problems of grammar from our schooling. Unfortunately, the approaches of school grammar, for either the native speaker of English or the individual learning English as a second language, are far from the concerns of modern linguistics. In fact, they are sufficiently remote from the research of contemporary linguistic scholarship that this familiarity may be as much a hindrance as a help in understanding grammar as studied within modern linguistics. Perhaps then you will forgive me if I ask you to suspend your familiarity with grammar for what follows.

To a modern linguist, the chief problem of grammar for a particular language, say English, is this. Each speaker has the ability to produce and understand a literally endless variety of sentences, the overwhelming majority of which he has never encountered as wholes before. Our amazing ability to deal with previously unencountered linguistic entities tends to obscure the fact that normal linguistic behavior does deal with unfamiliar sentences. You probably have not noticed at all that you have never before encountered these sentences. The problem of linguistics is thus to explain this amazing "creative" property of linguistic activity, to explain the fact that knowledge of language permits us to create novel sentences and to understand the novel sentences created by others, provided only that these are drawn from a language we know.

It is clear that with only the finite storage capacity of the human brain one cannot have learned an infinite set of sentences *directly,* the way most words are learned. It follows that linguistic knowledge, though literally endless in the sense that it encompasses an infinite set of sentences, must nonetheless be representable in a finite form to explain its internalization. There is no real puzzle here. Many kinds of finite systems describe infinite sets of things. One example is the rules of arithmetic learned in school. There is a finite number of such rules, but one who learns them knows how to perform an infinite set of calculations. There is no theoretical limit on the length of a list of numbers that we know how to add. In the same way, language provides no theoretical limit on the length of sentences that we can create or understand. However, practical limitations of memory, energy, and so forth restrict our ability to use this knowledge to a subpart of the objects defined by the theoretical knowledge of either arithmetic or language.

Based on considerations like these, the linguist today assumes an individual's linguistic knowledge is to be accounted for by positing that the individual has learned some finite system of principles, this system defining the endless class of sentences of his language. Such a system is referred to as a *grammar*. The linguist's goal is to specify as precisely and fully as possible the character of this grammatical system. On a more general level, one must also be concerned with universal grammar, with ascertaining how much of the overall structure of distinct linguistic systems is common and thus attributable to an innate aspect of human nature rather than to historical or cultural diversities.

Grammar encompasses three areas: phonology, syntax, and semantics. Phonology deals with the realm of sound and semantics with the realm of meaning. My present concern is with syntax, the part of grammar that concerns how sentences are constructed.

A key notion in the contemporary study of grammar is the idea of *rule*. The term is not unfamiliar, again because of acquaintance with school grammar. But, interpreted as part of the study of the finite grammars that underlie the infinite linguistic knowledge typical of human beings, the notion takes on new aspects. A concern arises to give a precise account of what kinds of rules natural languages can have, what kinds are impossible, what are the possible relations between rules, what rules are universal, and so on. These questions have not been of central concern to past epochs of grammatical study. It would, for instance, be foreign to the tradition of school grammar to say anything about the kinds of rules that languages *cannot* have. But such characterizations teach us something about language, and many restrictions are clear. For instance, no language can have a rule requiring all sentences to have an even rather than an odd number of words, or a rule requiring the first half of every sentence to rhyme with the second half. Ultimately, such facts must be explained by constructing a substantive theory of grammar that excludes the possibilities of a human language having rules of these types. Before questions about grammatical rules can be raised intelligently, however, one must consider the *function* that such rules have.

The rules of syntax define the set of sentences of the language. They specify what are sentences and what are not. For instance, for English the rules must say that *Harriet is proud of her son* is a sentence but that *Harriet is proud of she son* is not. Anyone who knows English is aware of such facts, and so the rules that make up their internalized grammar must have such facts as consequences. Here the relevant rules are obviously those having to do with choice of the case forms for pronouns. Furthermore, the rules of the grammar must describe for each sentence the particular structure it has. Such a description must specify the parts of the sentence, their order, other relations between them, and so on. These structural descriptions will provide, among other things, an account of the similarities and differences between different sentences.

The structural descriptions assigned to sentences by a grammar must also predict correctly a variety of special properties. For instance, the grammar must predict that some sentences are ambiguous, have two distinct meanings or interpretations. An example is *what annoyed Max was being investigated by congress*. This sentence means either that Max was being investigated by congress and this fact annoyed him, or, that something annoyed Max and this thing was being investigated by congress. A grammar of English must say that this sentence has these two distinct interpretations. On the other hand, the grammar must say that a sentence like *the law that annoyed Max was being investigated by congress* has only one of the two interpretations of the first sentence. The grammar must also say that in the phrase *who said he knew me,* the words *who* and *he* can refer to the same individual. But in the sentence *who did he say I knew* the words *who* and *he* necessarily refer to different individuals. These are just a handful of the many kinds of sentential properties that must be assigned correctly by a grammar of the language.

A study of grammatical rules is thus in part dependent on an understanding of the sorts of things sentences are. Here ordinary ideas about language, or those of school grammar, are in sharp conflict with the conception of modern grammatical study. Our ordinary conception tells us that a sentence is a string of elements called *words.* Roughly a word is an independently pronounceable part of a sentence. School grammar adds to this an analysis of words into categories; these are the famous parts of speech: noun, verb, adjective, and so on. School grammar also says that certain strings of words are organized into larger groups called *phrases,* and has a set of terms to describe some of the relations between words in phrases, words like *subject* and *object.* Taken together, such ideas provide a definite, if not completely clear, notion of what kind of a thing a sentence in a human language is.

Modern grammatical research certainly does not deny that sentences are things of this sort, or that their structure may be described in terms like the above, provided the ideas are extended and clarified. However, it has become evident that, questions of detail and elaboration aside, ideas like those just mentioned can in principle describe only a portion of sentence structure, and only the most superficial portion. Suppose we refer to those aspects of sentence form that can be described in terms of the familiar ideas as *surface structure.* Each sentence certainly has one and only one surface structure; to this all grammarians would agree. However, it has become clear that one must also assume that each sentence has at least one other type of grammatical structure. This has come to be called *deep structure,* and an increasingly wide group of grammarians now agree that each sentence must also be regarded as having a deep structure quite distinct from its surface structure.

The facts suggesting the existence of deep structure are varied in nature and vast in scope. Space limitations permit only a brief survey. Let us consider the two sentences: *Harry is willing to help* and *Harry is difficult to help*. In terms of the surface concepts of school and traditional grammar, these sentences are identical except for the two adjectives, *willing* and *difficult*. Each consists of a string of five words, beginning with the noun, *Harry*, followed by the verb *is*, the adjective, then the infinitive marker *to*, and finally the verb *help*. Thus, in traditional terms, these sentences differ grammatically only in choice of adjectives. They differ no more than do sentences like *Harry is sad* and *Harry is happy*. However, if one examines the sentences more closely, one perceives some striking differences not explained by the surface similarities. We observe that in the sentence with *willing*, the noun *Harry* is understood as designating the individual who is going to do the helping. That is, in the sentence *Harry is willing to help,* Harry is the helper. Technically, the noun *Harry* is said to be the *Agent* of the verb *help*. In the sentence with *difficult*, however, the noun *Harry* is understood as designating the individual who gets helped. Technically, *Harry* in the sentence *Harry is difficult to help* is the *Patient* of the verb *help*.

Thus in these two superficially similar sentences the noun *Harry* bears two distinct relations to the verb *help*. These relations are not expressed in the surface structure. It is the postulation of distinct deep structures for these sentences that offers the possibility of representing the differences. Notice that the sentence with *willing* is understood identically to a sentence like *Harry is willing to help one* whereas a sentence like the original with *difficult* is understood identically to a sentence like *Harry is difficult for one to help*. This suggests that the deep structure of the sentences without the word *one* in them will be the same as those in which this word occurs, despite their difference in surface structures. However, the sentence *Harry is willing to help* will have a deep structure like the sentence *Harry is willing to help one,* whereas the sentence *Harry is difficult to help* will have a deep structure like the sentence *Harry is difficult for one to help*. That is, the deep structures of the original sentences will differ in the positions of the pronominal element *one*.

These remarks immediately suggest one type of grammatical rule that will be necessary in a grammar that assigns sentences both deep and surface structures. There must be rules that delete elements from deep structures to yield the appropriate surface structures. In this case, English must have one or more rules that delete the pronominal element *one*. Such deletion rules are a special subtype of a general class of rules called *grammatical transformations,* or just *transformations.* These rules assign each deep structure its appropriate surface structure form by changing it in various ways. Consequently, there must be another type of rule—call them *base rules*—that describes the correct set of deep structures. The notion of deep structure thus leads naturally to a two-part conception of grammar in which one set of rules generates the set of deep structures, and another set of transformational rules assigns to each deep structure a proper surface structure realization.

Returning to our original two examples with *willing* and *difficult,* the different positions of the pronominal element *one* are not the only ways the deep structures of these sentences will differ. Observe that the sentence *Harry is difficult to help* is understood almost exactly as is the sentence *it is difficult to help Harry*. This identity is preserved when the pronominal form *one* is added to each, yielding *Harry is difficult for one to help,* which is the same as *it is difficult for one to help Harry*. It is the latter structure that provides the clearest picture of the deep structure of the original sentence with *difficult*. One reason for this is that the string *it is difficult to help Harry* contains as a subpart the clause *for one to help Harry*. In this the noun *Harry* occurs directly after the verb *help*. But post-verbal position is typical for nouns interpreted as Patients of verbs in English, and recall that the noun *Harry* was interpreted as Patient of *help* in the original sentence with *difficult*. Therefore, by deriving the original sentence from a deep structure like that of the sentence *it is difficult for one to help Harry,* we can account for the relational properties of the original in terms of the general principle of English grammar that correlates

Patient interpretation with post-verbal position. This principle is thus defined not on surface structures but on deep structures. Or, to put it differently, the noun *Harry* is understood as the Patient of the verb *help* in the sentence *Harry is difficult to help* because this noun occurs in post-verbal, Patient position in the deep structure of this sentence.

The difference between the surface structure and deep structure positions of *Harry* in such sentences reveals the existence of another transformation, one that moves the noun from its deep structure position in the subordinate clause to its surface structure position. Thus, while some transformations delete material, still others rearrange the position of items.

The original sentence with *difficult* has an analogue that begins with the word *it*. The original sentence with *willing*, however, has no such related sentence. A string like *it is willing for Harry to help one* is *ill-formed* or *ungrammatical*, that is, not an English sentence. This means that the deep structure of the *willing* sentence will be quite different from that of the *difficult* sentence, which was similar to its analogue beginning with *it*. The deep structure of the *willing* sentence will be like *Harry is willing for Harry to help one*. This also seems ungrammatical, but deep structures are not sentences; that is, they are not surface structures. They represent certain properties of sentences. The posited deep structure of the sentence *Harry is willing to help*, containing two occurrences of the noun element *Harry*, explains the relations understood in the original. There are, moreover, sentences like *Harry is willing for Max to help*, which are parallel to the deep structure we posited except for having two different nouns instead of two the same like the deep structure. But the sentence *Harry is willing for Max to help* is understood exactly parallel to the sentence *Harry is willing to help*, differing in involving willingness by one person and helping by a second, where the first involves willingness and helping by the same individual.

The parallelism in interpretation is explained by parallel deep structures, assuming a transformational rule that deletes the second instance of the noun in structures like *Harry is willing for Harry to help one* if it refers to the same individual as the first instance. This important rule is of very general relevance in English. It explains why we say *I want to go,* not *I want me to go,* parallel to *I want Bill to go;* it explains why we say *I am anxious to leave,* not *I am anxious for me to leave,* parallel to *I am anxious for you to leave;* and so on. Let us refer to this rule as IDENTICAL SUBJECT DELETION.

Given the deep structure posited for the sentence *Harry is willing to help,* namely, *Harry is willing for Harry to help one,* IDENTICAL SUBJECT DELETION must apply to derive the surface structure. This rule does not apply in the derivation of the sentence *Harry is difficult to help,* given the deep structure we posited for this, namely, *it is difficult for one to help Harry,* since this structure does not contain identical subjects. However, the contrast between two instances of *Harry* in the deep structure of the *willing* sentence but only one instance in the deep structure of the *difficult* sentence corresponds to the way the sentences are understood. That is, in the sentence *Harry is willing to help,* the noun *Harry* is understood as designating both the Agent of the verb *help* and the entity that experiences the willingness. *Harry* thus plays two roles in this sentence, a fact explicated by the occurrence of two instances of the noun in the deep structure that was posited. However, in the sentence *Harry is difficult to help,* *Harry* plays only a single role, Patient of *help.* *Harry* is not understood as bearing any direct relation to *difficult,* a fact explicated by the deep structure which provides only a single occurrence of *Harry* in this case, as shown by the fact that the deep structure is similar to that of the sentence *it is difficult for one to help Harry.*

Some further examples will help illustrate the properties of an approach to grammar that assigns deep structures to sentences and relates these to the surface forms of sentences by way of transformational rules. In English we can say things like *a friend of Lucy's, that friend of Lucy's,* with any of the various articles, *a, some, this, that, any, each, every.* There is, however, one exception. One cannot say *the friend of Lucy's.* This form is ungrammatical. Thus with the definite article *the,* a quite general pattern for forming possessive constructions is broken. There exist, however, unique forms like *Lucy's friend,* in which the possessive form occurs before the noun it modifies, rather than after it, as in the first construction. It would be quite natural to derive the latter type of example from a deep structure that would otherwise yield the banned forms with the definite article. This could be done by transformations that move the possessive noun to the front, while deleting the preposition *of*. A subsequent rule would then delete the article *the*.

Evidence that this plausible analysis is right is of several sorts. First, note that it at once explains both the gap in the original set of forms and the existence of the special class of expressions with prenominal possessives, like *Lucy's friend*. Second, the derivation from underlying forms with definite articles predicts that expressions like *Lucy's friend* should have properties like other forms with the definite article. And this is in fact true. One such property is that the definite article can occur with superlative adjectives. Thus we can say *the biggest doll*, but not *a biggest doll*, or *some biggest doll*; similarly, we can say *the tallest girl*, but not *any tallest girl*, nor *that tallest girl*. Notice, however, that expressions like *Lucy's biggest doll* are perfectly well-formed, showing that constructions with prenominal possessives behave as if they had definite articles, which is just what our proposed derivation gives them in their deep structures. As a last argument in favor of the derivation of forms like *Lucy's house* from a deep structure like *the house of Lucy's*, one can observe that, although the latter expression is ill-formed alone, it is all right if followed by a relative clause. That is, it is well-formed English to say *the house of Lucy's which was destroyed by the hurricane*. This fact is explicable if we assume that the rule that preposes possessive nouns and deletes the preposition *of* only works when there is no following relative clause. With a following clause, the rule is blocked and the original deep structure order of forms is maintained even with a definite article.

All this seems very complicated when we try to describe it precisely, but anyone who knows English can recognize immediately which forms are acceptable and which are not. It is of great psychological interest that we can "know" such rules in the sense that our speech conforms to them, yet we find it so difficult to explain exactly what it is that we know. And, of course, these examples merely hint at the further complexities that are revealed by still more detailed analysis.

For a final example, consider pairs of sentences like *that Steven lost is surprising* and *it is surprising that Steven lost*. Despite their surface differences, such examples are understood in exactly the same way. In each case, the clause *that Steven lost* bears the same relation to the predicate *is surprising*. We can account for this fact by positing that such sentences have identical deep structures, structures that are like the first sentence, *that Steven lost is surprising*. One must then assume that there is a rule that can move the clause to the end of the sentence. This rule is now generally called EXTRAPOSITION. When EXTRAPOSITION applies, another rule must insure that the form *it* occurs in the position where the clause would have been if it had not been moved. This analysis explains why the form *it* is the only word that can occur in the relevant position in examples like *it is surprising that Max lost*. Other words can occur before *is surprising* in other contexts, giving sentences like *that is surprising, that idea is surprising,* and so on. But when EXTRAPOSITION applies, only *it* can occur in the original position. The analysis explains this since it says that originally the moved clause filled the position, and that this is replaced only by the marker *it* when the clause moves away through application of the EXTRAPOSITION transformation.

EXTRAPOSITION illustrates an important property of transformational rules, namely, some of them are optional and some obligatory. Thus, in the examples given to illustrate the existence of EXTRAPOSITION, we see that well-formed sentences result regardless of whether the rule is applied or not. In fact, however, the situation is more complicated than this, since the same rule may be optional in some contexts but obligatory in others. This is true for EXTRAPOSITION. Although this rule is optional in the examples given so far, it is obligatory with verbs like *seem* in many contexts. Thus we say *it seems to me that Harry is mistaken* but never *that Harry is mistaken seems to me*. So in such positions we must say that EXTRAPOSITION is obligatory. To begin to see really a hint of the extraordinary depth and complexity of the grammar of a language, one need only note next that EXTRAPOSITION is optional even with the verb *seem* when further elements follow, as in sentences like *it seems obvious to me that Harry is mistaken,* which has an analogue where EXTRAPOSITION has not applied, namely, *that Harry is mistaken seems obvious to me.*

Finally, EXTRAPOSITION can be used to illustrate an important deep principle of grammar, which may well be an aspect of universal grammar. At any rate, it is certainly a principle operative in English and many other languages. This principle prevents the movement of elements by transformational rules out of phrases *that are the subjects of clauses,* although the same rules may apply to like phrases if these are not subjects. Observe that English has rules that move such words as *who, what, when, where, why,* and so on in both questions and relative clauses. These words are moved to the far left of a clause. The principle just noted, however, prevents such words from being moved out of subject phrases. Thus we can say things like *who did you see, who did you think you saw, who did Bill say you saw,* and so on, in each of which the word *who,* which is understood as the Patient of the verb *saw,* and would normally occur directly after it, is moved to the far left.

Now, EXTRAPOSITION is relevant to the principle that prevents movement of elements out of subject phrases simply because, as we have already observed, operation of EXTRAPOSITION takes an element that would otherwise show up as a subject and throws it to the end of a sentence, leaving an *it* behind in the subject position. The principle of grammar under discussion should thus predict that elements such as *who* can be moved out of a subject clause if it undergoes EXTRAPOSITION and is moved to the end of a sentence but should not be subject to such movement if EXTRAPOSITION is not applied. But this is correct. Notice that we can form sentences like *it is generally accepted that the president visited someone,* which are the extraposed versions of sentences like *that the president visited someone is generally accepted.* However, a question form with a moved *who* corresponds only to the sentence that has undergone EXTRAPOSITION. That is, we can say things like: *who is it generally accepted that the president visited,* where *who* moves out of the extraposed clause.

But we cannot say at all things like *who is that the president visited generally accepted*. Such examples are utterly unacceptable. The reason is that they violate the principle that precludes transformations from moving elements out of subject phrases. The importance of this principle is that it can be shown to control a wide variety of distinct rules in English, as well as other languages. Thus it is a reasonable candidate for the kind of deep underlying principle of grammar that does not need to be learned, but is rather part of innate human linguistic capacity. The role of such a principle in partly determining well-formed and non-well-formed sentences in English through its interaction with such particular rules of English as EXTRAPOSITION reveals that a human language cannot be regarded as a system that is either totally learned, or totally innate. Rather, it appears that all languages are a complex amalgam of innate principles and culturally institutionalized patterns. This shows that the study of individual grammars cannot proceed independently of the study of universal grammar, any more than the study of universal grammar can proceed independently of the investigation of the grammars of particular languages.

In summary, I have tried to suggest that each sentence in a natural language must be regarded as having a deep structure in addition to its traditionally studied and accepted surface structure. Deep structures are connected to surface structures by transformational rules that delete elements, rearrange elements, occasionally add elements, and so on. A grammar of a language must thus be regarded as having a binary structure, one set of rules to generate the set of deep structures, another set of transformational rules that determine the appropriate surface form for deep structures. The study of deep grammar is really only in its infancy and, as even the facts briefly discussed here may indicate, the idea we get from school grammar that the syntax of a language like English is already well known and well understood cannot stand up to serious scrutiny. The grammar of English, understood as the study of the finite system that defines the infinite linguistic knowledge of English speakers, remains largely unknown. Part of the reason for this, but only part, was illustrated in the discussion of the principle that prohibits transformational movement of elements out of subject phrases. That is, the study of English grammar is not at all separate from the study of the nature of grammar in general, and no full account of the principles of English grammar is possible without an understanding of the principles of universal grammar.

4 THE REALM OF MEANING

Jerrold J. Katz

Grammar encompasses three areas of linguistics: phonology, syntax, and semantics. Phonology concerns the pronunciation of sentences. Syntax concerns the way they are built up out of their constituents. Semantics concerns the literal meaning of sentences and their constituents.

For phonology and syntax, nothing more specific has to be said to indicate, at the outset, what subjects we are talking about. Theory construction has proceeded far enough in these areas, and has become familiar enough, at least in general terms, for us to have a fairly clear idea of the subjects. However, the uncontroversial characterization that semantics concerns meaning is uninformative. There are too many theories of meaning, each talking about something different, and none sufficiently articulate to make clear to which aspect of language it is addressed. So, instead of having a semantic theory to which we can appeal for clarification of the subject, we must seek clarification first in order to get a theory.

If semantics concerns meaning, its big question must be "What is meaning?" How do we go about trying to answer so big a question? In the past, linguists, psychologists, and philosophers have attempted to answer this question directly. We find, historically, a variety of direct answers, including Plato's answer that meanings are eternal archetypes, John Locke's answer that meanings are the mental ideas for which words stand as ex-

This work was supported by the National Institute of Mental Health, under Grant 5 PO1 MH 13390-07.

ternal signs, the answer that meanings are the things in the world to which words refer, Wittgenstein's answer that meaning is use, the behaviorist's answer that meanings are the stimuli that elicit verbal responses, the introspectionist's answer that meanings are mental images associated with verbal behavior, and so on. But every attempt to give a direct answer has failed. Some, such as the Platonic answer, proved too vague and speculative. Others gave the wrong answer.

For example, consider the doctrine that the meaning of a word is the thing to which it refers. Although it has the advantage of bringing meanings out into the open and making them no more mysterious than ordinary objects, persons, and places, it gives the wrong account of semantic relations like synonymy. This doctrine says that two expressions are synonymous if and only if they refer to the same thing(s), but, as Frege pointed out, two expressions, like "creature with a heart" and "creature with a kidney," refer to the same things without being the same in meaning. To take another example, the doctrine that the meaning of a word is the mental image that accompanies its use gives the wrong account of the distinction between meaningful and meaningless expressions. Words like "possibility," "randomness," "chance," "therefore," "ineffability," and so forth, are falsely predicted to be meaningless, whereas expressions like Lewis Carroll's "slithy toves" count as meaningful.

As an unfortunate result of the failure of such direct attempts, semantics has gained the undeserved reputation of being an irretrievably dreary discipline. However, it is not semantics that deserves this unsavory reputation, but rather the approaches to semantics that insist at the very outset on a direct answer so the question, "What is meaning?" Imagine what would have happened if astronomers had insisted on knowing what sorts of things planets are before trying to describe their movements. If mathematicians had insisted on a direct answer to the question, "What are numbers?" before they tried to explain arithmetic properties and relations like "is the sum of," "is the square root of," and "is a prime number," we would now be without arithmetic.

Therefore, I propose to adopt an approach that is just the opposite of the one followed in the past. I will try to answer the big question of semantics by *not* trying to answer it.

This is not as paradoxical as it sounds. Generally in science one begins an inquiry by breaking down big questions into little ones, which are more specific and thus more manageable, but which are still components of the big question. Such smaller, more modest questions tell us what properties and relations comprise our subject matter and so set guidelines for theory construction. They provide us with the necessary pretheoretic conception of our subject from which theory construction can begin.

Accordingly, we ought to try to break down "What is meaning?" into a number of smaller, more modest questions, the answer to each of which is a part of the answer to the big question. Proceeding in this way, we obtain the following sample of smaller questions about semantic properties and relations:

(1) What is the difference between meaningfulness and meaninglessness?
(2) What is sameness of meaning? What is the difference between synonymy and nonsynonymy?
(3) What is multiplicity of meaning or ambiguity?
(4) What is truth by virtue of meaning and what is falsehood by virtue of meaning?
(5) What is semantic redundancy?
(6) What is entailment by virtue of meaning?
(7) What is presupposition?
(8) What is superordination?
(9) What is incompatibility in meaning?
(10) What is a self-answered question?

The semantic properties and relations asked about in these questions may be illustrated by some examples. The contrast between meaningfulness and meaninglessness is seen in comparing "Open jars empty quickly" with "Waterproof shadows empty foolishly." The contrast between sameness and difference of meaning is seen in comparing the synonymous expressions "my sister" and "a female offspring of my parents other than myself" with the nonsynonymous expressions "my brother" and "a broken chair in my attic." Ambiguity is illustrated by the example, "I took the photo," which means, among other things, that the speaker photographed something and that he stole a photograph. "Uncles are male" is true by virtue of its meaning and "Aunts are male" is false by virtue of its meaning. Semantic redundancy is exhibited by the expression "naked nude." The sentence "Monarchs are anachronistic" entails the sentence "Kings are anachronistic": the inference from the former to the latter is justified by their meaning alone. The question asked by the interrogative "When did you stop beating your wife?" presupposes that the person addressed has been beating his wife but has stopped the practice. The superordination relation is exhibited by such pairs of words as "finger" and "thumb," "tree" and "oak," and "dwelling" and "cottage." The meanings of the words in the pairs "open" and "close," "whisper" and "shout," and "boy" and "girl" are incompatible. Finally, interrogatives like "Is breakfast a meal?" and "What is the color of a red car?" express self-answered questions in that they provide their own answers.

Taken together, these semantic properties and relations provide a reasonably good initial conception of the subject matter of semantics. They circumscribe an area of grammatical phenomena, beyond both phonology and syntax, for which a theory is needed, even though the properties and relations asked about in these questions represent only a sample of the full range of those with which semantics must ultimately deal. Semantic theory should explain the nature of these properties and relations, and any others to which its principles extend.

Thus, we will begin by trying to answer these smaller, more manageable questions. Once a theory has been built that successfully answers a reasonably large number of them, we may tackle the big question. Then we can base our answer to "What is meaning?" on what our theory had to assume about meaning in order to provide explanations for these semantic properties and relations. This approach is in the spirit of the one used in astronomy to discover the nature of the planets. Astronomers discovered that the planets are physical objects by first developing the theory that the movements of the planets obey familiar mechanical laws.

How do we frame a theory that will explain semantic properties and relations? Once again, I suggest that we take our cue from science.

Historians of science tell us that sciences begin with common sense reflection, then proceed by systematic reformulations to highly abstract theories. Some common sense reflections about language are: what makes an expression or sentence ambiguous is that it has more than one sense, what makes an expression or sentence meaningful is that it has a sense, what makes one meaningless is that it does not have a sense, what makes two expressions or sentences synonymous is that they have a sense in common, and what makes a modifier redundant is that its sense is already contained in the sense of the head with which it is in construction. To proceed from these common sense definitions to a theory that explains the nature of ambiguity, meaningfulness, synonymy, redundancy, and so forth, we must find some way to reconstruct formally such definitions within a theory of grammar.

Consider how the theory of grammar formalizes syntactic properties and relations. A generative grammar has a level of syntactic representation. At this level the organization of sentences is described by phrase markers, whose nonterminal portion represents the "positions" that morphemes, words, phrases, and clauses can occupy and whose terminal portion represents assignments of sentential constituents to such "positions." The common sense definition of the relation "x is the same part of speech as y," as understood in conventional school grammar, means that x and y can, in general, occupy the same positions in sentences. This common sense relation can be formally defined over the set of phrase markers by the following:

x is the same part of speech as y if, and only if, for any phrase markers M_i and M_j (not necessarily distinct) which represent the parsing of sentences in which x and y occur, x and y are dominated by nodes bearing the same major category label (for example, "Noun," "Verb," etc.) in M_i and M_j.

Notice two aspects of this formalization. First, since the phrase markers of a sentence represent that sentence's syntactic structure, the definition says that constituents belong to the same part-of-speech category by virtue of their syntactic form. Second, the defining condition is formal because the phrase markers to which it refers are formal. Accordingly, since an expression or sentence has a certain semantic property or bears a certain semantic relation to another by virtue of its meaning, we might reasonably try to give definitions of semantic properties and relations in terms of representations of meaning that, like phrase markers, are formal objects generated by the grammar.

So, the desire for formal reconstructions of common sense definitions of semantic properties and relations leads us to set up a level of semantic representation. At this level there will be formal objects whose structure can be utilized to define semantic properties and relations in the same way that the structure of phrase markers is used to define syntactic relations like "x is the same part of speech as y." That is to say, we are led to set up a semantic level of representation in order to replace *in*formal definitions like "x and y have a sense in common" by formal ones in the same way that informal definitions like "x and y occupy the same positions in sentences" are replaced by formal ones in the theory of syntax.

The initial step is to find some means of representing the senses of words formally. As a first guess, we might say that a particular sense of a morpheme or lexical item is represented by a single formal symbol, and that different senses of the same or other lexical item(s) are represented by distinct formal symbols. But this hypothesis is easily proven wrong. Semantically redundant expressions like "male boy," "female aunt," "unmarried bachelor," and so forth, show that we cannot take the sense of a lexical item to be an undifferentiated, monolithic whole, as is assumed by representing it with a single symbol. The proper generalization about these redundancies is that the whole sense of the modifier is included as part of the sense of its head. In order to express this generalization, we at least have to analyze the sense of such nouns as "boy," "aunt," and "bachelor" into the component that is identical to the sense of such a modifier and the component that is different. Therefore, the single symbols in semantic representations must stand for parts of senses, or as we shall say, for the *concepts* out of which senses are formed. If we carry this analysis to its logical conclusion, the semantic representations of senses, both of lexical

41

items and syntactically complex constituents, will consist of configurations of single symbols, each of which stands for an atomic concept. These single symbols will be referred to as *primitive semantic markers*. These symbols, together with representations of other concepts definable in terms of them, will be referred to as *semantic markers*.

We cannot set forth the primitive semantic markers of a natural language like English in the way that a logician sets forth the primitives of a formalized language. As Frege once observed, ". . . something logically simple is no more given us at the outset than most of the chemical elements are; it is reached only by means of scientific work." We hope eventually to reach the semantic simples of natural language, but that must be our goal, not our starting point. For the time being, we have to formalize the semantic representations of lexical items in terms of semantic markers, without making any assumption about their final status in semantic theory.

Accordingly, we might represent one sense of "bachelor" with the following configuration of semantic markers: "(Object)," "(Physical)," "(Human)," "(Adult)," "(Male)," and "(Never Married)." Semantic representations that take the form of strings of semantic markers are called *readings*. We distinguish between *lexical* and *derived* readings, depending on whether the reading is assigned to a lexical item or to a syntactically complex constituent. Each lexical item must be listed with an appropriate set of lexical readings.

How does the semantic component of a grammar assign derived readings to represent the senses of syntactically complex constituents? We not only want to represent the meaning of syntactic atoms like "boy," "a," "run," "the," "under," and "short," but also the meanings of syntactically complex expressions and sentences like "the short run of the short boy" and "the boy ran under a short boy," which the syntactic rules construct out of such atoms. Complex expressions, after all, exhibit the same range of semantic properties and relations as syntactic atoms. Here, however, we cannot simply list each expression and assign each a reading. Syntactic rules generate complex expressions, and hence sentences, by a process that can go on infinitely. That is to say, it is always possible, in principle, to continue a sentence, no matter how long it is already, and thereby form a longer one. For example, "I know a story that begins I know a story that begins. . . ." Since there is no longest expression or sentence, nor a most complex one, there is no possibility of listing cases one by one. A complete "dictionary of sentences" is impossible in principle.

But now we can avail ourselves of a traditional principle of semantics, namely, the principle of compositionality. This principle says that the meaning of a syntactically complex constituent, including sentences, is a compositional function of the meanings of its parts. Unless some such principle were part of the linguistic competence of the speakers of a language it would be impossible to explain how they are able, in principle, to produce or understand infinitely many sentences when the storage capacity of their brains is finite. If we assume such a principle to be part of their internalized competence, we can suppose that people store only the meanings of the finitely many lexical items of their language and that they obtain the meanings of the constructions containing these lexical items by using the compositional principle. Moreover, idioms, such as "shoot the breeze," "stir up trouble," "give hell to," and so forth, which are the only exceptions to compositionality, are exceptions that prove the rule, since unless the rest of the language were compositional, they could not be defined as special cases where the sense of the whole is not a function of the senses of its parts.

In order to obtain a representation of the meanings of sentences compositionally from the meanings of their smallest syntactic parts, we require both a *dictionary* and a *projection rule*. The dictionary lists each lexical item of the language and pairs each item with a set of lexical readings, the number of lexical readings reflecting the item's degree of ambiguity. The projection rule specifies how lexical readings for the syntactic atoms can be combined to form derived readings for a whole expression or sentence.

Two things are presupposed here. First, that the projection rule will receive an account of all of the constituents that make up a sentence, and, second, that it will be told the grammatical relations among these constituents. Clearly, the projection rule cannot get a representation of the meaning of a sentence from representations of the meanings of its constituents if it is not provided with a full enumeration of such constituents. And since the same constituents in different grammatical relations to one another can mean different things, as for instance in

John thought he had left Mary alone
Mary alone thought he had left John
Had he alone thought Mary left John

the projection rule must be provided with a full statement of such grammatical relations.

At this point we find a remarkable coincidence between what the semantic component demands and what the syntactic component supplies. For the phrase markers generated by the base rules of syntax—the phrase markers that represent deep syntactic structure—seem to supply exactly the information required by the projection rule. These phrase markers, called *underlying phrase markers*, specify all the constituents of a sentence and their grammatical relations. Therefore, by having the dictionary and the projection rule apply to the underlying phrase markers we satisfy both of the demands of the semantic component.

Thus, the process of forming and assigning semantic representations will work as follows: The underlying phrase marker(s) of a sentence will provide input to the semantic component of a grammar, which is composed of a dictionary and a projection rule. First, the dictionary will assign a set of lexical readings to each lexical item of the sentence by associating each terminal symbol of an underlying phrase marker with just those lexical readings from its dictionary entry that are compatible with its syntactic description in the phrase marker. Second, the projection rule will combine lexical readings, then combine the derived readings that result from such combinations, and so on, until a set of readings is associated with each constituent of the sentence, including the whole sentence itself. These combinations will be made only in case constituents are grammatically related. The type of combination is determined by the type of grammatical relation obtaining between the constituents whose readings are to be combined.

This process of combination must also weed out unacceptable

readings. If we count the number of senses of all the lexical items in an ordinary sentence of fifteen or twenty words and compute the total number of possible combinations that could be formed from them when they are paired up in accord with the grammatical relations of the sentence, the number of possible senses usually runs into the hundreds. Since no sentence of a natural language has anywhere near this many different senses, and some have none at all, a rather severe form of selection must be going on in the process of producing derived readings.

Some sentences have no sense, even though their individual words are meaningful, for example, "Shadows are waterproof." Such meaninglessness—the absence of any sense—is the limit of the same selectional process that must restrict ambiguity. To put the point another way: degree of ambiguity, from one sense (zero degree of ambiguity) to any number of senses less than the total possible on the basis of all available combinations of the lexical senses, is the case where the selectional process stops short of the limit. This indicates that our reconstruction of the selection process can be based on the same kind of semantic irregularities that produce meaningless sentences.

Here we can make use of some traditional philosophical ideas about meaninglessness. Since Aristotle, it has been recognized that concepts fall into categories, and that the category of a concept specifies the other concepts with which it can combine in order to assert something; the category of a concept specifies its range of predication. If, by virtue of the flexibility of syntax, a concept is combined with one outside its category, the sentence that puts them into combination will be conceptually absurd, or meaningless, as in the case of "waterproof shadows." Hence, to reconstruct such selection, we have to build this notion of category into our representations of lexical senses.

To say that something is waterproof means that water cannot pass through its surface to the inside. Since a surface is the exterior of a physical object, the concept of a physical object is the category of the concept waterproof. Thus, being waterproof can be attributed to physical objects like coats, cars, and cigarettes, but not to things like afterimages, reflections, and shadows, which are not in the category of physical objects. The category in which a thing must fall in order for a concept to be predicated of it will appear among the concepts in the definition of the word that refers to it. For example, the concept *physical object* appears among the concepts *physical object, artifact, outer garment, fits the upper part of the body* that define "coat." As we recall, the lexical reading of a word will contain a semantic marker to represent each atomic concept out of which its sense is formed. Therefore, it is natural to reconstruct the selectional feature that prevents "waterproof shadows" from receiving a sense by requiring that the nouns "waterproof" modifies have the semantic marker "(Physical Object)" in their reading in order that the reading of "waterproof" and the reading of its nominal head can combine to form a reading for the higher constituent of which the adjective and its nominal head are parts. This requirement can be stated as part of the lexical reading of "waterproof." Such requirements, called *selection restrictions,* are found in almost all lexical items.

Given such selection restrictions, therefore, the projection rule will produce only those derived readings that represent real senses of the constituents to which they are assigned. If we assume that the projection rule works from the syntactically minimal to the syntactically maximal constituents of a sentence, then the derived readings assigned to its constituents reflect its compositional senses. The result of the operation of the projection rule will be a pairing of a set of readings with each node of the phrase marker, where the readings in the set represent the senses of the constituent dominated by that node. Such pairings we call a *semantically interpreted phrase marker.*

We have considered the nature of semantic representation because we found that in order to formalize common sense definitions of semantic properties and relations we needed to refer to formal features of these representations. Consider now some examples of how common sense definitions are replaced by definitions stated in terms of formal features of semantic representations.

Let "C" be any constituent of a sentence, including the whole sentence, then:

C is semantically ambiguous in the sentence S just in case the set of readings assigned to C in the semantically interpreted underlying phrase marker for S has two or more members.

C is meaningful in the sentence S just in case the set of readings assigned to C in the semantically interpreted underlying phrase marker for S has at least one member.

C is meaningless in the sentence S just in case the set of readings assigned to C in the semantically interpreted underlying phrase marker for S is empty.

C in the sentence S is synonymous with C′ in the sentence S′ (not necessarily distinct from S) just in case the set of readings assigned to C and the set of readings assigned to C′ have a common member.

C is redundant in the sentence S just in case a reading of C in the semantically interpreted underlying phrase marker of S has been formed from a reading of a modifier c_1 and a reading of its head c_2 and the reading of c_1 contains only semantic markers that appear in the reading of c_2.

Formal definitions of other semantic properties and relations depend on constructing more revealing forms of semantic representation. Indeed, progress in semantics depends on the *mutual* development of semantic representations and of definitions of semantic properties and relations. We certainly cannot make progress in defining semantic properties and relations without developing deeper and more revealing representations of meaning, because such definitions are framed in terms of the formal structure of such representations. Nor can we have deeper and more revealing representations of meaning without further and more sophisticated definitions. The reason is simple. The formal makeup of a semantic representation has to be justified on the grounds that it reflects semantic structure, and such justification can come only from the intuitions of native speakers about the semantic structure of the words, phrases, clauses, and sentences for which semantic representations are given. Thus, the evidence for a semantic representation must take the form of a claim that such intuitions support the hypothesis that the semantic representation assigned to a linguistic construction correctly represents its semantic structure. But semantic intuitions always take the form of judgments that the construction has one or another semantic property or relation! So in order to tell whether such intuitions do support an hypothesis, we must know what predictions the semantic representation makes about the semantic properties and relations of the construction to which it is assigned, and whether they agree with the speakers' judgments about them. Because definitions of semantic properties and relations tell us what predictions the semantic representation makes about the construction, they provide an essential step in empirical justification, without which progress toward deeper and more revealing semantic representations is impossible.

How far such a mutual development of semantic representations (in grammars) and definitions of semantic properties and relations (in the theory of grammar) has to progress before we are in a position to seriously address ourselves to the big question "What is Meaning?" is anybody's guess at present. The only thing that is clear is that further development is necessary. Nonetheless, present research in semantics has succeeded in making contributions to theory of grammar, to the study of the relation between logic and language, to the philosophy of language, and to psycholinguistics. Perhaps, what this shows is that semantics may soon become a branch of the science of language (with interdisciplinary connections to related subjects) independent of philosophy and that the big question will come to occupy only those philosophers concerned with the foundations of this science, in much the same way that the question "What are numbers?" now occupies only philosophers concerned with the foundations of mathematics.

5 BIOLOGICAL ASPECTS OF LANGUAGE

Eric H. Lenneberg

The biological study of language is primarily concerned with the human brain. How does our brain make it possible for us to learn a language such as Turkish, English, or Russian? Is there something new or unique in man's brain? What is lacking in the brains of dogs or monkeys that keeps them from understanding any sentences in these natural languages? Research to answer these questions might take either of two directions: we might begin by surveying what is known about the human brain and then try to apply this knowledge to the study of language; or we might first study language thoroughly and then see whether the findings help us in understanding how the brain works. Both approaches have been found to be useful, often simultaneously. For instance, we might study patients who have something wrong with their brains and then see what effects disease has on language performance. In this example we start with a guess (usually supported by clinical evidence) of where the injury (lesion) is located. The next step in the logic of our argument might be to propose a mechanism of cerebral processes and to say how these processes have been disrupted by the disease. Thus, one might·tentatively say of a given case: "The injury destroyed fibers between the reception stations for vision and for audition (that is, for sight and sound); therefore auditory information (words) can no longer be associated with visual information (objects), and this, in turn, should make it impossible for the patient to learn any new words." This, then, would become our working hypothesis, and our research would be concerned with obtaining data that either support or disprove the hypothesis. The hypothesis makes assumptions of two kinds: about the mechanisms of the brain, and about the nature of language. Now we are ready to examine the patient. Is it true that he can no longer learn to name objects? Suppose we found that our patient does have trouble in telling us what the names of the objects are that we hold up to him; can we also discover just what the nature of the trouble is? Is there evidence that sight and sound can no longer come together? Or that earlier associations between specific visual and auditory patterns have now been disrupted—have been cut apart? In most cases, we will find that unless the patient has lost his power of clear thinking, he can still learn the names of the doctors in the hospital or learn the meaning of new words. His trouble is, for instance, that he either cannot say or cannot think of the word when he ought to, although he recognizes the word when he hears it. Further, his trouble is always of a general nature, that is, it is not restricted to just certain words. If he cannot name things readily, the difficulty extends to naming in general. Both of these discoveries argue against our first hypothesis, that the effect of the injury was simply to block the flow of information from visual to auditory centers. Now we might turn to the student of language for further help. One of the first things modern linguists will tell us is that the operation of language cannot be characterized as a process in which things are cemented together, but rather as an operation in which something is being computed, analyzed, figured out. Apart from the details, the linguist's information will help the student of the brain, in that he might now reformulate his working hypothesis in one way or another. In alternating between studies of the brain and studies of language, we hope to narrow the gap between our knowledge of the function of the brain and our knowledge of the function of language. By exploiting nature's abnormalities for research purposes, we hope to emerge with a unified theory of language. The importance of this work is clear: it is relevant to the treatment of people who can not speak, and it helps us to understand how man's brain is different from the brains of other animals.

One of the most outstanding features of man's brain is its

enormous size. We might ask, therefore, whether our ability to speak has anything to do with this aspect, the sheer volume of the brain or the large number of its cells. The answer appears to be *no*. There are human beings who have failed to grow and who, in consequence, have brains no larger than that of a chimpanzee. The particular condition that I have in mind is an inherited form of dwarfism—sometimes called bird-headed dwarfs. Many of these unfortunate people have perfect language. In fact, some are known to have spoken several foreign languages in addition to their native tongue. There are several famous dwarfs who stood no taller than two and a half feet (about 85 cm), with heads the size of a tiny baby's, who traveled all over the world to entertain royalty and presidents. Observations of this sort indicate that it is not the quantity of brain that is responsible for language but probably the quality, or, more correctly, the way in which the human brain functions.

It is useful to make a distinction between speech and language. Let us call *speech* the skills of making special noises, namely of shaping the muscles in and around the mouth and in the voice box in such a way as to produce speech sounds; and let us call *language* the capacity to understand what is being said and the capacity to construct sentences. Both speech and language are dependent on the existence of biological (or rather, physiological) mechanisms in the central nervous system. Either of these specialized mechanisms may be destroyed by disease, interfering selectively with one or the other skill. However, the two are not equally important for verbal communication. Language is much more basic than speech—there are many instances in which patients cannot speak but do continue to have language and are therefore not cut off from the rest of society. One of the most important discoveries of recent years has been that even children who have never been able to speak may nevertheless develop the capacity for language. I have studied a number of children who suffered some minor brain damage before or shortly after birth that interfered with their coordination for speech. Because of this they cannot make the normal babbling sounds of babyhood and never are able to say anything that can be understood. If these children grow up in an environment where they hear people talking to each other and, even more importantly, if they are spoken to frequently and normally, one can eventually show that they have acquired language without speaking it. To demonstrate this, one gives the child a number of commands, asking him to do things, using progressively more complex language. To be sure that the patient is really understanding the sentences, one must avoid all gestures and one must ask him to do things with objects around him (such as: "Pick up the pencil and put it in the big box"). Sentences such as "Wave bye-bye" or "Stick out your tongue" are not useful for our research. They might be responded to as a simple conditioned reflex, that is, the subject may have a small repertoire of fixed, unchangeable tricks; dogs have the ability to respond to such verbal commands though they can be shown to lack the ability to understand sentences such as "Pick up the stick and put it on the table." One may also ask the child to answer questions by simply nodding *yes* or *no*. Very often the language capacity of a child is not examined properly, and this may have disastrous consequences. Children who do not speak are often treated as if they were mentally retarded. However, if they *do* have the capacity for language, one might give them a different kind of education and thus dramatically change their outlook for a useful life.

The distinction between speech and language (and the relative unimportance of speech) is also illustrated by a study of children with cleft palates or children without tongues. Most of these patients have no trouble at all in learning language, even though they do not have the means for speaking. From illustrations of this sort, we see that man's capacity for verbal communication is primarily dependent upon the operation of his brain—not upon the outer mechanisms. Once this is understood, we become much more cautious in our claims about the language capacities of cats or chimpanzees. Suppose, for instance, we wanted to find out whether a monkey can acquire a form of human language. The primary question is not whether he can learn to *say* words like *mamma* or *cup*, but whether he can learn to *understand* simple sentences. The vocabulary may be kept quite small in such a test, say 25 words. But with these 25 words it is possible to form thousands of sentences, questions, or commands. Will the animal, after appropriate training, give evidence of understanding such a simplified language? Will he do the things he is asked to do verbally, that is in the form of sentences, or be able to nod *yes* or *no*? The answer to this question is not yet known.

To illustrate the extraordinary skills that small children have in the acquisition of language, we might briefly turn to language development in children born either deaf or blind. Naturally, a deaf child fails to acquire language at the usual age. Unless he gets special instruction he will, in fact, never learn language at all. In America there are two basic forms of education of the deaf. One is the so-called oral approach, in which attempts are made to teach the child to lip-read and to make sounds that are intelligible to the hearing population. The other approach uses sign language. Both forms of education rely heavily on the teaching of reading and writing. The remarkable thing is that despite the great handicap of deafness, all deaf children still acquire language with comparative ease and can subsequently communicate with the hearing world very effectively (usually by writing and reading). They differ from the monkeys in that they have a human brain, which is biologically set to deal with words and sentences in highly specific, human ways.

The same point is shown by a study of the blind. Children who cannot see still develop language, and at the same age as sighted children. In fact, after a careful study I have convinced myself that they have no special difficulty whatever, and that there are very few words that they ever misuse. This is particularly amazing because one may assume that the conceptual world of the blind is somewhat different from that of seeing people. Moreover, one would think that most of what we talk about refers to objects or conditions that we *see* or *have seen* at some time. Why is it that the blind child is not more confused about the meanings and significance of verbal communication?

This puzzle gets even deeper when we turn to children who are mentally retarded. These children are deficient in their intelligence, and there are many patients whose intellectual capacities do not seem much better than those of a chimpanzee.

Language deficits are very common among retardates; however, it is interesting that most of the patients have *some* beginnings of language, and that these beginnings are always the same as the normal first stages in the language development of healthy children. Their understanding is always better than their own speech production, and most of them understand simple sentences and can answer simple questions.

Thus our capacity for learning language is not due to special brain connections between sight and hearing; nor is it due to a simple increase in the size of the brain or in general intelligence. Something must be going on in our brain that is just lacking in the brains of other species. We do not yet know what this "something" is; but we can start asking questions by a careful analysis of the language process itself.

Let us examine a simple sentence like, "Put the shoe on the bed." Children of a year and a half can understand this, and so can feeble-minded individuals. But what does this understanding involve?

Let us assume for a moment that it is clear what is meant by the words *shoe* and *bed*. But what is meant by *put* and *on*? Suppose we had to construct a machine that would recognize patterns and objects; every time it encountered an object such as *shoe,* it would ring a bell. With a little imagination, we might conceive of mechanisms that could—at least in theory—accomplish the task. Let us now turn the machine into a robot or a mechanical model of a language-learning child. How would we program the machine to recognize *put* and *on*? The words do not refer to any tangible objects or concrete patterns but to complex sets of interrelationships *between* objects. Again, with imagination we can conceive of an apparatus that might solve tasks of this kind, but it also becomes clear that the machine is no longer simply responding to "what it sees." It must *operate* on what it sees—must perform a sequence of computations before it can decide whether a given event was or was not an example of *put* and of *on*. A machine that recognizes *put* and *on* in nature is more complicated than one that recognizes *shoe* and *bed*. However, the machine is not yet complicated enough to learn language; it must be able to cope with yet more abstract relationships. For instance, it must be sensitive to such differences as *shoe on bed* as against *bed on shoe.* Further, it must be able to recognize situations to which the sentence *You put the shoe on the bed* applies, but the sentence *He puts the shoe on the bed* does not apply.

So far we have been discussing the machine's capacities to make computations upon the physical world. Understanding sentences involves, further, the extraction of all the logical relationships that are implied by syntactic structures. For example, in most languages of the world there are special ways of signaling whether the elements *you, put, shoe, on, bed* constitute simply a declarative statement—the listener is simply informed of some fact—or imply a command or a question, calling for very different activities in the receiver. Thus these syntactic marking devices signal a further dimension of relationships, namely, the relationship between the speaker and the listener.

The important point of this discussion is that the subject matter of verbal communications is abstract relationships—nothing that can be directly observed. To detect these relationships, the brain must first operate on input, must make computations upon data. Understanding language involves two separate sets of computations, each one designed to extract a separate kind of relationship. It involves the extraction of relationships between objects and energies of the physical world; and it involves the extraction of relationships that are implied in sentences. Execution of a verbal command such as *Put the shoe on the bed* requires, further, that the two kinds of computations be matched appropriately.

All of these considerations have important implications for theories of the brain and its mechanisms for language. Let us look at what happens to language when certain parts of the brain are injured and how our knowledge of language helps us to interpret these disorders. Let us begin with patients who sustain injuries in adult life.

Curiously enough, it is only the left side of our brain that is involved with language. Further, we can point to special regions on the left side that affect language skills in special ways, whereas injuries in other regions leave language unaffected. Patients who have had a stroke may, for instance, be unable to get any word out although they still understand everything that is said to them; they can still read and sometimes even write with their left hand (the right side of their body is usually paralyzed in these cases). If one asks them questions they nod *yes* or *no* in reply, and by this means one can find out how they feel (or whether they know what they want to say). Some patients are less severely affected and can still formulate words, but it requires a great effort on their part and the words come slowly and belaboredly. This condition is caused by a lesion that is located in a spot called Broca's area after the neurologist who first described this brain-and-behavior relationship. Other injuries may cause the patient to produce an uncontrollable flow of speech—he appears to have difficulty in stopping his talk; however, what he says is not like a talkative person's discourse but is, for the most part, incomprehensible hash-talk; sometimes the first few words seem to be to the point but soon the utterance deteriorates to nothing but gibberish. These individuals usually also have difficulties in understanding what is said to them, and they appear unable either to read or to write sensibly. In rare instances a patient can still express himself (though with many oddities) but is totally unable to understand the spoken word (although he is not deaf), and sometimes patients have disproportionately greater difficulty with either reading or writing than with the other aspects of language. A still different kind of symptom (but an extremely common one) is an inability to think of the right word at the right moment. This may be so bad that the patient can virtually say nothing. He still understands everything, and if one supplies the word that he is obviously groping for at the moment, he immediately repeats it with ease.

When we look at the entire range of symptoms that occur in the clinic, we may discern certain general patterns and principles. The most important one is that the destruction of tissue does not cause the loss of selected language items. For instance, one cannot just lose certain words or certain rules of grammar but keep others. In fact, disease cannot abolish the knowledge of language, allowing the patient to be normal in every other respect. The most remarkable aspect of all language disorders, collectively called *aphasias,* is that language knowledge never disappears totally; only its normal function and its use are disarranged. The computational processes underlying language have gone haywire; the equilibrium and correct timing that existed between the processes are disturbed, resulting in a lack of coordination, or integration.

That aphasia is due to interference with ongoing processes rather than being due to the specific loss of certain learned items may also be seen from the fact that similar symptoms may be produced temporarily by drugs, by fever, or by electrical stimulation of the surface of the brain. All of this leads to an important conclusion. When a patient has an aphasia due to the destruction of tissues, he is not like a treasury or a file from which a few things have disappeared; rather, he is comparable to an electronic computer whose inner mechanisms have been partially destroyed so that its logic is altered, causing it to make mistakes in its computations. Therefore, we must not think that we can simply restore language to the aphasic patient by teaching him as one teaches a foreign language in school. Instead, one should see what kinds of skills are still relatively intact in the patient and try to use these skills, perhaps develop them, in such a way that they may substitute for the patient's language disorders, which can never be restored if they are due to fixed, permanent lesions.

The biological approach to language also concerns the discovery of how language skills develop in the growing child. Obviously the child cannot acquire language unless he grows up among people who speak to him and to each other. In that sense, language must be learned. But this is not the same as saying that language must be *taught*. Unless the child has the biological capacity to acquire language, the "teachers" of language are totally powerless. We still don't know how the child acquires language nor, in fact, how we could teach it. Most adults are competent speakers (that is, speak in such a way as to be judged native speakers of their mother tongue) without knowing how they do it. This is, of course, true of many other skills. As everyone knows, a healthy child begins to speak at a certain time of its development, and even though children speak different languages, the mode of onset is the same everywhere in the world. The onset of language is regulated by states of maturation in the brain. Between the ages of two and ten or twelve, our brain is in an optimal condition for acquiring language. This facility declines, and by the late teens something has occurred in the brain that makes it very difficult or impossible to acquire language if one hasn't learned to speak yet. Evidence for this comes from different sources. Take, for instance, feeble-minded children. In many of these children the rate of physical maturation is slowed down, due to different causes, and it is totally arrested in the middle teens. Consequently, the children start late with language and make only slow progress during childhood. Once their physical maturation stops, their language development also stops. Thus the patient goes through the rest of his life with just those language skills that developed before puberty. Such individuals can still learn new words or say things they have never said before. But whatever they do is done by the means at their disposal, that is, follows the simple and incomplete set of relational rules that they attained by the time of their adolescence, causing them to speak a sort of baby talk forever after. A similar picture is obtained by a systematic study of aphasia in childhood. In the adult brain, destruction of certain brain tissues causes language disorders that are irreversible, that is, that never improve again. However, a similar injury in children interferes with language for only a short time; soon language is re-established. Permanent aphasias first make their appearance only in young adults. There are many indications that suggest that the brain is not quite mature as long as language is learned with ease; but once it has matured, functions are locked into position, so to say, and no readjustment can take place after destruction. Mechanisms of this sort are well known in biology and are related to embryological histories of tissues. During development, tissues and cells become more and more specialized, and the same is true of the physiological functions these tissues serve. This is called differentiation. Undifferentiated tissues often have a capacity for readjustment, whereas the end of differentiation marks the loss of such plasticity. The readjustment process and the final fixing are known among embryologists as regulation and determination, respectively.

The association between language acquisition and man's natural history of maturation strongly suggests, also, that the capacity for language is indirectly connected to the action of genes. This is so because all maturational phenomena are under the control of genetic factors. This genetic control accounts for the fact that normal children all over the world go through the same sequence of developmental stages as they learn to talk, even though they may be acquiring very different languages. Support for this genetic hypothesis may be found in the many language disorders that run in families. Very careful studies have been made in many parts of the world in which it has been shown that quite specific language skills are inherited as Mendelian traits. The reference to genes, however, should not mislead anyone into thinking that environmental influences are unimportant. Genes merely dictate (and this, incidentally, in very roundabout ways) what is to be done with the building blocks provided by the environment. We speak to a child, but the child is programmed in such a way as to cause it to make a particular use of this treatment. It does not simply repeat, that is, mirror back what it receives; it does not imitate like a parrot. Rather, its brain analyzes the sentence it receives, abstracts the principles of formation, and then puts these principles to work, thus making sentences all its own.

You may have noticed that nothing has been said about the origin of language. From a biological point of view, the concept of "origins" does not make much sense. Biological phenomena always have a transformational history; they do not suddenly emerge from nothing, but must be regarded as transformations from some earlier form or function. In this picture of constant change, nothing has a clear-cut beginning or end. The impression of a "sudden" emergence of language in the course of human evolution is merely the consequence of a very incomplete historical record. There is still little agreement on what the biological antecedents of modern human language were. Some scientists believe that the types of communication that may be observed in contemporary animals are the ancestors of human verbal communication, but, so far, there is no direct evidence to support this view. My own theory is that language is intimately related to human forms of cognition and perception. This means that the history of human language can only be told in connection with the history of the human forms of knowing the world. The biologist, however, can contribute very little to this historical research.

6 THE BRAIN AND LANGUAGE

Norman Geschwind, M.D.

Experimental studies of animals permit us to investigate many aspects of the physiology of the nervous system, or of the effects of brain damage on behavior. This means of investigation fails, however, when we consider the problem of language in relation to the brain. As far as we know, no animal has language in the human sense, and indeed, even if forerunners of this ability exist, they must be very rudimentary. Our knowledge of the neurological bases of language has been derived overwhelmingly from the effects of disease on the brain of man.

The term "aphasia" is used to describe disorders of language resulting from damage to the brain. The aphasias are, unfortunately, very common disorders, and occur very frequently as the result of the disease of the blood vessels supplying the brain. There are literally millions of people throughout the world suffering from aphasia. Consequently, this disorder has great theoretical interest as the major source of knowledge of the brain mechanisms involved in language. It is also a great practical problem for which we have as yet no very satisfactory solution. Research in this area therefore has a double motivation: as we increase our knowledge of how the brain functions in language we may be able to devise more rational approaches to the treatment of these disorders.

As was the case with many other branches of science, the foundations of our knowledge of aphasia were established in the last half of the nineteenth century. The history of this field began in the early 1860s when a French physician named Paul Broca described a patient who had lost his faculty of speech, and whose brain became available after his death. Broca found destruction of an area in the lower and posterior part of the left frontal lobe of the brain. This area lies a short distance above and in front of the left ear. To this region, later named Broca's area, he ascribed the faculty of articulate speech. This discovery set off a tremendous wave of interest throughout the medical world, and disorders of speech became a major concern of the young field of clinical neurology. In the next few years Broca's discovery was confirmed repeatedly and important new observations were added. Broca himself pointed out that disorders of language seemed to result almost exclusively from damage to the left half of the brain. This discovery of the dominance of the left half of the brain for language also represents a distinctive feature of the human brain. In no other animal of the mammalian series has dominance been described. We will return later to a further discussion of cerebral dominance.

Students of aphasia pointed out early that aphasic patients were suffering from a language disorder and not from a loss of speech as the result of paralysis, since it could be readily observed that the organs of speech could be used adequately for other functions. These patients had instead lost the ability to use the speech organs for language. This dramatic discrepancy can be observed repeatedly in the clinic. A patient who will stumble over the attempt to answer even the simplest question may correctly sing the melody, but not the words, of a song.

By 1874 the simple view that aphasia was the result of damage to Broca's area could no longer account for all the data. Schmidt in Germany and Bastian in England had described disorders of the comprehension of language, but their neurological basis was not known. Furthermore, even in some cases with disorders in language output, damage had been found not in Broca's area in the left frontal lobe but rather in the left temporal lobe.

The situation was clarified in a remarkable paper published in 1874 entitled, "The Symptom-Complex of Aphasia." The author, Carl Wernicke, was only twenty-six years old and completely unknown. Wernicke's paper was a remarkable blending of clinical observation and anatomical facts, and was to set the major pattern of the study of aphasia over the next fifty years. He pointed out for the first time a major linguistic distinction between two different forms of aphasia which corresponded to differences in anatomical localization. Earlier observers had already noted, as I mentioned before, the presence of aphasia after damage to the left temporal lobe. Wernicke pointed out that in aphasia resulting from temporal damage the patient had fluent speech which was well articulated. Despite this the patient had a great deal of difficulty in finding words. We thus have a form of fluent, well-articulated speech, with the essential melody and grammatical structure being preserved, but with many failures to find words and therefore many circumlocutory phrases. The patient also shows many errors of two types. There are substitutions of sound, for example, "spoot" for "spoon," which are called literal or phonemic paraphasias. On the other hand he may substitute one word for another, for example, "fork" for "spoon," which is called a verbal paraphasia. In some instances the words are completely neologistic, that is, totally unrecognizable as being related to any word in the language, for example, "flieber" or "sodent."

This linguistic pattern, in which grammatical form is preserved and articulation is correct, was associated in Wernicke's cases with a severe deficit in writing and in the comprehension of spoken and written language. This aphasic syndrome is now called Wernicke's aphasia, and the affected region, in the posterior and superior portion of the temporal lobe, a bit behind and above the left ear, is called Wernicke's area. This syndrome stands in sharp contrast to Broca's aphasia, in which articulation is poor, speech is slow and effortful, and sentences are grossly ungrammatical. However, patients with Broca's aphasia are relatively much more capable of finding single substantive words. Thus the Wernicke's aphasic describing the weather may say, "It's like it was on the other one," from which one might deduce, if there were enough contextual information, that the patient meant that it was raining, just as it had been on another day recently. The Broca's aphasic may respond with "Weather—raining" and may fail to produce a full sentence even with the greatest urging. Even when the examiner says the full sentence the patient will often repeat it with omission of the small grammatical words. The Broca's aphasic will also show similar abnormalities in writing but will show good preservation of the comprehension of written and spoken language. Wernicke not only called attention to these linguistic differences in the spoken language, but also succeeded for the first time in making students of aphasia aware of the existence of forms of aphasia in which comprehension difficulty was prominent.

Wernicke carried his analysis further, however, in the attempt to understand how the brain was organized for language. He pointed out that Broca's area lay just in front of the area in which lay the representation of the mouth, tongue, and palate, that is, of the speech organs. It thus seemed reasonable that Broca's area could be considered a storehouse of the sequences of movements necessary for speech. In contemporary terminology one could say that Broca's area contained the programs for articulate language. Wernicke's area, by contrast, was located next to the cortical region in which lay the representation of hearing. Wernicke hypothesized that this area contained the representations of spoken words, that is, the rules by which the continuous flow of speech was divided into separate patterns. It thus followed that damage to this region would lead to difficulty in comprehension. Wernicke thought it reasonable that language originated in this region and was transmitted forward to Broca's area where it was, so to speak, recoded into patterns of movement of the articulatory muscles. It was thus reasonable that a disorder of spoken language would also result from damage to Wernicke's area. He argued further that people normally learned to read by translating written language into its spoken form. It followed that damage to this region would also lead to failure of comprehension of the written word.

Why did this paper, the first publication of a young unknown, have so great an impact? Wernicke had pointed out important clinical distinctions that were rapidly verified by other students of aphasia. He had linked these to localizations that were repeatedly confirmed by other investigators. These alone would have been major contributions. His work, however, had a further importance. He had provided a theoretical framework that could be experimentally tested. From the scheme outlined by Wernicke one could predict the existence of other kinds of aphasic disorder. On the other hand, one could predict the site of the brain damage in patients presenting clinical forms of aphasia that had never been seen before.

It should be remembered that many remarkable men devoted their attention to aphasia, and made important contributions. Wernicke was the only one, however, to present a theory capable of being tested for its ability to predict and explain new phenomena—a theory that has stood up to repeated testing for nearly a century. Over the forty years after this paper was published further syndromes were discovered, many of them remarkable because the disorders of language were so limited. In 1892 Dejerine, the great French neurologist, described the postmortem examination of the brain of a highly intelligent patient who had lost the ability to read, but who had normal visual functions for other activities and who could write and speak normally. The disorder was remarkably isolated. Although the patient could not understand written language he could copy the words he did not understand, thus proving that he could see the words correctly. In dramatic contrast he could read numbers without difficulty and could identify complicated objects. He could, for example, name a whole series of instruments in a scientific catalogue. When the patient died, Dejerine examined the brain. He found two areas of damage. The visual region of the left half of the brain had been destroyed. Hence visual information could reach only the right half of the brain. Since language capacities are not present on the right side, the printed word must be transferred to the speech regions in the left side of the brain. This transfer takes place over the corpus callosum, the large body of nerve fibers connecting the two hemispheres. Dejerine's patient had, however, a second area of damage in that small portion of the corpus callosum that connects the visual regions of the two halves of the brain. As a result of this combination of damaged areas the words seen on the right side of the brain could never reach the language areas. Many further cases of this type have been seen with the same findings in the brain. Wernicke's pupil, Liepmann, published the first report of the examination of the brain of a case of pure word-deafness, in which the patient speaks, reads, and writes normally, but fails to comprehend spoken language although he has normal hearing by the usual tests that do not employ language.

Perhaps the most remarkable prediction was that of Liepmann, who published in the early 1900s a case in which he predicted that extensive damage to the corpus callosum would be found, a prediction confirmed when the patient died several years later. Liepmann found from his examination that information could not be transmitted between the right and left hemispheres of the brain, although each half of the brain alone could function essentially normally. Liepmann correctly concluded that this meant damage to the corpus callosum, which, as we have already noted, is the main body of nerve fibers connecting the two hemispheres. He confirmed these findings in other cases, and by the beginning of the First World War several other investigators had also been able to describe similar cases, all proven by examination of the brain after death. The contributions of Dejerine and Liepmann had thus clearly established the importance of the corpus callosum in transmitting information between the hemispheres. Although these were two great and well-known figures, the information they and their followers had accumulated was almost forgotten. Animal experiments failed to find any effects of cutting the corpus callosum, which contributed to the loss of interest in this important work. Surgical cases in humans which confirmed the earlier clinical findings were published by Ford in 1937 and Maspes in 1948, but even these were overlooked. It was not until the 1950s, when Myers and Sperry published the first cases of positive experiments in animals, and 1961, when Geschwind and Kaplan reported the first modern case of human callosal disconnection, that interest again revived in this long-neglected area. It is remarkable that this important body of knowledge concerning the corpus callosum was almost completely forgotten for nearly half a century. The modern work I have mentioned has again confirmed the correctness of Liepmann's clinical and anatomical findings.

Another of Wernicke's pupils, Otfried Foerster, was a pioneer in the field of brain surgery and in particular in the treatment of epileptic seizures by removal of scars. In the course of these operations he gained important further information about language by stimulating different areas electrically. Dr. Wilder Penfield and his colleagues in Montreal have conducted the most detailed series of investigations of the speech areas by means of stimulation at operation.

Let us now discuss somewhat further the phenomenon of cerebral dominance. Long before the period of modern knowledge of the brain one aspect of dominance was well known, that is, the fact that the majority of humans are right-handed. When it was discovered that one half of the brain controls the motor functions of the opposite half of the body it became obvious that in some sense the left side of the brain was the dominant one for handedness. What was totally unexpected was the discovery that the left side of the brain was also dominant for speech in most people.

As we have already mentioned, among the mammals dominance appears to be confined to man. Let us specify somewhat more closely the absence of dominance in animals. It is true that monkeys will show a preference for the use of one hand. While about 93 percent of humans are right-handed, in monkeys right- and left-hand preferences are more or less equally frequent. Human right-handedness is, however, more than just preference for one hand. Hugo Liepmann discovered another very important fact which has not received adequate recognition. He brought evidence to show that the left hemisphere is the primary storehouse of patterns of learned movement. Clinical experience supports this strongly since the loss of patterns of learned movement follows certain types of damage to the left but not the right hemisphere. It is remarkable that two of the most important evolutionary acquisitions of man, that is, language and the use of tools, seem to depend on structures that are usually present on the left side of the brain.

Dominance is thus not merely a preference for one side of the brain. It also means that the learning of certain kinds of material is crucially dependent on one half of the brain. At this time there is no known case in which damage confined to one half of the brain of a monkey abolishes learning in any sphere. Thus a monkey does not appear to possess dominance in the human sense.

The beginnings of dominance are already present at birth. If a newborn infant is placed on his back he will turn his head to one side. As Gesell and Ames pointed out some years ago, approximately 95 percent of children will turn their heads to the right. They also showed that the direction of head-turning was closely related to the later development of hand preference. Although hand preference may become evident early in infancy the consistent use of one hand may not be clearly established until a few years later.

In adult life about 93 percent of people are right-handed. The remaining 7 percent are referred to as non-right-handers, which includes those who are more or less ambidextrous as well as the frankly left-handed. Women tend to be right-handed somewhat more frequently than men. Left-sided dominance is even more striking for speech than for handedness. Right-handers are almost invariably left-brained for speech. About 60 percent of left-handers are also left-brained for speech, while about 40 percent have right dominance. Thus about 96 percent of the population have left dominance for speech.

Until recently it was not possible to determine which half of the brain was dominant for speech until someone had suffered brain damage. In recent years it has become possible to determine speech dominance in people who have not suffered damage to the speech areas. Wada, now in Vancouver, devised a technique by which sodium amytal, which is a sedative drug, is injected into the main artery serving one half of the brain. This produces a temporary paralysis of that half of the brain. If speech is lost at the same time, it is clear that the injected hemisphere is dominant for language. This technique is of great value to brain surgeons in deciding on operative procedures, since they wish to avoid producing damage to the speech regions. Kimura has shown recently that in adults the right ear is usually superior to the left in perception of language. It should eventually be possible with further refinement of this important technique to determine speech dominance in the intact normal person.

In the adult significant damage to the speech regions on the left side usually leaves a permanent disorder of language. In children, however, there is frequently excellent recovery of language even after very extensive damage to these regions. This means that the right hemisphere is endowed with the potential of developing speech. However, it appears to take over language functions, with rare exceptions, only after damage to the left hemisphere in childhood. Why this capacity is lost in adult life has long remained one of the mysteries of the study of aphasia.

For many years it was believed that the left half of the brain was completely dominant, and that the right hemisphere was totally subordinate. So strong was this belief that the terms "left hemisphere" and "dominant hemisphere" have generally been used as synonyms. In recent years it has become clear that the right hemisphere is not subservient to the left for all functions. The right hemisphere is obviously dominant for certain abilities. De Renzi, Vignolo, and their colleagues in Milan have summarized these differences in a very simple formulation. While the left hemisphere appears to be involved in learning associations between stimuli, the right hemisphere appears to be better in elementary perceptual tasks. Thus the right hemisphere is superior in picking out small differences between complex stimuli, such as differences in faces, or fine gradations of color. It appears to have superior musical abilities, and to perform better in certain tasks requiring spatial perception. Another striking feature of the right hemisphere is its involvement in emotional behavior. Thus after damage to the left hemisphere patients are usually depressed. After damage to the right hemisphere patients often show a remarkable loss of emotional reactivity. In brief the right hemisphere appears to be more involved in perception, spatial sense, music, and emotional reactivity, while the left side is involved in language, complex patterns of movement, and generally in learning associations between stimuli.

What is at the basis of cerebral dominance? It is very often stated in the scientific literature that the two halves of the human brain are completely symmetrical. According to this commonly accepted view, cerebral dominance is based on some subtle physiological difference between the two halves of the brain. Although this view is widely accepted, more recent evidence suggests that it is not correct. My colleague, Dr. Walter Levitsky, and I decided a few years ago to reinvestigate the possible anatomical basis of cerebral dominance for speech. We found that several earlier authors had suggested that there were anatomical differences between the hemispheres. We followed up these leads and found that there were striking differences between the two halves of the brain. Wernicke's area, the speech region that lies in the upper and posterior portion of the temporal lobe, is considerably larger in most cases than the corresponding region on the right side, and this difference is readily visible to the naked eye. In only a small number of cases is the right side larger than the left. More recently, Dr. Wada of Vancouver, following up our work, has studied these anatomical regions in the brains of newborn infants. The anatomical differences between the right and left sides were found to be just as common as in adults. These data strongly support the view that speech dominance is determined by anatomical differences that are genetically determined. These anatomical differences do not mean that only the left side is capable of acquiring speech, but that, because of its larger size, it leads the opposite side.

The only definite anatomical difference between the hemispheres that can account for any aspect of dominance is the one we have just described. It seems very likely, however, that with further careful searching we may be able to find other anatomical asymmetries that may help to account for aspects of dominance.

The dominant side is the one that acquires language more rapidly, but since the other side has the potential it is not difficult to understand why after destruction of the left side the child can recover by use of the right half of the brain. Why then does the adult not recover by means of his nondominant side? It may be, of course, that this ability is permanently lost once maturity is reached. On the other hand, it is possible that this capacity is always retained, but is somehow suppressed. If this is the case, then we should be able to learn how to remove the suppression, and to free the nondominant hemisphere. This is a very hopeful possibility since it suggests that there may be a means to provide help to the many millions of people throughout the world who now suffer permanently from disorders of language as the result of brain disease.

Let me review briefly what we have covered. Although systems of communication exist in lower animals it is only man who possesses a system of communication that could deserve the name language in the full sense of that term. As a result, most of our knowledge of the relationship of language to the brain has been based on our study of the effects of localized damage to the human brain. A remarkable feature of the human brain is that language capacities are localized in the adult in only one half of the brain, most commonly the left side. We have discussed some of the aspects of this phenomenon of cerebral dominance.

Even within the left hemisphere the regions involved in speech make up only a small portion of the total area. There appear to be two major areas involved in language. One is Wernicke's area, which lies in the posterior and superior portion of the temporal lobe, adjacent to the cortical region for hearing. This area seems to be of focal importance for language, and is apparently involved in the recognition of the auditory patterns of language. Damage to this region produces a severe difficulty of comprehension of language in all its forms. This region is also involved in formulating the linguistic message which is then sent forward to Broca's area. Damage to Wernicke's area thus also produces a disorder of the output of language. The speech is fluent, well articulated, with a normal rhythm and melody, and with preservation of the basic grammatical structure, but with a marked tendency to incorrect word usage and circumlocution.

The second major language area is Broca's area which lies in front of the cortical representation of the muscles of speech and which seems to be involved in recoding the message received from Wernicke's area into its articulated form. It also seems to be involved in the grammatical structure of language. Damage here leads to speech that is poorly articulated, is produced slowly and with great effort, and is marked by loss of the small grammatical words and endings.

Beginning with these two areas, we can, on the basis of their anatomical connections, and of their connections with other brain areas, predict the occurrence of many other kinds of language disorder, including some that are limited to one sensory sphere or even to one half of the body.

Many subjects of great interest, such as the evolutionary changes in the brain which make possible the appearance of language in man, have been omitted, but I hope that I have at least made clear that a knowledge of the anatomical foundations of language is both of great importance to the student of language, and of potential value in providing clues for the relief of one of mankind's most distressing disorders.

7 SPEECH DEVELOPMENT AND BIRD SONG: ARE THERE ANY PARALLELS?

Peter Marler

Ever since Aesop, animals have served as a kind of mirror for man, although the reflections, such as they be, are usually viewed with some sense of condescension on our part. It is obvious to anyone who thinks even half seriously about the matter that man and the animals are fundamentally different, or so we are told. But two recent popular books that were high on the best-seller list in the United States for many weeks—Desmond Morris' *The Naked Ape* and Robert Ardrey's *The Territorial Imperative*—have raised a nagging question in the minds of many of their readers. These books renew the ancient plea that the chances of solving some of the questions that plague us about human behavior may be increased if we remind ourselves that man still has much in common with his animal ancestry. Some of our confusion about the position to take vis-à-vis our animal ancestors surely stems from uncertainty concerning the appropriate questions to ask about the causes of our own behavior. These authors argue persuasively that if we can only achieve a more thorough understanding of the rules that govern the behavior of animals, we may then be in a better position to develop more revealing hypotheses about ourselves.

But there are others who are still unconvinced of the relevance of animal studies to man, at least at the psychological level. At the level of cellular biology, and physiology, even that of the nervous system, we all accept the many parallels between animals and man, and much of the science of medicine is based on the assumption that studies on rats, dogs, and monkeys have a bearing on human medicine. But the same notion seems much harder to accept at the psychological level. We are tempted to think that the extent to which our behavior is shaped by cultural influences in general—and by language in particular —removes us so far from the condition in other organisms that any parallels are remote and essentially irrelevant to the understanding of the behavior of anyone more mature than a babe in arms. My own view is that animal studies are as relevant in the psychological realms as in physiology, in understanding the human condition. If this is not yet obvious, I believe it is because our understanding of animals is still so incomplete.

I am a biologist who has spent a good deal of time studying the behavior of birds. The results we have are not of any great direct human import, but I would like to present some of them within the framework of a comparison with our own language, to try to convince you that there are some parallels worthy of comment. Specifically, I want to suggest that the processes by which speech develops in children have several properties that are echoed in animals.

If one were looking for parallels with the process of human vocal learning, the most obvious place to look would be in our closest surviving relatives, the apes and monkeys. Surprisingly, no one has yet discovered a nonhuman primate with any facility for vocal imitation. It is true that several apes have been taught a few words of human speech. In a famous experiment conducted in the thirties two young psychologists took a baby chimpanzee into their home and raised it as a child. One of their primary aims was to teach this young female chimpanzee, Viki, to utter some words of human speech. After considerable labor they were successful. However, if you study the methods that were necessary to accomplish these few words, "mama," "papa," and "cup," it becomes clear that this was accomplished not by imitation in the usual sense but by gradual shaping of the separate movements of lips and jaw that produce the words. The labor and concentration involved, both for experimenter and for the subject, are on a quite different scale from the effortless mimicry of the human infant. Thus Viki's vocal accomplishments are interesting, but do not shed any light on the processes involved in speech development.

In searching for parallels, it is in fact necessary to go beyond other primates and, with the possible exception of dolphins, even beyond other mammals, to the birds, to find any facility for vocal imitation at all. We have been studying the processes involved, and I want to try to convince you that they have something in common with speech development. First, in both our own species and in certain birds, learning of young from adult plays a major role in the development of natural patterns of vocalizations. Second, in both cases dialects arise as a consequence of that learning. And third, there is in both a certain critical period of life during which the ability for vocal learning is at its maximum. I shall present evidence that we can see in both child and bird certain predispositions emerging during this critical period which have the effect of guiding the learning in certain directions. We can show that hearing plays a special role in both cases, not only to allow the young organism to hear sounds of adults of its species, but also in allowing it to hear its own voice, as a vital factor in normal development. There are early stages of vocal development, the so-called babbling of infants, and what we call subsong in birds, which have a number of properties in common which are probably not coincidental. There are reasons for supposing that the process of vocal imitation is in both cases essentially self-reinforcing, and is basically independent of any kind of reward by the parent. And finally, there is a remarkable parallel in the tendency for one side of the brain to assume dominant control of the sound-producing equipment, the larynx in man, the syrinx in birds.

Parrots and mynahbirds are commonly kept in homes because their ability to mimic sounds amuses their owners. Several investigators have been convinced that study of speech learning in mynahbirds might illuminate our understanding of human speech development. Some of the results are interesting but I am convinced that the inferences to be drawn from trying to teach birds human sounds are very limited. Would it not be more illuminating to find a species in which learning plays a key role in the normal vocal development and attempt to analyze the processes involved there, before attempting a comparison with ourselves? We have tried to do this with several species of wild birds, and I would like to summarize the results with just one of them, namely, the white-crowned sparrow, a small finch we studied in central California.

First a little natural history about the use of sounds by animals, and birds in particular, for social communication. If we record the sounds that a species uses in the course of its life cycle and analyze them by electronic methods, the sounds can be arranged in categories according to their physical structure. From such an analysis it is possible to estimate the size of the acoustical repertoire for a species. Although our knowledge is still very limited, some generalizations are beginning to emerge. The largest repertoires to be found among birds and mammals are considerably greater than those of frogs and fish and invertebrate animals. As far as one can tell there is no great difference between birds and mammals in this regard. For example, an estimate of the number of basic vocalizations in the adult repertoires of animals might reveal a range of from five to fourteen sounds in birds and from five to seventeen in various monkeys and apes. Actually such comparisons can be deceptive, since in some species the sounds are organized in discrete, nonoverlapping categories while in others the sounds grade into one another with a variety of subtle distinctions that probably have significance to the animals themselves. In such cases, it is difficult to derive a meaningful estimate of repertoire size by descriptive analysis alone.

However in most birds there is usually no difficulty in distinguishing between a variety of sounds or calls, in which the fundamental acoustical unit is short, and the song, in which sequences of sounds are given in a more or less highly organized pattern. The song is usually the prerogative of the male. It is often the loudest sound in the repertoire. As we shall see, learning plays little part in the development of calls, but is often very important in the development of the male song.

A consideration of the situations in which birds utter sounds may help in understanding why calls and song might differ in their development. As with other behavior so the sounds of birds are given in more or less well-defined contexts. Some are characteristic of a particular age. Some vocalizations are heard the year around while others are restricted to birds in breeding condition. For example, adult chaffinches in nonreproductive condition commonly use only two vocalizations, a flight call and a social call. These two calls evidently suffice for adequate organization of behavior in the winter flock.

In the spring the flock breaks up, males stake out territories, each is typically joined by a female, and they raise a brood. As the level of sex hormones in the circulation rises several new vocalizations enter the repertoire, especially that of the male.

Some of the new sounds that herald spring and the coming breeding season—such as the courtship and alarm calls—occur only in a particular situation, for example, the approach of the mate or the appearance of a predator. This is not true of the male song. Although it sometimes occurs in response to social stimulation, it more often seems to occur spontaneously.

The male song serves both to attract and retain a mate and to maintain the spacing of territorial males, both functions that require the male to broadcast evidence of his presence more or less continuously. By the same token, the male song serves for communication over long distances. In line with these functions, it is perhaps not surprising that in the breeding season of many bird species, the sound with the greatest volume and the highest frequency of utterance is the song of the male.

Now if we probe a little further into the different functions served by the song and some of the calls we can perhaps speculate about the rates of change that might be required in the course of evolution, if the functions are to be served efficiently. For example, we have found the alarm calls used by various woodland birds to be very similar, and this resemblance surely correlates with their frequent use in the interspecific communication of danger. There is little for neighbors to gain by evolving very different alarm calls if they are endangered by the same predators. Thus in the case of alarm calls efficient functioning requires only a minimum of specific divergence in the course of evolution. Quite the reverse is true of the male song. To attract a female white-crowned sparrow and to repel other male white-crowns it is important that there be no danger of confusion with the songs of other species. It is surely no accident that even close relatives usually have highly divergent song patterns.

When we reflect on the recent multiplication of the numbers of species of song birds, such that many species are to be heard in any given area, it becomes clear that the functions of song require a high rate of structural change in the course of evolution. This may be important to maintain separation not only from other species, but even from separate populations of the same species. With different rates of change required for different vocalizations within the repertoire, the stage is set for some radical innovation in the mechanisms of development. If there is a dominant role for learning in the development of the male song of some birds, this may perhaps be viewed as a response to this kind of evolutionary demand for rapid change.

We find that the song of the male white-crowned sparrow, which has a distinctive and elaborate acoustical pattern, is normally learned in nature. A male raised in social isolation from five days of age with no opportunity to hear other sparrows develops an abnormal song. To correct the sequence of development into normal channels, it is sufficient, under the same experimental conditions, to play recorded songs to the young male, about sixty songs a day for three weeks. He will subsequently develop normal song. Field study reveals that the learning generates local dialects in the songs, so that groups of birds only a few miles apart have song patterns that are in certain respects distinctively and consistently different from one another.

On exploring the nature of the learning processes involved, by varying the age at which the young male is exposed to recorded song, we find that there are certain constraints upon the time of life at which learning will take place, and constraints on what sounds will be learned. A period from ten to fifty days of age seems to be critical in learning a song pattern to which a male is exposed. Whether song develops normally or abnormally, further auditory experience has no further effect.

Another kind of constraint emerges if we present during this period recordings not of one sound but of two, his own specific song and the song of another species. Under these conditions he learns his own and rejects the other. If he is exposed only to alien song during this period, it is again rejected and song develops as in an isolated bird. With another kind of approach, we find that the ability of the bird to hear itself has a special role. There is normally a delay of several months between learning and singing. If we deafen the bird during this interval, he subsequently develops a highly abnormal song. Thus he has to be able to hear himself if he is to translate what is learned into the motor pattern of song. If on the other hand the deafening is postponed until song development is complete, then it has little or no effect on the motor pattern. Here and elsewhere, I hope that you already perceive some distant but intriguing parallels with human speech development.

I am also trying to make another point: that if we had set out to try to teach sparrows human speech, or to teach children bird song for that matter, the results would have been negative. This would have of course told us something, but something, in my opinion, of limited value. As it is, we have made some progress in understanding how learning plays a part in vocal development in this species and we find it makes sense in terms of the general biology of the species. This may in turn serve to remind us that human language too is a biological phenomenon that must have an evolutionary history.

Let me just run quickly over some of these parallels between avian and human vocal development again. In both speech development and song development, a certain kind of acoustical stimulation plays an unexpectedly large role in determining the future structure of the behavior. I have mentioned the critical periods of life when the ability for the particular kind of learning involved is at its height. Especially interesting are the predispositions that are brought to the task of vocal learning.

In the sparrows these play a prominent role in determining the course that development will take. And if we think back to the environmental situation in which learning occurs, it becomes clear that such predispositions are very important if the learning process is not to lead to the incorporation into the repertoire of biologically inappropriate sounds. In the habitat in which these sparrows are common, one can stand by the nest, and as often as not the closest singing bird will be a member of another species, namely, the song sparrow. A male white-crowned sparrow who had learned the song sparrow song would be a social misfit. At best, he might waste a great deal of time before finding a deaf female white-crowned sparrow for a mate; at worst he might have to make do with a female song sparrow and run the risk of infertile offspring. Viewed in this light, it seems natural, indeed almost inevitable, that a species would evolve constraints on the learning process. We are prone to forget that the very openness that learning brings with it can lead to biological hazards as well as advantages.

Predispositions for learning human language have frequently been invoked to explain the course of speech development in children (see Chapter 10). It is surely no accident that children learn speech rather than the multitude of other sounds that impinge on them. Predispositions to develop certain kinds of deep grammatical structure in language have also been postulated.

Hearing one's own voice plays a double role in vocal communication. It is important both for the development of vocal communication in the young and also for the monitoring and maintenance of vocal behavior in the adult. We have considered the importance of hearing in development. What about the *other* kind of role for audition? In both birds and man, the reliance on auditory feedback, so critical for normal development, becomes to some extent redundant as vocal development is completed. A man deafened after speech has developed maintains much of the basic structure unchanged in spite of the slurring of consonants, the monotonous tone and the sudden changes of volume.

With regard to the nature of the learning process involved, there are psychologists who seem to believe that learning occurs only as a result of having been rewarded, that is to say, only when the behavior being learned is reinforced, perhaps by food, or social stimulation. In the case we are considering here, the white-crowned sparrow, there seems no need to invoke extrinsic reward to explain song learning occurring within a soundproof box, in which the playback of sounds bears no contingent relation with food, water, or social stimulation. I gather that some students of speech development feel that the act of matching vocalization with sounds heard may also have some intrinsic reinforcing properties for children, in addition to any direct rewarding that may occur.

As a final point, the structure of subsong, which is a series of acoustical transformations appearing in the sparrow before the development of song, is in some ways reminiscent of the babbling stage of speech development. It may represent a phase in which the organism is acquiring skills in matching vocal output to learned sounds by auditory feedback, in a sense, then, learning to use the vocal equipment. Perhaps something very similar occurs in both species.

I am obviously in danger of pressing these parallels too far. The point nevertheless is a relatively simple one, that any species whose biology depends in any fundamental way upon a series of complex learning processes can ill afford to leave to chance the direction in which learning will take place. The capacity for learning can be as biologically harmful as it can be advantageous, in the wrong circumstances. Human language is the pedestal on which much of our biology is based, and just as it makes sense that song learning would be guided by a set of well-defined constraints, it seems to me almost inevitable that the same would be true of human language, with constraints in time, and constraints on what will be learned, and perhaps even special predispositions to guide the abstraction of syntax from what the child hears. In this sense then I suggest that comparative study of song development in a bird and of speech development in a child can be illuminating. It is not that it tells us anything specific about how speech develops. The two organisms are so distantly related that the chances of detailed parallels would be very slim indeed. But it should at least prepare us for the possibility that the child approaching the task of speech acquisition is in no sense a blank slate, a tabula rasa, and probably could not develop language if it were.

Although avian and human anatomy are different in so many ways, there may even be some parallels in the organization of nervous control of the sound-producing organs. It is well known that there is functional asymmetry in the brain mechanisms that control human speech. Each person has a dominant hemisphere and damage to that side of the brain has much more drastic effects upon speech than damage to the other side.

My colleague Dr. Fernando Nottebohm has found what may be a remarkable parallel in birds. Although the syrinx of a chaffinch is symmetrical as far as one can see, with nerves coming to it from both sides of the brain, the effects of severing these nerves on the right and left side are strikingly different. A male chaffinch in full song who is subjected to this minor operation on the right side either suffers no change in his song or two or three of the simplest acoustical elements are lost. The rest of the song remains intact. The same operation on the left side, however, has more drastic effects. One of two things may happen. The majority of the elements of the song may be lost, so that when the male sings, their place in the song sequence is now vacant while a few others remain intact. As an alternative consequence all components of the song may become highly modified so that in the place of tuneful, structured notes there are short bursts of noise or other very simple sounds. Once lost, the capacity for normal singing is not regained.

If, instead of performing this operation on an adult bird already in full song, we do the same thing with a young male who has not yet come into full song the result is very different. Dr. Nottebohm finds that such a bird can develop a complete pattern of song with the nerves on the left side cut. In fact it can develop song quite normally as long as one or the other side remains intact.

As you are perhaps aware, this is another curious reminder of the human condition, for if damage to the dominant hemisphere of a child's brain occurs early in life, the hemisphere that is not usually dominant is still capable of sustaining normal speech. Nottebohm's discovery does not of course convince us in any way that birds have language. The phenomenom of neural lateralization may again be an adaptive characteristic with more general significance than we usually acknowledge. If a structure in the midline, such as the larynx or the syrinx, is required to make the very subtle and complex behavioral adjustments that vocal learning must involve, it may be difficult to accomplish with symmetrical nerves from two sides of the brain each vying for control. It may well be more efficient for the dominance of one side to be fore-ordained, to take a leading role in control of sound production, while the other side takes a subordinate role. It is not inconceivable that we will find other organ systems in the midline, whose function requires complex neural control, in which lateralization of physiological control has occurred.

This then is the point, as I see it, of comparisons such as these between the behavior and underlying physiology of a pattern of human behavior, and the analogous processes and structures in an animal. We are quite naturally and intensely preoccupied with those traits that are unique to us as a species. However, it is very easy to confuse those that are truly unique with those that exist in animals but have yet to be described. By drawing attention to these many parallels between speech development and song development, we establish the point that the development of our language almost certainly takes place within a well-defined biological framework—it would be very surprising if it were not so. Within that framework, learning has a great deal of freedom in modifying our behavior. But there must be limits to the extent of modifiability, and I entertain the hope that our understanding of those limits of modifiability, whether in our speech or in our social behavior, may be improved by a careful study of similar processes in our animal relatives.

8 PRIMATE COMMUNICATION

Stuart A. Altmann

Let us suppose for the moment that we are in a grove of acacia trees on the savannahs of East Africa. In the trees above our heads there is a group of the common African green monkey, sometimes called the vervet. Suddenly, a martial eagle swoops down on the vervets. The first vervet that sees the approaching eagle gives an alarm bark. At the sound of this vocalization all the vervet monkeys suddenly drop from the branches of the trees to the dense undergrowth, where they are safe from the attack of the eagle.

Here is a vocalization given by one member of a social group that is heard and responded to by other members of his group. Such vocalizations are obviously used for communication. But can we call this kind of communication a "language"?

On these same savannahs of East Africa, baboons, which are large, ground-living monkeys, are fairly abundant. At night, these animals sleep either in trees or on cliff faces. The small infant baboon sleeps huddled against its mother.

As the infant becomes older, however, the mother becomes progressively more reluctant to allow the infant to sleep next to her. This rejection by the mother seems to be a traumatic situation for the infant, and in the evening, as a group of baboons approaches their sleeping trees, the repeated cooing and screeching of a rejected infant can be heard. Sometimes the infant's calling is successful and the mother allows the infant to sleep next to her.

As a final example, in the rain forest of Central and South America there is a monkey, called the howler monkey, that produces one of the loudest sounds in the animal kingdom. When two groups of howler monkeys come together, the calling of the adult males between the two groups can be heard for a great distance. The males do not wait for the appearance of another group before giving their call, however. They howl each morning at about sunrise and at other times of the day as well, even though no other group of howler monkeys is visible through the dense foliage. This howling vocalization seems to serve as a proclamation of an occupied territory and each group tends to avoid those areas from which the howls of other males come.

Each species of monkey or ape has a small repertoire of such socially significant vocalizations. For example, the green monkey and the howler monkey each have about twenty distinct calls in their repertoire. And each of these vocalizations generally elicits a distinct response in the other members of the social group.

Should we refer to such systems of vocalizations as languages? One's immediate response to this question is *no*—that only people have the ability to use language, to speak. But if we ask ourselves what it is that distinguishes the speech of humans from the kinds of vocalizations that we have heard in these monkeys, the answer is not a simple one. Thus, one reason for looking closely at the communication systems of other animals is that we may sharpen our ideas of what is unique about human language.

Man is a primate; that is, he belongs to the group of animals that includes the monkeys, the apes, and the prosimians. And so, for evolutionary reasons this group of animals is of particular importance for comparisons with man: we share a common heritage with the nonhuman primates and for that reason they bear many similarities to us in the chemical composition of their bodies, their anatomy, their behavior, and so forth. Perhaps they have inherited systems of social signaling that are similar to our language. Thus another reason for studying the communication of nonhuman primates is that we may learn something about the evolution of man's ability to speak.

In addition, these primate signaling systems are interesting in their own right. These animals live in complex social groups. The coordination of group activities depends upon the ability of the animals in the group to communicate with each other. We therefore have an unusual opportunity to study the relationship between the social behavior of individuals and the kind of social system that they live in.

Unfortunately for the sake of such comparisons, the study of behavior and social communication in nonhuman primates is in its infancy. More time and effort have been devoted to the study of any of a number of human languages, such as Navaho, than have been spent on all the rest of the primate species put together. Only within the last few years have there been any concerted attempts to understand the social signals of these animals. Nevertheless, from what is now known about communication in the monkeys and apes, we can make some interesting comparisons with our own language.

We have already said that many nonhuman primates are able to communicate by means of vocalizations and that these vocalizations may trigger responses in other members of their group. In this respect, their vocal communication is like human speech. In addition, these animals, like man, communicate by various nonvocal signals, including visual signals such as gestures, postures, and facial expressions, by various odors emitted by scent glands, and so forth. As with human speech, most of the social communication of nonhuman primates is specialized, in that this signaling behavior serves no function other than social communication.

A classical way of distinguishing human speech from the communication of other animals is to say that man uses symbols. But exactly what does it mean to say that we use symbols? Or to put it the other way around, if there were an animal that could use symbols, how would we know it?

Unfortunately the term "symbol" is too ambiguous to be very useful here: it has come to mean too many different things to different people. But certainly, a central property of what most people mean when they talk about symbols is to say that there is some kind of fixed association between the symbol and some object or event in the real world. Such messages are called "semantic messages" and in some sense a semantic message stands for the object or event.

There are examples of semantic messages in the social signals of nonhuman primates. For example, the alarm calls of vervet monkeys are semantic, in that a vervet monkey gives essentially the same response to the sound of the alarm call as it gives to the sight of an approaching eagle: in both cases, the animal drops from the branches of the tree into the undergrowth.

For the most part, however, the social signals of monkeys and apes are not semantic: the messages do not stand for something else. They are simply social signals to which a response is given. In this they are much more like the cry of a newborn infant than they are like the speech of human adults.

A striking characteristic of human speech is that we often talk about things that are not immediately present. We may talk about events that occurred in a different place or at some remote period in time. This characteristic of human speech—that these semantic messages are often markedly displaced in time or space from whatever objects or events they stand for—is an extremely important property. It gives us the flexibility of discussing things that are not present at the moment. We can therefore readily discuss past events and use our experience with such past events to plan for the future. For example, if you want to talk about whether or not to buy a cow, you do not need to have a cow in front of you in order to use the word "cow." Similarly, the person to whom you are talking does not need to have a cow there in order to understand what you mean by that word. Nonhuman primates seem to have a much more limited capacity to displace their semantic messages in time or space from whatever the messages stand for. These animals are much more tied to their immediate sensory environment.

Perhaps the most important characteristic of human speech is that it enables us to communicate about everything, even if we must create new words or sentences to do so. We have names for all the things that are familiar to us and if we encounter something new we can make up a new name for it. In fact, hundreds of new words are introduced into our language every year. Similarly, we can make up whatever sentences we need in order to say what we mean. We are not limited to those sentences with which we are already familiar.

This ability to generate new sentences grows out of the

process by which each human child learns to speak during the first few years of its life. The child does not simply memorize a number of sentences that are then used at the appropriate time or place. Rather, the child somehow acquires the ability to combine the various words in its vocabulary into meaningful sentences. Some of these sentences may never before have been used by anyone, yet they can be understood.

This remarkable ability to produce countless new words and new sentences, and to use this ability to talk about anything, is not present in the social signaling of any nonhuman primate. Of course, new vocalizations must evolve within primate societies from time to time. There is no other way to account for the present diversity in vocalizations that we find in species of monkeys and apes. But each such change probably involves a considerable change in the genetics of the population. The evolution of such primate vocalizations is therefore limited by the rate at which such genetic changes can take place.

Human language is not subject to any such restriction. Our ability to make up or learn new words and to transmit these new words to other members of our society means that human language can evolve independently of any further genetic changes. The same is true of our ability to produce countless new sentences.

Each of us was born with the ability to learn a language—not just the particular language of our parents but any language spoken by any human beings. If, for example, an Indian child were raised in a Spanish-speaking family he would grow up speaking Spanish. Thus, each human child is born with the potential for becoming a speaker and understander of any human language despite great differences in the vocabularies and the grammars of languages. But the monkey infant has no such flexibility. An infant monkey that is raised with monkeys of another and very different species still gives for the most part just those social signals that are characteristic of its own species, though it may come to understand those of the species with which it lives. This would seem to indicate that monkeys, at least, have much more flexibility at understanding foreign social signals than they do at using them. As is often the case with human behavior, recognition is easier than recall and reproduction.

We have indicated that human languages are universal, in that we can speak about anything, and that this universality depends upon our ability to coin endless new words and to generate new sentences apparently without limit, so that no matter what new situation arises we are able to talk about it. If the universality of our language depends upon language being constantly open to the introduction of new words and new sentences, and if this universality is lacking in the social signaling systems of monkeys and apes, then it might be worth looking carefully at those characteristics of man that enable him to have an open signaling system.

The ability of a child to learn a large number of words, even words that are newly introduced into the vocabulary, requires a good memory. Undoubtedly the evolution of language went hand-in-hand with the evolution of man's learning capacity. The number of words in any human's vocabulary is immensely larger than the number of vocalizations or other social signals in the repertoire of any monkey or ape. Even so, a new word can always be introduced into our vocabulary.

By what trick are we able to generate an endless string of new sentences? When we speak, we string together a number of sounds into a word and then a number of words into a sentence. The sounds that make up a word have no meaning of their own, but they are essential in enabling us to distinguish one word from another. For example, the English words "pan" and "ban" have very different meanings, yet they differ structurally only in that one begins with the sound that we represent with the letter "p" and the other begins with the sound that we represent with the letter "b." But these sounds by themselves have no meaning. We recombine a fairly small number of basic sound units, called "phonemes," into a very large number of words or word stems, which linguists call "morphemes." Similarly, we string words together in different ways to form different sentences.

Of course, not every string of words forms a meaningful statement. This is to say that our language has a certain grammatical structure or syntax to it. Even with this restriction, however, our sentences are sufficiently long that the number of meaningful word combinations that are available to us is probably so large as to be inexhaustible during our lifetime. If, in addition, we recognize that there is no upper limit to sentence length, then we can generate an indefinitely large number of meaningful sentences.

In recent years there have been some attempts to see whether or not a monkey or an ape could learn a set of arbitrary signals like those of human language and could acquire the ability to recombine these in ways that were new to the primate and that were still meaningful. In Chapter 9 Edward Klima and Ursula Bellugi describe some attempts at doing this with chimpanzees. The chimpanzee, like many other animals, has some ability to learn arbitrary social signals. There is now some evidence that a chimpanzee can be taught to understand combinations of such social signals. Under the right conditions it may spontaneously generate new, meaningful combinations and may thereby communicate in novel ways. These are the rudiments of a form of communication that resembles human speech.

Such natural abilities of chimpanzees might have been intensified through natural selection to the point where chimpanzees would now speak. But in fact, they do not: there is no evidence from recent field studies of chimpanzees that these animals make much use of these latent abilities. This raises an interesting question about the evolution of man. What conditions were present in the evolution of early man that selected for the ability to communicate by means of the unique signaling system that we call "language"? For that question we still have no good answer.

So much, then, for our comparison of primate signaling systems with human language. In what follows we shall look briefly into some of the ways in which these primate signaling systems adapt these remarkable animals to the environment in which they live.

The more one looks at the social displays of primates, the more one is impressed with the adaptive significance of these social signals. Recall, for instance, the vocalization of the howler monkey that we mentioned at the beginning of this chapter. It is no accident that this vocalization—which is apparently a proclamation of occupied territory—is of low pitch. The physics of sound is such that very low-pitched vocalizations are not reflected or absorbed unless they encounter very large objects. Such sound waves flow around things and consequently they will penetrate deeply through the trees. In a dense tropical forest, where long-range communication by visual display is often impossible because of intervening foliage, such deep-pitched vocalizations are highly adapted to the difficulties of communication between distant groups. Thus the structure of some primate social signals is adapted to special physical characteristics of the environment.

These low-pitched vocalizations are of great importance in the lives of howler monkeys and thus there has been strong selection for those adult males that were best able to give such deep vocalizations. This selection has led to extensive evolutionary changes in the entire anatomy of the voice apparatus in these primates.

Now let us go back to the vervet monkeys. We mentioned the response of these animals to an eagle, but the same animals give very different calls when approached by a ground-living predator, such as a leopard. When vervets hear this second type of alarm call, they go higher into the trees and are thereby safe from a predator approaching on the ground.

We have, therefore, two distinct alarm calls in these monkeys. The first is given to a predator approaching through the air, and the response of the vervet monkeys is to drop from the trees into the undergrowth. The other alarm call is given when a predator approaches on the ground, and the response of the monkeys is to scamper high into the trees.

It is obviously important that the monkeys never confuse these two vocalizations. In fact, when we listen to them, it is apparent that these two vocalizations are very different from each other. This is no coincidence. There would be strong selection against any variation in either of these vocalizations that resulted in its being responded to as if it were any other vocalization. In other words, the distinctiveness of primate social signals is the end product of natural selection against ambiguous intermediate signals.

In the social life of monkeys and apes, each individual has a unique role in the social organization, and each individual is recognized and responded to differently by other members of the social group. This is not the case with all animals, however. For example, in a hive of bees, there is no indication of individual recognition, and each worker bee is responded to on the basis of its behavior.

In order for one monkey or ape to recognize another, there must be some cues that can be used for such recognition. These cues may be essentially permanent, like postures, ways of walking, facial patterns, and so forth. Other recognition cues may be part of transient social signals.

In a group of human mothers, each mother can distinguish or recognize the cry of her particular infant. It may be that the monkey mother can do the same. If so, then there would be selection for sufficient variability that each infant has a distinctive and recognizable cry. On the other hand, the cries of infants must not become so variable that they are confused with other kinds of calls. Here, as in so many other situations, evolution is the result of a balance between several selective factors.

Individual recognition is important, not only in the relations between mother and infant, but also in dominance hierarchies. In a group of macaque monkeys, for example, the males differ in their social status. Males of higher status have priority of access to receptive females, to shade trees, to food, and other natural resources.

Another advantage of high dominance status is that a high-ranking adult male can communicate with much greater efficiency. Other members of the group are unusually responsive to what such a male does, and even a mild threat from such a male can be very effective. Thus, one of the great advantages of high dominance status in a group of monkeys or apes is that it conveys an efficiency of communication that enables these dominant individuals to accomplish the same results with far less expenditure of energy.

It would be very wasteful of time and energy if each male had to reassert his status at each new encounter with another male. In fact, macaque monkeys have signals of social status. For example, the dominant rhesus male of a group characteristically walks about with his tail held upwards, in an S-shaped curve.

We have described a variety of different social vocalizations in vervets, baboons, and macaque monkeys. These species are members of a large ensemble of closely related monkeys that are found throughout much of Africa and Asia. If one looks closely at the social signals of old-world monkeys, it is surprising how similar these behavior patterns are from one species to another. Although some monkeys have peculiar behavior patterns that are characteristic of the species, most of the behavior patterns in each species are part of a repertoire of behavior patterns that is common to all of them.

Yet despite this great similarity in basic social signals, there are striking differences in social organization. Even within a single, closely related group of species, such as the African baboons, social systems may be markedly different. For example, the yellow baboons of the African savannahs live in groups that contain several males, several females, and their offspring. These are essentially permanent groups, and most individuals spend their entire lives in the group in which they were born. In contrast, the Hamadryas baboons of Ethiopia live in groups that characteristically contain a single adult male and his harem of associated females. Whereas a female in a group of yellow baboons may mate with any of a number of adult males in her group, a female Hamadryas baboon mates only with her one male "overlord."

The Hamadryas baboon harem is maintained in a curious way. The young female Hamadryas is adopted by a male, who threatens or attacks her whenever she shows any sign of leaving him. Gradually, the female comes to respond appropriately to these threats of the male. That is, she responds to the threat of her male overlord by approaching him, rather than running away from him. This is exactly the opposite of the response given by a female yellow baboon, who flees from the threat or attack of an adult male. In both species, however, the basic patterns of threat and attack are essentially the same.

We have, then, the curious fact that the social systems of old-world monkeys differ more than do the patterns of signaling behavior upon which the social systems are based. In these primates it appears that evolution of social behavior has been not so much an evolution of the basic signaling patterns as it has been an evolution of the uses to which these patterns were put.

9 TEACHING APES TO COMMUNICATE

Edward S. Klima and Ursula Bellugi

Over the past few years, many interesting facts have come to light about the ways animals communicate in their natural state. Certain of these facts suggest properties usually associated only with human language. The bees have a dance whose choreography communicates to the other members of the colony the direction, distance, and richness of the pollen source discovered minutes earlier. Thus in no sense is the bee's message an immediate reaction to its environment of the moment, but more a relating of certain aspects of a past experience. Certain birds, like the white-crowned sparrow, have an elaborate song whose mature shape is determined by the particular dialect it is exposed to at a critical period in its infancy. Thus there are significant aspects of the sparrow song that do not simply go along with being a sparrow, but rather are dependent on early experience. The apes in the wild display an elaborate system of communication combining gestures, facial expressions, and sounds into a composite signal in which the significance of one type of signal—a particular gesture, for example—is dependent on what particular facial expressions and sounds accompany it. The full significance of a signal may, in addition, be determined by the relative social positions of the participants in the communication act. Thus certain aspects, at least, of the system of animal communication do not have a simple one-to-one relationship between unit signal and significance, but depend, rather, on selected aspects of the accompanying signals as well as of the social context.

While too little is known *in detail* about the system of animal communication to provide a deep analysis of its basic elements, the observed complexity of the systems may suggest that they are "languages," similar in principle to human languages but simpler in vocabulary and in the number and complexity of combinations, and, of course, not necessarily vocalized. The assumption that human language is intimately related to the signal systems of the apes and monkeys has appeared especially attractive, since human language could thereby claim the communication system of the nonhuman primates as its evolutionary predecessor.

But, in fact, it is the consensus of opinion among linguists, anthropologists, and psychologists that this is a deceptively loose use of the word "language"—that the natural systems of animal communication are different *in essence* from human language. The scholarly position is expressed plainly by Jane Lancaster when she says:

> The interest in human evolution and in the origin of human language has distorted the study of the communication systems of nonhuman primates. These systems are not steps toward language, and have much more in common with the communication of other mammals than with human language. The more that is known about the communication systems of nonhuman primates the more obvious it is that these systems have little relationship with human language, but much with the ways human beings express emotion through gesture, facial expression, and tone of voice. There is no evidence that human displays expressing emotion, such as laughing, crying, smiling, are any more or less complex than are displays of monkeys and apes or that they differ in form or function.

There is, however, a second question that can be asked about animals and language: a line of inquiry that parallels that of the relationship between animal communication in the wild and human language. That question is: What aspects of human language will a higher animal, like the monkey or the ape, learn under conditions of extended exposure to a language, or even when subjected to intensive training? This, of course, is not a question of the animal's *natural* behavior in its *natural* environment but rather a question of its capabilities in an environment that is manipulated in varyingly *unnatural* ways.

In the last forty years there have been several attempts by

American psychologists to raise a chimpanzee in a homelike atmosphere in the hope that given an environment resembling that of a child, another species might be able to learn our language, along with other aspects of human behavior. The Kelloggs raised Gua, a female infant chimpanzee, with their own son Donald who was about the same age, for about nine months. Gua did not learn to speak, but did learn during the course of the training period to respond to more than sixty different English sentences. Some years later, Keith and Cathy Hayes adopted a female chimpanzee, Viki, when she was three days old, and worked with her intensively for six and a half years. Viki learned to make only four sounds that were sometimes recognizable as approximations of English words. These were learned only with the greatest difficulty, and even afterwards there were sometimes confusions and inappropriate uses.

These experiences make it seem that a vocal language is not appropriate for a chimpanzee. We know that there are distinct differences between the articulatory apparatus of the nonhuman primates and that of man, most recently from the work of Philip Lieberman at Haskins Laboratory. Lieberman argued that the vocal mechanisms of the nonprimates are not capable of producing human speech sounds, a result of an anatomical lack of tongue mobility, among other things. It seems that nonhuman primates cannot change the shape of their vocal tract to control the necessary variety of sounds, the way human beings can for the thousands of languages of the world.

From field reports of anthropologists like Jane Goodall, we learn that chimpanzees vocalize primarily under conditions of great excitement in their natural habitat. Perhaps this adds to the difficulty of attempting to train them to control their vocalizations. But does this necessarily mean that it is next to impossible to teach them to communicate with us? It has seemed so, until the past few years when two psychologists at the University of Nevada, Allen and Beatrice Gardner, decided to take a fresh approach to the question of teaching language to a home-raised chimpanzee. They reasoned that the use of the hands is a prominent feature in the behavior of chimpanzees, who have a rich repertoire of gestures both in the wild and in captivity. They undertook to teach an infant chimpanzee a language based on gesture, the American Sign Language of the deaf. They obtained a chimpanzee (Washoe) from the wild when she was about a year old, and worked with her for more than three years. By comparison with the four words that Viki learned to speak, Washoe's progress in sign language is spectacular. By about four years of age, she had learned to make reliably more than eighty different signs. One estimate suggests that she can respond appropriately to more than five hundred different utterances in sign language—a remarkable achievement for a chimpanzee. The Gardners, and all those who were with the chimpanzee, used only signs to communicate with her. They learned signs largely from a dictionary of American Sign Language. They used gestures and manual configurations to represent the concepts in sign language and avoided the use of finger spelling as much as possible.

The sign for *flower,* for example, is made by holding the fingers of one hand extended and brought together at the tip as if holding a flower, and touching this first to one nostril and then to the other. This is a gesture we might use in smelling a flower. The sign for *girl* is made with a closed fist and the thumb extended upward from the fist. Keeping this hand position, the thumb is placed about the middle of the cheek but a few inches away and moved downward to the lower part of the cheek, still maintaining the same distance. On seeing the sign for the first time, it would be difficult to guess its meaning; historically, it derives from an old French sign for *girl,* which was made with two hands, the thumbs on either side of the face outlining the strings of a French girl's bonnet.

The Gardners have made intensive and deliberate attempts to teach Washoe a great number of signs, but they also sign to her in sentences as they prepare her meals, dress her, and play with her, in the same way that parents chatter to their children. The signed sequences produced by the Gardners, who are not native signers, are like English sentences with certain elements left out (articles, inflections, auxiliary verbs). A literal translation into English of some of the Gardners' utterances to Washoe might be: *What you want? You not yet hide, You catch me,* and *Me catch you.*

It seems clear from this experiment that Washoe not only has learned to make manual gestures, but makes them in ways that clearly refer to aspects of her external environment. Her ability to name has a development that in many respects is similar to that of a young child. She first learned the sign for *open* with a particular door. She then extended the use of that sign far beyond the original training, first to all closed doors, then to closed containers such as the refrigerator, cupboards, drawers, briefcases, boxes, and jars. Eventually she spontaneously used the sign for *open* to request opening of the water faucet and of a closed bottle of soda pop. She learned a sign for *cat* and a sign for *dog*, originally with pictures of each, and she used the signs appropriately while looking through magazines or books as well as for real cats and dogs. She made the sign for *dog* even when someone drew a caricature of a dog for her, and also when she heard a dog that she could not see barking in the distance.

She sometimes overextends the use of signs in ways that resemble children's early overextensions. Washoe learned the sign for *listen* for an alarm clock which signals meal time. She used the sign for other bells, for the sounds of people walking outside her trailer door, and for watches and clocks. She signed *listen* spontaneously when she found a broken watchband, and then when she saw a flashlight that blinks on and off. Washoe has a sign for *hurt* which she learned first with scratches or bruises. Later she used the sign also for red stains, for a decal on the back of a person's hand, and the first time she saw a person's navel.

Washoe first learned the sign for *flower*, which we have already described, and eventually made it apply to a large variety of flowers and pictures of flowers. As the flower sign became more frequent, the Gardners noticed that she made the sign in several inappropriate contexts which all seemed to include smells— when opening a tobacco pouch, or entering a kitchen filled with cooking smells. They introduced a new sign to her for *smell*, and gradually she began to use it in the contexts where she had formerly used the *flower* sign incorrectly. She now partitions the domain of *flowers* and *odors* in the same way that we do. These examples are all characteristic of the range and extensions of words used by children in the process of learning a language.

Washoe has more than eighty signs which she makes reliably. To give some idea of the range of concepts, we can indicate some rough English equivalents of her signs. She has some request signs: *come-gimme, open, tickle, hug, help, ride-wagon, sit-chair;* some signs that are primarily names of objects: *dog, cat, flower, shoes, key, book, banana;* some signs that represent properties of objects: *red, white;* some that indicate direction or location: *up, out, down;* some name-signs of people who are with her often: *Roger, Dr. Gardner, Mrs. Gardner* (and a sign for *Washoe*); and the signs for *you* and *me,* which are made by pointing to the chest of another person or oneself. While these signs represent concepts that are not always bounded in the same way as their English word translation, one can see that this vocabulary is rich enough to allow for communication in a variety of situations.

At first, Washoe used signs singly, like *open* and *more.* Then, as soon as she knew eight or ten signs, the Gardners report that she began using combinations of signs in sequences. They note that it is not too difficult to define what constitutes a sequence for her by observing something like the relaxation of her hands after making several signs. This is like our intonation contours, which make us feel that someone has finished a sentence or stopped speaking. At first, Washoe combined signs only two at a time, but by the time she was four years old (and had been trained for three years) there were sometimes three or more signs in a sequence. The Gardners specifically trained Washoe to make individual signs; they did not train her to make sequences. It should be interesting then to look at the characteristics of the combinations of signs that she makes, without being specifically taught.

But before describing Washoe's combinations, let us give perspective to her accomplishments by comparing her progress with that of a child. Washoe produced her first combination of signs (*gimme sweet*) when she was about twenty months old. After that, the Gardners kept complete records of every new sign combination they observed. Fourteen months afterwards, they had recorded a total of 330 different combinations of signs used by Washoe. We have the same sort of information for one hearing child, Gregory, provided by the psychologist Martin Braine.

Gregory first produced an utterance that combined two words when he was eighteen months old, and his parents recorded all new combinations thereafter. Seven months later, he had produced more than 2,500 different combinations; his parents could no longer reasonably keep track. Certainly there is an enormous difference in sheer productivity, but the crucial differences are more profound than this.

A good example of Washoe's combinations involves the sign for *open*, which was one of the first Washoe learned to use, and she used it frequently. When she had learned other signs, she eventually began combining them with *open* and produced the following sequences, for example:

> *open out*   (when standing in front of a trailer door)
> *open flower*   (to be let through the gate to the flower garden)
> *open drink*   (for the water faucet)
> *food open hurry*   (at the refrigerator door)
> *key open please blanket*   (at the bedding cupboard)
> *open key clean*   (at the soap cupboard)

These are all appropriate combinations, relevant to a particular context; some may not be copies of sentences she has seen other people sign, that is, may be original for Washoe. She does produce names that are fitting to a particular situation, and she combines them in sequences—spontaneously.

The Gardners report, however, that most signs occur in many or all orders, that order seems irrelevant in Washoe's signed sequences. For example, she has produced *open drink* and *drink open*; *key open* and *open key*; *more open* and *open more*; the three-sign sequence, *please sweet drink,* has been produced in all possible orders. Let us take one example where it is clear that a change in the order of signs usually occurs for different situations, at least in the way the Gardners sign to Washoe. She loves to be tickled and also likes to tickle the people around her. In the sign language Washoe uses, *I* and *me* are made in the same way, so we will use *me* as the English equivalent. The Gardners sign to Washoe *me tickle you* when they are about to tickle her, and *you tickle me* as a request that she perform the action. Washoe instead has used all possible orders of these signs and did not distinguish one situation from the other.

Washoe signed *me tickle* when she wanted someone to tickle her and when she was going to tickle someone. She requested tickling by signing either *you tickle* or *tickle you*. Her combinations, from this and other evidence, seem like unordered sequences of names for aspects of a situation. It is rather like a kind of complex naming (signs, in any order and combination, that are appropriate to a context). This does not have the basic characteristics of our sentences—hierarchical organization, internal structure, certain degree of explicitness, and the expression of basic grammatical relations. In addition, there is no evidence that Washoe asks questions or makes any negative statements.

It seems to us that Washoe's meager production of combinations should not be allowed to result in overhasty conclusions about limitations in what she has the ability to communicate. Washoe's impressive performance in learning to assign names to things, or classes of things, comes as a result of specific training designed to teach her that very task. It should be remembered that Washoe did not naturally start signing in the way that children start phonating (or indeed as the children of the deaf start signing). She was induced to make signs, by reward, by modeling, and so forth. The question was not, Would a chimpanzee naturally copy elements of a manual language to which it was regularly exposed? The question was, rather, Could a chimpanzee be taught selective elements of a manual language and then use these productively, that is, for novel instances? The answer turned out affirmatively when the elements taught corresponded to individual wordlike elements—the signs for *flower*, for *tickling*, for *cat*. That Washoe did not spontaneously capture the relationships implicit between the signs in the sentences to which she was exposed should not be surprising. What was demonstrated with Washoe's impressive naming was that she could be taught to associate a visual-manual token with a certain object or event and could subsequently generalize the use of the token to similar objects or events, though, of course, we do not know by precisely what criterion of similarity.

The reason for the interest in Washoe's multi-sign message formations is that this is the context in which the differing roles of the various signs are specified with respect to the total picture.

It seems clear that Washoe can be taught to perform simple naming; her own behavior indicates that she can similarly perform complex naming, emit a string of tokens jointly associated with a situation. It is quite another question whether she can be taught to distinguish, in the *form* of the message, between such differing relations as actor versus acted on—the sort of thing that some languages (like English) accomplish with word order in differentiating *John tickles Mary* from *Mary tickles John*, and that other languages accomplish with different formal devices.

Recently Professor David Premack, a psychologist at the University of California, has been pursuing precisely this sort of question, namely, Can a chimpanzee be taught to code differences in relationship between tokens occurring in combination? In an address to the American Psychological Association in September 1969, Professor Premack outlined an experiment underway on a chimpanzee named Sarah. The mode of communication is manual-visual, as with Washoe, but rather than actually forming the signals, Sarah has at her disposal ready-made tokens, in the form of plastic pieces of varying size, shape, and color. She is trained to associate distinct tokens with selected parts of her experience within the narrow object-world of the experiment: a token for *apples,* another for *bananas,* one for *pail,* one for each of four differently colored chips of wood, a token for her own name, and one for each of the three experimenters. A combination of four tokens is associated with Sarah's handing Mary an apple, for example. Included in such a combination are the tokens already associated with apple, Sarah, and Mary. The tokens that are used by Sarah and her experimenter to form a message are placed on a magnetized slate, vertically when a combination of tokens is required. The experimenters have intentionally avoided any physical relationship between the form of the token and what the token is associated with. For example, the tokens with which the differently colored, but otherwise identical, chips of wood are associated are themselves colorless and differ rather in shape. Like Washoe's signs, Sarah's tokens are trained (as opposed to spontaneous) and arbitrary (as opposed to representational). But rather than emphasizing the number of tokens that Sarah can use, as in the Gardner experiment, Professor Premack is exploring the chimpanzee's ability to associate the selection of tokens and their order in combinations with subtler functional differences.

As of August 1969, Sarah had command of sixty different tokens, all used in combinations of three or four tokens. So the total number of different routines in her command is in the hundreds. Let us examine briefly a sample of the training procedure and the chimpanzee's subsequent productive variations on the procedure. After having been familiarized with the tokens individually, Sarah is taught a four-token sequence, like *Sarah-insert-banana-pail,* in a routine in which the chimpanzee constructs the sequence by placing the four tokens in a vertical row on the slate and at another time acts out putting a banana in a pail. Then she is tested for her ability to extend the pattern to tokens already mastered but not explicitly trained in this particular routine. Thus, if she had previously mastered the use of the token for *apple* in the four-token sequence *Mary-give-apple-Jim,* she would subsequently be tested for her ability *creatively* to associate the novel four-token sequence *Sarah-insert-apple-pail* with the situation in which Sarah is inserting an apple in a pail. Similarly, having been trained to associate different tokens with four differently colored cards (blue, green, yellow, red) Sarah is then taught to associate the three-token sequence *Red-on-Green* with a red card on a green card. Then she will be tested on her ability to extend this training *creatively* to new instances, for example *Blue-on-Yellow.*

So far there have been very strict controls imposed on Sarah's behavior in these routines. Once a combination has been taught in a particular routine, a response consisting of a single token— though adequate in terms of communication—is not accepted, that is, not rewarded. Moreover, the choice of tokens put within Sarah's reach for any particular routine has been very strictly limited. Sometimes she has within reach only those tokens that will ultimately form the correct sequence when ordered in the correct way. So there has been a difference more profound in the training of Washoe and Sarah than just emphasis on vocabulary with Washoe and emphasis on functionally significant combinations with Sarah. Washoe, since she herself ultimately forms her signs, has all of them available at any given moment. Her behavior can more nearly be approached as communication, and can hardly be called just collections of learned routines, particularly since she uses her manual signs outside of the training situation. Moreover, Washoe was permitted and even encouraged to let her own inclinations dictate how she would use her signs. This spontaneous, apparently innovative, and often unexpected behavior on the part of Washoe raises fascinating questions above and beyond those of her success in the training routines.

The experiment with Sarah was much more ambitious in the questions that it was designed to answer. It must still be viewed as in its preliminary stages, where the various controls and procedures used in the routines may well have influenced her performance in ways that have not been taken into account. Once the training has progressed to a sufficient degree that the controls can be loosened and the number of tokens available for any single act of combining made large enough so that she must choose among many possibilities, then we can better assess to what degree Sarah's combinations are communication, and what languagelike properties they display. In evaluating the success of attempts to teach animals to communicate, we must recall that, after all, pets and circus animals can be taught, when given signals, to perform a great number of complicated tricks.

In conclusion, let us return to a theme that has emerged several times in the preceding discussion—a theme that has to do with so-called *languagelike* characteristics of the trained visual-manual communication of Washoe and Sarah. The claim is nowhere made that these chimps have been taught a language —but only that what they *have* been taught displays some significantly languagelike characteristics—notably having to do with the productive or creative use of arbitrary signs. Washoe demonstrated· that she could use names productively—that is, that having been taught to associate a given sign with particular real examples of an object, property, or process, she would extend the sign to novel instances not found in the training procedure —apparently giving the same name to objects that shared certain properties. The experiment with Sarah, if successful beyond its present preliminary stage, may indicate that she is able to associate differences of function with variations in the order of tokens—and treat these differences in order of tokens *productively*; that is, in novel cases. But it is very important to recognize an *essential* difference between the sort of productivity that we would ascribe to the behavior of Washoe and Sarah and that that appears to be its counterpart in human language. In human language this productivity, though unlimited, is unlimited only within the tight limits set up by a shared system of special constraints—a grammar—which is reflected by our feeling for what counts as a well-formed expression in our native language. The linguistic productivity that we are referring to is not the metaphorical use of words or the invention of new words, nor is it fanciful distortions of syntax; the linguistic productivity we are referring to is that that characterizes our ability to produce indefinitely many sentences never heard before, whose meanings can be understood (as precisely as they are expressed) by anyone else who shares the system; that is, by anyone who knows the language. It is this coupling of *productivity* with interpretability provided precisely by a shared system of grammar that makes human language such a versatile system of communication—so versatile that not only can we express things that are outside of our immediate experience, we can even express the inconceivable. Not only can we relate past events and predict future ones, not only can we lie and indeed create whole fictitious worlds, but we can even communicate our most irrational fantasies.

10 THE DEVELOPMENT OF LANGUAGE IN CHILDREN

Roger Brown

In 1967 Mr. Benny Blount went to Nyanza Province in Kenya in East Central Africa to make a study of the development of language in childhood. The language spoken by about one million people in Nyanza Province is Luo. His study was comparable with studies already made in the United States and Britain and in progress in several other places. Mr. Blount took with him a copy of the *Field Manual* written to guide such studies by Daniel Slobin and his associates at the University of California at Berkeley. While this *Manual* describes some experimental methods for investigating child speech the central procedure is the collection, on a regular schedule, of large samples of the spontaneous speech of the children being studied. When my associates and I originated this kind of study with three American children in 1962 we found that we could obtain from any of our children several hundred utterances in about half an hour's time. Among the Luo, Mr. Blount found things rather more difficult. In his first fifty-four visits, of half an hour or longer, he obtained a total of only two hundred sentences. The problem was primarily one of Luo etiquette which requires that small children be silent when adults come to visit, and the small children Mr. Blount visited could not throw off their etiquette even though their parents entreated them to speak for the visiting "European," as Mr. Blount was called.

In the end, happily, Mr. Blount was able to learn quite a bit about the speech of Luo children, and what he learned, once he got past the difference of etiquette, was mostly familiar. Familiar to him and to other students of child speech, from work already done with children learning languages having no historical relation to Luo, languages like English, Russian, Finnish, and Samoan. And this is perhaps the most exciting news to emerge from the modern study of child speech. It looks as if child speech is, in some respects, the same everywhere in the world. As if it had some universal properties, as if there were some universal stages of development.

Let me begin by outlining the range of evidence now available. There have been studies covering the preschool years of about a dozen American children. There is a study not yet complete of three children living in the United States but learning Finnish as their first language. There are field studies of children learning Samoan, of children in the highlands of Mexico learning the Mayan language called Tzeltal, and of children learning Japanese. All these studies are operating within a single tradition, using large samples of spontaneous speech, asking the same questions, and operating with the same analytic tools. There are also studies from outside this tradition that provide valuable data—for instance, Werner Leopold's account of the progress of his daughter Hildegard who learned English and German at the same time; A. N. Gvozdev's account of his son Zhenya's learning of Russian; Antoine Grégoire's account of his two sons' learning of French; and several others. In sum, enough evidence to take seriously if not quite enough to establish universality.

The most interesting universal generalizations concern the grammar or syntax of child speech. When I speak of grammar I do not refer to the relatively trivial business of "speaking correctly," as people put it, which usually means following the rules of some dominant region and social class. I refer instead to the very important and impressive business of using some rules, whatever rules are made available in the speech of parents and older children, to construct sentences one has never heard before. And this is something all normal children unquestionably learn to do between the ages of eighteen months and five years. They do not simply commit to memory the sentences they hear other people speak. They extract from other people's speech a set of rules of construction that enable them to produce indefinitely numerous new sentences that will be correctly understood in their language community. This staggeringly impressive accomplishment has so captured the imagination of present-day students of language development that most of our energies have gone into the study of grammar or the sentence construction process.

Curiously enough the clearest indications, in the everyday speech of children, that they are learning construction rules are to be found in the mistakes they make. Let us consider just one. Most American children learning English, when they are about four years old use the form *hisself* rather than *himself*. How do they come by it? It can be shown that they use it when no one else in the family uses it and when they have not heard it outside the home. In circumstances, therefore, where the form is certainly not copied or imitated but must have been constructed or invented by the child himself. Why does he invent what is, from the adult point of view, the wrong form? To answer that, we must recall the set of words most similar to the reflexive pronoun *himself*. They are such other reflexive pronouns as *myself, yourself,* and *herself*. But all these others, we see, are constructed by combining the possessive pronoun, *my, your,* or *her,* with *self*. The masculine possessive pronoun is *his,* and if the English language were consistent at this point, the reflexive would be *hisself*. As it happens, English is inconsistent or irregular at this point, as all languages, for accidental historical reasons, are at some points, and the approved masculine reflexive is *himself*. Children, by inventing *hisself* and often insisting on it for quite a period, "iron out" or correct the irregularity of the language—and incidentally reveal to us the fact that what they are learning is general rules of construction, not just the words and phrases they hear. Examples of this kind are common in children learning any language and are one of the most interesting things to watch for in one's own children.

When I say that children learn rules of grammar I do not, of course, mean that they learn them in any explicit form. Preschool children cannot describe the rules they follow. The knowledge they have is implicit. Rules that are used but cannot be formulated or expressed are known implicitly. Not until they are in school and study grammar do children learn any explicit rules. We must suppose, however, that almost everything taught to them in grammar classes is already known on a certain level, the implicit level, the level of use.

For examples of the universal properties of child grammar let us turn to the first stage in sentence construction. Stage I is defined as beginning when the child produces any utterances at all that are made up of more than one word. When that happens the average length of his sentences (a measure we call "mean length of utterance") will rise above 1.0. The end of Stage I is defined by the attainment of a mean length of utterance of 2.0. When the mean is 2.0 there will be many utterances of one, two, and three words, a few of four, and an upper limit of about five. The mean length of utterance is a good index of grammatical development because for several years practically everything the child learns about the structure of his language has the effect of increasing the length of his sentences. Mean length of utterance is a better index of level of grammatical development than is chronological age because there is substantial individual variation in the rate of development.

The remarkable fact is that Stage I, defined by the external index of utterance length, is definable also in terms of a universal set of internal characteristics. Stage I speech is marked by the absence of grammatical function forms; Stage I speech expresses some nine semantic operations and relations; the major syntactic device of Stage I speech is word order.

Grammatical function forms are little words like *the, a, in, on, and, but, will, can,* and inflections like the plural "s" of *cats* or possessive "s" of *Daddy's chair* or the past tense "ed" of *walked.* They are articles, prepositions, conjunctions, auxiliary verbs, inflections, and affixes. Forms that are few in number but frequent in use, forms that do not name places, things, or processes but that express subtle relational and often quite psychological meanings. Grammatical forms are called "function words" by contrast with "content words" which are nouns, verbs, and adjectives. Stage I speech universally lacks function words even in contexts where they are obligatory in the adult language. Whether Finnish or English or Samoan, Stage I speech is a speech of content words and chiefly nouns and verbs.

The absence of grammatical forms is only a descriptive fact, though a general one, and it awaits a good explanation. Are grammatical forms missing because they are not heavily stressed in pronunciation and so not perceptually striking, or because their use is elaborately contingent and tied to the classification of other words, or because the concepts expressed are, in some sense, psychologically complex? Whatever the general set of reasons it is clear that function words are not all at the same level of difficulty. In all languages a few begin to be used by Stage II, but in all languages the control of the full set requires several years for its accomplishment. Function words are not one problem but many.

About 75 percent of the sentences at Stage I seem, in any language, to express a limited set of semantic operations and relations. For example, there are three common operations of reference: *nomination, nonexistence,* and *recurrence.* Nomination involves naming a referent when the referent itself is present and also speaking some pointer word such as, in English, *that* or *see.* As when a child, pointing or looking, says *that dog* or *that book* or, even, among the Luo, *that lion.* Nonexistence expresses the disappearance or failure to appear when expected of some referent. As, in English, *dog all gone* or *no more dog.* Recurrence comments on or requests the reappearance of a referent, as, in English, *more dog, more book.*

Then there are the relations of location, possession, and attribution. Locations seem to be expressed simply by putting together the name of a movable object and its locus without full specification of the nature of the locative relations, whether *in, on, over, under,* or what not. And so, in child English, we have constructions like *sweater chair* where the sweater is on the chair and *pencil cup* where the pencil is in the cup. Possessives or genitives express a primitive sense of property and territory. Certain objects and spaces seem always to be assigned to particular family members, and the child learns this early. In English the child's possessives always omit the possessive inflection and simply come out as *Daddy chair* or *Mommy dress.* Attributives, normally an adjective and a noun in English, take the same referent and specify the value of an attribute which goes unspecified in the referent name itself. Thus, in English, *yellow truck* or *big book.*

There are also the relations agent-action, action-object, and

111

agent-object. The agent is the initiator of an action and the object receives the force of the action. The Stage I child, sounding very strange to adults, also makes sentences of agent and object alone without any action. Thus *Mommy sock* when Mommy was mending the socks. It is as if the most obvious thing about this situation was to him the interaction of a person and a thing, the former being the source of causality, with the particular *quality* of the interaction being a more advanced abstraction.

It may reasonably be asked What could the child talk about except the relations and operations described? What else is there? Well, really quite a lot. He could talk about time and about number and about identity and subordination and causality, implication, disjunction, and so on. In fact there are a great many operations and relations expressed in the adult language that are not expressed at Stage I.

What makes us think, when the Stage I child produces two or three words in succession, that he intends to express certain relations between or operations upon ideas? Why should we not suppose that he is simply naming in temporal succession various aspects of a situation as these aspects attract his notice, without meaning to relate them in any particular way at all? Why should not the child's content words be like the *leitmotiven* in Richard Wagner's later operas: elements having a certain semanticity occurring in associative chains but not in such definite relations as are called agent and action or action and object? The most important reason for thinking the child intends relations is the fact that his words are produced in a particular order and that that order is almost always appropriate to the relation that is suggested by the nonlinguistic setting.

For example, imagine a case in which a cat is biting a dog. A Stage I child learning English might say: *cat bite dog* or perhaps only *cat bite* or *bite dog* or even *cat dog*. What he would never say in these circumstances but would say in circumstances where the roles were reversed is *dog bite cat,* or *dog bite* or *bite cat* or *dog cat*. The two sets of possible responses are nonoverlapping. It is this kind of discrimination, this discrimination with respect to order, that shows that the Stage I child has in mind not only certain animals, persons, things, qualities, and actions, but definite structural relations among them.

It is of parenthetical interest that a word order appropriate to the reference setting, which is universally the first manifestation of syntax in children, is just the characteristic lacking in a most interesting comparison case. The comparison case is a chimpanzee named Washoe, who was raised at home by Allen and Beatrice Gardner (see Chapter 9). From the first the Gardners attempted to teach Washoe the American Sign Language, the sign language of the deaf in North America. And to the amazement of linguistic scientists everywhere Washoe made great progress. She even strings signs together to make what may be short sentences. What these sentences still lacked in 1969 to make them just like the Stage I sentences of childhood is appropriate word order. Washoe tends to use her signs in all possible orders and without discernible connection with the structure of the reference setting. It would be rash, however, to guess what the limits of Washoe's linguistic capacity could prove to be.

Rules of word order vary from language to language, and Stage I speech reflects the local rules whatever they may be. In English, for example, the relation of possession is expressed by naming first the person who possesses and second the object possessed. In Samoan, the order is just the reverse. In both languages adults mark the construction with grammatical forms as well as word order. What do Stage I children do? Whether English-speaking or Samoan-speaking they drop the grammatical form. If English-speaking they use the order possessor-possessed, and if Samoan-speaking, the reverse.

The semantic operations and structural relations that account for the meaning of most Stage I sentences seem to me to develop directly out of the sensory-motor intelligence, which has been shown by the great developmental psychologist, Jean Piaget, to be the major attainment of the first eighteen months of life. Piaget's studies of this period have convinced him that the infant does not at first conceive of objects and persons as permanently existing, independently of himself, in a single space with himself. Neither does he recognize that persons and objects are all potential "sources of causality" as well as potential recipients of force. In the first eighteen to twenty-four months, in Piaget's view, the infant "constructs" the world of enduring objects and immediate space and time. The meanings of the first sentences, coming just after eighteen months, seem to me to presuppose the attainments of sensory-motor intelligence but also to go beyond it. For sensory-motor intelligence is an intelligence of action, not thought; its aim is practical success, not truth. What the Stage I child can do that the sensory-motor child cannot is propositionalize about the sensory-motor world. He can create assertions which can be tested for truth. Somehow that capacity, which goes beyond sensory-motor intelligence, also develops in the first eighteen months.

The complications of structure that follow Stage I almost all add to the length of sentences. However, it is probably not the number of words that limits what the child can do at a particular time but rather the grammatical complexity of the construction. There is rather clear evidence of this in our studies of Adam, Eve, and Sarah deriving from the difficulty the child has with what are called tag questions. Tag questions are requests for confirmation, communication checks like *n'est-ce pas?* or *nicht wahr?* except that the grammar of English tags is more complex. One can add a tag to any statement. Thus: *John will be late, won't he? His wife can drive, can't she?* And so on. The form of the tag varies with the form of the sentence to which it is added. The tag itself is very short: three or four words long. Which means that as far as superficial length is concerned it would even be within the capacity of the child at the end of Stage I. In fact, however, tags are not to be heard before Stage V, some two or three years later, when some sentences are as long as fifteen words or even more. What delays their appearance until this time?

The form of the tag varies with the form of the sentence to which it is added and, as a matter of fact, the tag is always a strict derivative of the sentence to which it is added. Suppose the basic sentence is *His wife can drive.* How do we get from this the tag *can't she?* It is in the first place necessary to make a pronoun of the subject. The subject is *his wife,* and so the pronoun must be feminine, third person, and since it is a subject the nominative; in fact *she*. The second step is to make the tag negative. In English this is done by adding *not* or the contraction *n't* to the auxiliary verb *can;* hence *can't*. The next step is to make the tag interrogative, since it is a question, and in English that is done by a permutation of order placing the auxiliary verb ahead of the subject. The final step is to delete all of the predicate of the base sentence except the first member, the auxiliary, and that at last yields *can't she* as a derivative of *His wife can drive*.

The derivation of tags since it is a completely determinate procedure could, in principle, be done by a machine. But it would have to be a machine that knew a large part of the grammar of English. The machine would have to be able to identify sentence subjects; replace subjects with pronouns, preserving number, gender, and so on; construct negatives; construct interrogatives; and do predicate deletions. Which, of course, is why children seldom produce tags before they are about five years old. We have been able to show that they do not produce them until they are able to carry out all the constituent operations like negation, interrogation, and so on, both singly and in simple combinations.

The idea of grammatical complexity has one fairly clear sense in linguistic theory. If you operate with a generative-transformational grammar of the kind introduced by Noam Chomsky in 1957, then the complexity of a construction might be indicated by the number of steps in its derivation. A derivation in transformational grammar is a kind of proof that a sentence belongs to a language, a proof that proceeds by showing that the rules of the language will generate the sentence and assign it the correct structure (see Chapter 3). Tags, though short of words, are exceedingly long of derivation. Most of us working on the development of language today are working with the linguistic theories of Chomsky and his associates. And it appears to be the case that the derivational complexity of English constructions within a generative grammar predicts fairly well the order in which the constructions will be acquired in childhood. Not invariably, not without some qualifications, but nevertheless quite generally. Affirmatives appear before negatives, declaratives before interrogatives, simple sentences before embedded sentences or coordinated sentences. Most predictions from derivational complexity are confirmed by the facts of development.

So substantive information about development in many languages is accumulating rapidly nowadays. What will it mean if, when much more evidence is in, it does indeed appear that the course of development is in important ways universal? It may mean, in the first place, that all the languages of the world have certain structural features in common, that there is a universal definition of language. In fact this much is already established by descriptive and theoretical linguistics. A universal order of development may furthermore mean that the brain of our species is programmed to operate in quite definite ways upon any materials that manifest the properties of language; that language materials set off programs of analysis which discover in these materials those structural properties that are not universal, the rules that are local and variable; and that rules of various kinds are sought in a fixed order. Initially, perhaps, grammatical function forms, however these may be universally defined, are disregarded and there is a search for whatever rules of order are used in the expression of basic semantic operations and relations.

Perhaps language use is to the human species as nut burying is to the squirrel. A squirrel raised in isolation from its kind and given no opportunity to learn how to bury nuts will, nonetheless, when it first encounters a nut or a nutlike object, undertake to dig a hole and tap it into the ground. It will attempt to carry out this fixed-action pattern even in very unaccommodating circumstances, as on a linoleum floor. Speaking English or Samoan or Luo or any particular language is certainly not a fixed-action pattern released in the human species by contact with the language. But perhaps there are fixed analytic patterns, processes of information analysis, which are released by any materials having the universal properties of language. And perhaps these processes succeed one another in a relatively fixed order and produce the invariant features of the development of language in children.

11 LEARNING TO READ

Jeanne Chall

My father, a great music lover who never himself had the opportunity to learn to play an instrument, took special delight in my diligent efforts at playing the piano. When I was eight years old, after about a year of instruction on the piano, he gleefully presented me with a surprise—a piano score for one of Beethoven's *Contra Dances*.

"Here," he said. "Play it for me." When I could recover somewhat from the shock, I murmured, "But I can't."

He would not accept my answer. "You can play, can't you?" he said.

"Yes," I hesitated.

"You can read notes, can't you?" he insisted.

"Yes," I managed to get out.

"Well," he said. "These are notes, why can't you play them?"

It was obvious to me, but not to him, that the notes he wanted me to play were too hard for me. Yes, I could read some notes—and I could play those I could read quite well. I could play a simplified version of the *Blue Danube* or *Twinkle, Twinkle, Little Star*. And I did well with my exercises. But a Beethoven *Contra Dance*! That was too much! Maybe in a few years—with faithful practice—but not now!

And so it is with reading. After a year of instruction and practice, the typical child in the first grade can read his primer and first reader and perhaps a simple fairy or folk tale. He may also be able to read his cousin's primer—if the words are like the ones in his own. But it will take many years before he will be able to read general literature—newspapers, magazines, and books written to inform him rather than to teach him *how* to read.

Reading, like playing an instrument, is a complex skill that is not learned *all at once*. It takes most people many years to achieve a skillful performance. And like piano playing there are wide variations among individuals exposed to the same amount of practice. Some may achieve in two or four years a level of proficiency that others may reach only in eight or more, or perhaps never.

What do we mean by reading? More specifically, what is the essential reading skill?

The essential skill in reading is getting meaning from a printed or written message. Thus, reading and listening have much in common—with language the common component of both. There are some differences between reading and under- standing spoken messages. The written message does not have the intonation, stress, and emphasis of the spoken message. But the written message has punctuation and other conventions of print to tell the reader when to pause, and what to emphasize.

Of course, reading (as listening to a spoken message) is much more than getting the literal meaning of the message itself— although even this is quite an accomplishment, when we stop to think about it. For as John B. Carroll so aptly put it, to get the literal meaning of a verbal message means that we have not only recognized the words themselves, but have interpreted them "in their particular grammatical functions. . . ." We have "unconsciously recognized what words or phrases constitute the subjects and predicates of the sentence, what words or phrases modify those subjects or predicates, and so on." (Carroll, 1970, p. 296). Moreover, each sentence has been interpreted seman- tically; that is to say, we have given the proper meaning to each of the key words in the sentence.

And mature reading implies even more than getting the literal meaning. It means evaluating the ideas for truth, validity, or importance. We do this by checking them against our own ex- perience or knowledge. We think of the implications for future actions. And we may make inferences or draw conclusions that go far beyond what is explicitly stated in the text. When this is done, we are really engaging in "reasoning" or "thinking."

And indeed, to read at the highest level of maturity means thinking and reasoning, and to have an advanced command of language, concept, and experience.

How is this high level of reading skill to be attained? What does the beginner have to learn in order to reach it?

If we assume that the beginner is a six-year-old, and that his task is to learn to read his native language, then he already comes to it with some knowledge of at least one aspect of the reading skill—the language. To be sure, his language is not as advanced as it will be when he is an adult, but it is quite extensive. Although there is some disagreement as to the number of words the typical six-year-old child understands or can use, a reasonable, and conservative, estimate is about four thousand words (Lorge and Chall, 1963), and so forth. In addition, linguists tell us that by the age of six, the typical child has good control over the major grammatical structures of his language.

Thus, he is quite proficient in receiving and producing verbal messages—simple directions, stories, descriptions. Obviously he will have to continue to grow in his language proficiency—in his command of vocabulary and concept, his knowledge of more advanced syntax. But this he will learn from experience, from school, and especially from his reading—for the strong relationship between language and reading is not necessarily from language to reading alone; it may indeed work the other way around too—from reading to language.

How then is he to begin? There has been considerable disagreement and debate about this question in the United States and in England. Essentially, although there has been no disagreement on the ultimate goal of reading—getting the meaning of written messages as efficiently as, or more efficiently than, getting the meaning from the same or similar messages when spoken—there has been a major disagreement on how the child is to be initiated into the reading skill. And essentially, it has to do with which of the two major aspects of reading is to be emphasized more at the beginning—whether the meaning (or language component) or the decoding (or word recognition) component.

In other words, the debate that has existed and continues to exist in the teaching of reading in the United States and in

England (and no doubt in other countries with similar writing systems) is how to program these two components of reading for the beginner.

In a recent study supported by the Carnegie Corporation of New York (Chall, 1967), more than twenty published beginning reading programs were analyzed. These included the two reading series most widely used in the United States during 1962 to 1965 (the time in which I did the study) as well as new programs either in print at that time or still in the experimental stage. From a rather extensive analysis of these programs, I found that they could be placed on a code- to meaning-emphasis continuum. At one end could be placed those that stressed the decoding component, with less emphasis on meaning, in the initial steps of learning to read. At the other end were those programs that stressed the meaning component, with less emphasis in the beginning on the alphabetic code.

The most popular reading series in use during 1962 to 1965 (and indeed since the 1930s) fell on the meaning-emphasis end of the continuum. In such reading programs, the child is viewed almost as a small adult, who, from the start, is asked to react in a meaningful way to the printed form of words, phrases, sentences, and stories. Most of the child's practice time (if his teacher follows the instructions in the manuals accompanying these readers) is devoted to answering questions on the pictures and on the content of what is read.

The words used in the beginning books are highly controlled, limited to the commonest in the English language, and judged to be within the child's understanding. Only a few "new" words are added in each lesson and the old ones are repeated often. After the child learns to recognize "as wholes" (that is, globally) about fifty different words, he is taught some skills in decoding —that is, what letters or letter combinations stand for what sounds. But this is secondary to learning to recognize words as wholes and to "reading for meaning."

Most of the new programs in the 1960s (and incidentally the trend appears to be even stronger in the 1970s) as well as those that were predominantly in use before the 1930s in the United States fell on the code-emphasis end of the continuum. Such programs give more attention, at the beginning, to the systematic teaching of the relation between the spoken and written forms of words. They usually teach the names and/or sounds of the letters *before* teaching the child to recognize whole words or *while* he is learning to recognize words.

Generally, code-emphasis programs view learning to read as a two-stage process—the first stage being mastery of the alphabetic code; the second, reading for meaning. Code-emphasis programs vary, and in my classification I included systematic phonics programs (most of which were synthetic, rather than analytic); the so-called "linguistic" approaches of Leonard Bloomfield and Charles C. Fries that limit the early reading vocabulary to regularly spelled words (for example, "man," "fan," "can," and "tan"); and schemes that use a modified alphabet with a more regular sound-to-letter correspondence for initial instruction, such as Pitman's Initial Teaching Alphabet (ITA).

Although the code-emphasis programs put early stress on learning the alphabetic code, they also have the beginner "read for meaning." But overall, as compared to meaning-emphasis programs, the child spends relatively less time at the beginning on "reading for meaning" and more on mastering the alphabetic principle.

Let me clarify the distinction between meaning emphasis and code emphasis. These are not either/or distinctions. They are relative positions. Actually, most beginning reading programs fall on a continuum with regard to the relative emphasis placed on either decoding or meaning practice. I found this distinction not only useful for classifying the different programs available in the United States in the early 1960s, but helpful in understanding research comparing the effectiveness of methods that went back to 1912. At that time, the beginning reading methods vying for adoption were championed under different labels that could be reclassified into the broader framework of the meaning- to code-emphasis continuum: "look-say" versus "phonics," "no phonics" versus "phonics," or "thought" versus "sounding." Later, in the 1930s, they were labeled "intrinsic phonics" versus "systematic phonics." And more recently they have been studied as "basal reader" versus "basal reader plus systematic phonics," "ita," or "linguistic."

Essentially, then, if the programs are classified as meaning- or code-emphasis in relation to each other, some continuity and thus some sense can be made out of this old research, which at first glance appears to be quite contradictory and very confusing.

What is the research evidence? Does the beginning emphasis make a difference? Do pupils do better when initiated into reading by a code emphasis or by a meaning emphasis? Does one or another of these approaches produce fewer failures?

The evidence from these various researches—classroom comparisons, laboratory experiments, clinical reports, and correlational studies—although not absolutely clear-cut, *did* indicate a definite trend: those programs that could be classified as having a code rather than a meaning emphasis tended to produce readers who were not only more advanced in word recognition and in spelling, but also in tests of reading for meaning. These advantages for the code-emphasis programs held at least through the grades for which sufficient evidence existed—the end of grade 3 or the beginning of grade 4. Too few researchers followed up the children beyond the fourth grade. However, on the basis of the evidence that did exist, I hypothesized that the advantages of an initial code emphasis would remain, if the reading program in the later grades was sufficiently advanced to challenge the early superior attainment of the children.

The analysis of the past research suggested a hierarchy of reading skills. While the "conventional wisdom" of American reading instruction from about 1930 on has been that word recognition and analysis (that is to say, the ability to recognize words and sound out others not recognized immediately) are only lower order skills, it appears that for the first few years at least, these lower order skills are essential to the higher order skills of comprehension and interpretation. Indeed, since the beginner's grasp of the language is, for the first few years of learning to read, significantly above his ability to recognize this same language in print, the decoding skills are essentially the key to comprehension, the ultimate, accepted mature skill. Stressing the alphabetic code, then, does not distract the child from the ultimate task but actually gives him the tools to achieve it.

There is some evidence, too, that the results of code emphasis are even more beneficial for children of average and lower ability, for children of low socioeconomic status, and for children who are "high risks," that is, those who have a high probability of failure.

The research to 1965 did not, however, indicate that any one code-emphasis approach was more effective than another. There was insufficient research evidence to say that systematic phonics was better than a "linguistic approach," that a linguistic approach was better than a modified alphabet approach such as ITA, and so on. Nor was there sufficient evidence to conclude that one particular *published* code-emphasis program was better than another, although some undoubtedly are.

The clinical studies tended to support the classroom comparisons. Although they did not present enough data to indicate whether the actual number of failures produced by either emphasis was greater, since children with reading problems were initially taught by both kinds of programs, it appeared that those initiated by a code emphasis had less serious difficulties that were more amenable to remediation. Thus, while a code emphasis does not guarantee that all children will learn to read easily, it does tend to produce fewer serious reading problems.

These trends were also supported by the laboratory experiments as well as by the correlational studies. Indeed, knowing the names (and sounds) of the letters in kindergarten or early in grade 1 came out as one of the strongest predictors of success at the end of grade 1 in different studies done as early as the 1930s, up through 1965, and also in the more recent large-scale methods studies sponsored by the U.S. Office of Education from 1966 to 1968.

Probably more classroom experiments comparing the effects of different initial reading programs have been conducted in the United States since 1965 than in the period 1912 to 1965 covered by the Carnegie Study. What are the results? Do they support or refute the conclusions I drew from the research to 1965?

Fortunately, Robert Dykstra, one of the coordinators of the U.S. Office of Education Cooperative Studies—there were twenty-seven such comparisons using similar instruments and observations in the first grade, with nearly half of these continued through the end of the second and third grades—has done this for us. He drew together specific data from these studies pertinent to the effectiveness of an initial code-emphasis versus a meaning-emphasis program. Following the classification scheme for beginning reading methods devised for the Carnegie Study, he categorized conventional basal reader programs as meaning-emphasis, and "linguistic" and phonics-first basal reading programs as code-emphasis.

After analyzing those studies that were relevant to the issue, he concluded:

> Data from the Cooperative Research Program in First Grade Reading Instruction tend to support Chall's conclusion that code-emphasis programs produce better over-all primary grade reading and spelling achievement than meaning-emphasis programs. This superiority is especially marked with respect to pronouncing words orally in isolation, spelling words from dictation, and identifying words in isolation on a silent reading test. It is apparent that concentrated teaching of the alphabetic code is associated with improved initial ability to encode and decode words. (Dykstra, 1968, p. 21)

Yet method does not account for all differences. Success within all methods is related to pupil characteristics, to the general school situation, and to teacher characteristics. Indeed, since larger differences were found between different school systems ostensibly following the same method than between the different methods in the same school system, Dykstra in an earlier summary that included also many programs that varied on other than the meaning- to code-emphasis continuum, concluded that the total instructional setting and the teacher were probably more important for reading achievement than the specific method used.

It is questionable whether such a conclusion can be drawn from the data since differences between schools could stem from differences in library facilities, money spent on reading and related instruction, the social, cultural, and intellectual characteristics of the pupils, the cooperation of parents, the amount of supervision and in-service training given to teachers, and so on. At any rate, although I question the validity of concluding that the teacher is of *greater* importance than the method, I believe there is sufficient evidence in the earlier as well as in the United States Office of Education studies to conclude that the teacher *is* an important factor.

This conclusion has support from one of the cooperative first-grade studies (Chall and Feldman, 1966). We attempted to find out what it is that the teacher *is* and *does* that makes a difference in pupil achievement. Detailed weekly observations of teachers who ostensibly were using the same basal reader (meaning emphasis) program showed considerable variation in the way they implemented it. Generally, we found little correspondence between what the teachers said they did and what they actually did when observed. When initial readiness characteristics of pupils were controlled, the following were related positively to reading achievement at the end of grade 1: over-all teacher competence, a thinking approach to learning, providing children with materials of suitable difficulty (not too easy nor too hard), and a greater emphasis on teaching the relation between sounds and letters (code emphasis).

What can we conclude from the research through 1965, and from the more recent studies? Certainly, that method itself is not a simple matter nor that it is a sufficient condition for achievement. Even without the evidence available from these experiments, it is reasonable to expect that teachers vary in their competence and skill in implementing any method; that children vary in their background, abilities, interests, and receptiveness to different learning tasks; and that schools vary in their expectations and facilities. Thus, any reading program, even if carried out exactly as the author prescribes, tends to vary in its effectiveness. It may well be that a less effective program in the hands of a good teacher may lead to better reading achievement than a more effective one in the hands of a poor teacher. But this does not deny the importance of method.

Let me summarize some of the main points made so far:

First, reading is a complex skill that is quite different at the beginning stage from what it is in its most mature form.

Second, reading at the beginning is essentially mastering the alphabetic code since the language development of beginners or adults who learn to read their native language is several years ahead of their ability to recognize the visual representations of these words.

Third, reading after the code has been broken (which for the typical child occurs after about three years of instruction) is essentially further development in language, concept, and reasoning ability. Generally, the child who is more advanced in language and cognitive development will, after mastering the alphabetic code, make greater strides than the one who is less advanced in language and cognitive development.

The next obvious question is, How can language and reasoning in reading, that is to say, reading comprehension, be best developed? Here there is so little hard knowledge that strong disagreement has not yet developed. Indeed, although most American children are subjected to annual standardized achievement tests that always include a test of reading comprehension, there is little explicit knowledge as to what these comprehension tests actually measure. Also, although most children in the middle- and upper-elementary grades go through hundreds of "comprehension" exercises in workbooks and "reading laboratories"—selections of increasing difficulty followed by multiple-choice questions designed to test the reader's understanding of the selection—there are no hard data as to the effectiveness of these exercises.

Although everyone agrees that reading comprehension is the whole purpose behind learning to read, no one seems to know exactly what to do in order to assure not only that all children reach a level of skill commensurate with their language and cognitive development, but that their language and cognition are improved through the development of reading comprehension.

True, many psychologists have asked such questions as: What is the nature of comprehension? How can it best be measured? How can it best be taught? Yet it seems to me that the clearest definition of these issues as well as attempts to answer them can be found in the writings of E. L. Thorndike as early as 1914. It is disheartening to realize that all the work over the past fifty years has not advanced our knowledge. Indeed the issues have been blurred.

It seems to me that this is the area that needs researching. It needs serious study now particularly because of the recent strides made in the knowledge as well as in the practice of beginning reading instruction. As more children succeed in learning to decode, it will become even more obvious that some are not progressing as they should at the "real reading task"—reading comprehension—the accepted ultimate goal of reading.

To make a dent in this area will take the concerted efforts of investigators from many disciplines—philosophy, cognitive psychology, linguistics, psycholinguistics, literary criticism, mass communication, psychometrics, as well as from the area of reading. But it should be worth it.

12 THE SPEECH CODE

Alvin M. Liberman

Speech is such an easy and convenient thing that most people are misled into thinking it must also be very simple. If it were really very simple, of course, there would not be very much to say about it. In fact, however, speech is one of the most complicated and intricate skills that we ever acquire, and there is a great deal that can be said about it. We can talk about the sentences we speak, or about the meanings they have, or about the purposes they serve. But even if we ignore all those complicated aspects of speech, there is still much left to say that is interesting about the way we speak and the way we hear speech.

How do we make the vowels and consonants of our language? This question is far more complex than it seems. Speech is very special. It bears a special relation to language. It uses a special set of sounds. It is processed by a special part of the nervous system. It is perceived in a special mode.

Now most people do not realize that speech is so special. The common assumption is that the sounds of speech are like the letters of an alphabet. As I hope to show, that assumption is entirely wrong. I would like, nevertheless, to discuss this erroneous view, because it is important to see just where the mistake lies.

Let us consider, then, what it means to represent language alphabetically. Suppose we wish to communicate a simple word —for example, "bag." To do that in writing, we must first appreciate that the word comprises three phonetic elements or segments: the first segment is the consonant we call "b," the second is the vowel "ae," and the third is the consonant "g."

To write the word, we have only to select the appropriate letters of the alphabet, one for each of the three phonetic segments, and set them down in the proper order. Thus we have the simplest possible relationship between the phonetic message and its written form: for each unit of the message there is a unit letter.

Nor is there anything special about the optical shapes that we use as letters. Indeed, the selection of letter shapes is a matter of perfectly arbitrary convention. If, like most speakers of English, the writer is accustomed to using a Roman alphabet, then he would certainly choose from among the optical shapes in that particular set. But he could as well communicate the word with letters of the Cyrillic alphabet, or, indeed, he might, if he wished, invent a new one. Any alphabet, old or new, need meet only two requirements: there must be a letter for every phonetic segment, and the letters must be easy to identify. But since we can identify indefinitely many optical shapes, we can have indefinitely many alphabets.

If speech were like alphabetic writing, then to say the same word, "bag," the speaker would select three sounds, appropriate for the three phonetic segments, and utter them in proper sequence. To carry the analogy with writing further, we should suppose that selecting the sounds would be a matter of social convention. It is commonly assumed, however, that there are very many of these sounds, and that each community of speakers chooses, quite arbitrarily, the particular set it wishes to use.

My point is that speech is not at all like that. Speech is not an arbitrary alphabet on the language. Rather speech is linked to language by way of a complex and especially efficient code. As a result of research on speech, most of which has been done in the last twenty years, we now know something about the characteristics of the speech code, and we are able to say in what ways and in how far it is special. Later I will summarize some of those research findings. But first I would remind you that, even without doing any research on the speech signal, we can find much evidence that the sounds of speech have a special relation to language. At the very least, they are privileged and uniquely efficient vehicles for the communication of linguistic information. To see that this is so we should continue our comparison of speech and writing, but now, instead of supposing that these two ways of communicating language are similar, we should consider in what quite obvious ways they are different.

The ability to speak and to perceive speech is universal; with the exception of people who are deaf or brain injured, everyone does it. Reading, on the other hand, is quite rare. Many languages do not have a written form, and even in literate societies there are, among those who speak and listen, many who cannot read and write.

Speech comes first in the history of the race, writing comes second. Indeed, writing is a comparatively recent development. Speech is a product of natural evolution, or so we should suppose if only because it is something that every human being does. Writing, on the other hand, is quite clearly an invention. Moreover, the easiest way of writing—that is, by an alphabet— is so far removed from man's biological base that it has been invented only once in all history.

Consider, too, that language survives blindness but not deafness. Children who are born blind develop language in a perfectly normal way. Being unable to see the world they talk about is, of course, a terrible handicap, but it does no harm to language. Nor is their language development impaired in any essential way by their inability to read. On the other hand, children who are born deaf suffer a severe linguistic disability. Now it is easy enough to understand why a deaf child should not learn to speak. Being unable to hear, he cannot properly control and correct the sounds he makes. It is, however, much less obvious why deaf children who do not acquire speech cannot easily be taught to read or write. If speech and writing are but equivalent representations of language, why is the spoken form prerequisite to the written? Why is it, in fact, so very difficult to substitute the optical shapes of an alphabet for the acoustical shapes of speech?

Putting all these readily available facts together, we might conclude that there is something special about speech. But first we must ask whether the obvious priority of speech over writing is owing to factors that are, from our point of view, trivial. Are there explanations for the superiority of speech that have nothing to do with man's capacity for language or its relation to speech? Let us consider the trivial reasons that might be advanced.

One might argue, first, that the superiority of speech can be explained by supposing that the ear is a better organ than the eye. But such an argument runs contrary to fact. By almost any standard we can think of, the eye is a wider and deeper channel of information transmission than the ear.

If we cannot argue that speech is better than print because the ear is the better organ, then we might try the argument that speech sounds are the better signal. Perhaps these acoustic signals are, by comparison with print, particularly clear or simple. Suppose that is so, and imagine then what would happen if we were to try to build two analogous machines: one to perceive speech, the other to perceive print. It would not be required of these machines that they understand the message, only that they respond differentially to the phonetic elements. If speech were the better signal, then the speech perceiver should be the easier to build. But the experience of engineers has run directly contrary to that expectation. Engineers have succeeded fairly well in building machines that read print, but they have had almost no success in building machines to perceive speech. It is important to emphasize that the failure in the case of speech is not for want of trying; some of the best engineers in the world have given their best efforts to the solution of this problem. The difference in difficulty is owing to the fact that the advantages of clarity and simplicity lie with print, not speech. Print presents the engineer with a very clean signal that bears a straightforward relation to the message it conveys. Speech, on the contrary, is a very murky signal and is related to the rest of language in a very complicated way, as we shall see shortly. For now it is enough merely to point to a most interesting fact: for machines, print is easy to perceive but speech is very hard, while for us human beings, it is just exactly the other way around.

Knowing that the speech signal is neither clear nor simple, let us now try the argument that the advantage of speech lies in the fact that it is sound, and that sound is the best vehicle for language because it always attracts attention. We don't have to be looking at sound in order to hear it, and we don't have earlids with which to shut it out. But if the advantage of speech over writing lay in this, then we might expect to find many sets of sounds that would work equally well. Though there are many different alphabets, and though none is as easy for human beings as speech, they are all equally good. It is the more interesting, therefore, to note that the situation in speech is very different: there is only one set of sounds—those of speech—that will work well. We know that this is so because of what happens when people try to substitute nonspeech sounds for speech. Consider the familiar dots and dashes of the Morse telegraphic code. After years of practice people can perceive these signals at rates hardly one-tenth those at which they easily perceive speech. Less familiar, perhaps, are the attempts to contrive nonspeech substitutes for speech in connection with the development of reading machines for the blind. These are devices that transform print into sound. But if you know the history of the attempt to build such devices, you know that the first one was constructed more than fifty years ago. You must then also know that in the many machines that have been developed since that time, many sound alphabets have been tried, yet none has ever been found that is better than the sounds of Morse, and Morse is less than one-tenth as good as speech.

Of course, we should have known all along that sound alphabets could not possibly be substituted for speech. Consider that in the case of speech we can perceive at rates that require us to take in as many as twenty-five or even thirty phonetic elements per second. If each of these elements were represented in speech as they are in the nonspeech alphabets, there would be a unit sound for each phonetic element. But surely twenty-five or thirty such sounds per second would merge into a tone or buzz. The ear does not, and indeed cannot, separate individual acoustic events that occur at that rate; rather it integrates or merges them to form a unitary sensation, just as it integrates the individual pressure pulses of a tone and converts the signal into what we describe subjectively as pitch. Speech somehow evades this limitation. We should suppose, therefore, that speech is not a sound alphabet.

These facts suggest that the sounds of speech are somehow special. They are uniquely efficient and natural carriers of linguistic information. This is not for trivial reasons. Rather, we must look to the possibility that speech is, in some interesting way, uniquely well matched to language and to man. But the match cannot be a simple one; that is, speech cannot be a sound alphabet on the language. With that as background, let us now look at speech and try to find out what it is.

We should begin with the production of speech and, for that purpose, return to the example we used before—the word "bag." If speech were like writing, then we should select three articulatory gestures, one for each of the phonetic segments, and string them end to end. But that is not what we do. The first segment of "bag"—the "b"—is made by closing the lips and then opening them. The second segment, "ae," is made by putting the tongue into a particular position. Now it is clear enough that we do not make these gestures in tandem, first one and then the other; rather we do both at the same time. That is, we put the tongue into position for the vowel "ae" at the same time that we close and open the lips for the consonant "b." The next segment, "g," requires that we close the vocal tract by putting the back of the tongue up against the roof of the mouth. Many component parts of that gesture can be also overlapped in time with movements characteristic of the vowel. In this way we organize the phonetic segments into syllables, like "bag," which is to say that we overlap the segments that constitute the syllable and transmit them at the same time.

Notice how very efficient this procedure is, especially by contrast with writing. In writing we must make the movements for one gesture and then the movements for the next. The rate at which we transmit the segments of the message is limited by the rate at which we can move our muscles. In speech we are, of course, also limited by the rate at which we move our muscles, but in speech we move muscles for several successive phonetic segments all at once.

From a physiological point of view, the kind of efficiency we achieve in speech is not easy to arrange. It requires, in fact, a great deal of organization and coordination. Not only are the articulatory movements made with great speed and accuracy, but, as we have seen, they are organized and overlapped in very complex ways. It is of considerable interest that such organization and coordination is not found in the vocalizations of animals other than man. Our closest primate relatives vocalize, but recent evidence indicates that they produce only variants of a single vowel-like sound, one approximating the neutral vowel "uh." There is no evidence that they can co-articulate in such a way as to produce consonant-vowel syllables of the kind that are found in every language of the world. Yet this complex co-articulation is so easy for us human beings that one-year-old infants do it quite expertly in their spontaneous babbling. We should suppose that the ability and tendency to speak in this way is a part of our biological nature.

Let us turn our attention now from production to perception and see that there is also great efficiency in the way language can be listened to. Because the phonetic segments are, as we saw, overlapped and shingled into syllabic packages, we can perceive speech faster than we could if there were a unit sound for each phonetic segment. Earlier I said that if speech were an alphabet on the phonetic structure—that is, if each phonetic segment were represented by a unit sound—then the sounds of speech would merge into an unanalyzable buzz at relatively low rates of speaking. We have seen, however, that the phonetic segments are organized in such a way that an entire syllable is transmitted as a whole in one burst of sound. As a consequence, the limit on the rate at which we can perceive speech is set, not by the number of phonetic segments, but by the number of syllables.

I cannot emphasize too strongly, however, that the gain in listening efficiency is achieved at a considerable cost: in order to transmit several phonetic segments at the same time, there has to be a very complex relation between those segments and the sound that conveys them. Let us see in what way this is so. We have noted that in the production of speech the component elements of a syllable are put onto more or less independent muscles and overlapped in time. From the standpoint of muscular control, this is a very complex situation. But the result in sound is even more complex. The additional complication arises because there are fewer independent dimensions of the sound signals than there are muscles of articulation. Consequently, the simultaneously active muscles, representing successive segments of the message, affect exactly the same part of the sound. We find then that the same piece of sound is, at every instant, transmitting information simultaneously about more than one segment of the phonetic message. Indeed, a single aspect of the sound will sometimes carry information about three successive phonetic segments, all at the same time.

The relation between sound and phonetic message is now complicated in two important respects. First, there is no simple correspondence between the segments of the sound signal and the segments of the message, either in the number of segments or in their structure. Therefore, the sound signal requires very complex processing before we can know how many phonetic segments are encoded into it. Second, the part of the sound that carries information about a particular segment, say "b," will necessarily be very different depending on what other segments come next. This requires further complex processing if we are to discover the identity of the segments. In both these respects, the sounds of speech are different from the letters of an alphabet. In the case of an alphabet there is a simple, one-to-one correspondence in segmentation—one letter for each phonetic segment—and the letter shape is the same regardless of the phonetic context. To borrow a distinction from cryptanalysis, we might say that a written alphabet is a simple substitution cipher, but that the sounds of speech are a form of very complex code. Yet, as we know, human beings perceive the complex code more readily than the simple cipher. We should suspect that this is so because human beings have physiological devices that are specifically designed to decode these complex sounds and recover the phonetic message.

There is now a great deal of evidence that we human beings do, in fact, possess a special speech decoder. We don't know yet exactly how this decoder works, but we know what it has to do, and we have indirect, but very strong, evidence for its existence.

First of all, the speech decoder must decode. It must recover the phonetic message from an acoustic signal into which it has been complexly encoded. In the case of our example, "bag," it must determine that there are three phonetic segments. From the standpoint of an engineer or cryptanalyst this is a very difficult thing to do, because the three phonetic segments have been merged into just one burst of sound. The decoder must also cope with the fact that the part of the sound that carries information about the consonant "b," for example, is vastly different for every context in which that consonant appears. The fact that we nevertheless hear the consonant "b," both in "bag" and in "boog," indicates that the speech decoder is some-how able to hear through the physical variations and perceive the consonant in its canonical form.

But decoding is not all that our special speech processing device must do. When one examines the speech sound he finds that the important linguistic information, carried largely by so-called formants, often constitutes only a relatively small part of the total sound energy. The important information does not stand out clearly, as in the case of printed letters. If we human beings nevertheless hear speech well, it is because our speech processor is somehow able to extract and attend to the very indistinct parts of the signal that carry the linguistic information.

Thus, we might suppose that we have a special speech device simply because the successful perception of speech implies that a special decoding has been accomplished, and also that the essential parts of the signal have been separated from the un-essential parts. But there is other, more direct evidence for the existence of such a special device.

If the physiological device for perceiving speech were special—that is, different, in some important respect, from the device that perceives nonspeech—then we might expect that speech would be heard in a special way. Let me describe one bit of evidence that fits that expectation. Consider, first, what we have recently discovered about the acoustic cues on the basis of which we distinguish speech sounds. The primary cue that enables us to tell "ba" from "ga," for example, is in the movement of a band of acoustic energy at the beginning of each syllable. In the case of "ba," this band moves upward on the frequency scale, but in the case of "ga" it moves downward. Now a band of acoustic energy that moves up in frequency would be heard normally as a pitch that rises—that is, as an up-going glissando—and a band that moves down, as a pitch that falls—a down-going glissando. By dealing with synthesized speech we are able to remove these bands from a speech context and listen to them in isolation. We then hear exactly what we might expect: a rising pitch in the case of the band taken from "ba," and a falling pitch for the band from "ga." But when we listen to exactly these same bands in their normal speech patterns, we cannot hear anything like pitch glides, no matter how hard we try. What we hear then is not an auditory event, like a rising or falling pitch, but speech. We hear "ba" or "ga." This is to say simply that "ba" and "ga" cannot be heard in auditory terms. We should suppose that this is so because our perception of these sounds is accomplished by a processor that is specialized to deal with speech. As a consequence there is, in the perception of sound, not only an auditory mode, but also, and quite separately, a mode in which we hear speech.

There are other research results that point even more directly to the existence of a special speech processor, but I will describe only one. Suppose we present a stop-consonant–vowel syllable—say "ba"—to one ear and a different nonsense syllable—say "ga" —to the other. If we do this many times, using all pairs of "ba," "da," "ga," "pa," "ta," and "ka," we find that most people hear better the nonsense syllables presented to the right ear. If we now do the same experiment, but instead of nonsense syllables, we present simple musical patterns, we get the opposite effect—that is, our listeners hear better the patterns presented to the left ear. Now we know that each ear is connected to both sides of the brain, but we also know that the connection is stronger to the opposite side. That is, the connection between the right ear and left brain is stronger than the connection between right ear and right brain. The right-ear advantage for speech and the left-ear advantage for music indicate, then, that these two kinds of signals want to be processed on opposite sides of the brain, speech on the left, and music on the right. Of course, it has long been known that higher-level language functions tend to be localized on the left side of the brain. What these newer experiments teach us is that phonetic perception is there, too. This reinforces the view that the lowest level of speech perception is an integral part of language. But it is more relevant to emphasize that perception of speech sounds is carried out in one part of the brain and perception of nonspeech in another. Surely this supports the assumption that speech and nonspeech sounds are perceived by different devices.

If the production and perception of speech are special, then we are left with at least one more important question: Is speech unique to man, and, if so, then in what sense? Nonhuman primates produce only a single vowel—the neutral "uh"—and no consonants. More important, they show no evidence of the highly coordinated overlapping of articulatory components that occurs in the prelinguistic babbling of human infants. How, then, do nonhuman primates hear speech? Unfortunately, we don't know. But if all that I have been arguing is correct, we should have to suppose that they cannot hear speech as we do, even at the lowest phonetic level. This is not to say that animals should be deaf to speech, or that they should fail to discriminate speech sounds, but only that their perception of speech should be different from ours. Recall that though the primary acoustic difference between "ba" and "ga" is in the direction of movement of a band of sound, we humans hear not pitch glides, but unanalyzable linguistic events we call "ba" and "ga." I would guess that if we could get inside the monkey's head we might discover that, lacking our speech-sound processor, he hears not "ba" and "ga" but pitch glides.

Is this to say that speech is, in every sense, unique to man? Not necessarily. To suppose that speech production and perception occur only in man is to make a statement about behavior, not about underlying mechanisms. It is possible, indeed likely, that the special devices that enable us to produce and perceive speech are special only in the particular end they achieve. The basic principles they represent may be very similar to those that produce other highly specialized behaviors in animals other than man. As an example, recall that the speech processor must be able to attend to the linguistically important parts of the speech signal, even though those parts often constitute a relatively small part of the total acoustic stream. Now we know that many animals have devices that are specialized to respond to particular patterned aspects of the animal's environment. There is, for example, the bug detector of the frog. Investigators have found that the frog has a perceptual device that responds specifically to objects that move across its visual field at particular rates. Thus, the frog is made sensitive to an aspect of the environment that is of particular importance to him as a source of food. Somewhat similar, though surely still more complicated, mechanisms may be put together in different ways to make us human beings particularly sensitive to the linguistically significant parts of the speech signal, an aspect of our environment that is as important to us as flying bugs are to a hungry frog. Of course, such a speech detector is only the first step in the processing of the speech signal, since it will succeed only in paying attention to those sound patterns that have linguistic significance. A device to decode the signal and recover the message is still necessary. But when we understand how that decoder works, we may again discover that the underlying principles are not entirely new, but are rather old ones turned to new purposes. If that proves to be so, we shall have discovered that what is unique about man is not that he alone possesses these interesting physiological mechanisms, but that only he is able to use them in vocal communication.

To summarize: There is evidence all around us to show that the sounds of speech are uniquely natural and efficient carriers of linguistic information. We might then expect to find that the speech signal is special in some interesting sense. When we do research on speech that expectation is confirmed. We discover that the sounds of speech do not bear a simple alphabetic relation to the phonetic message they convey, but are rather a complex and special code. The essence of the code is that information about two or more successive phonetic segments is carried simultaneously on the same piece of sound. This makes for rapid transmission of information, but at the cost of a complex relation between the sounds and the message. Speech is nevertheless easy to perceive because we human beings have ready access to physiological devices that are specialized to decode the sound and recover the linguistic message. In this sense speech is a special system of communication; it is well matched to man and forms a significant part of his unique capacity for language.

13 ARTIFICIAL SPEECH

Edward E. David, Jr.

Artificial speech—speech generated by machine—fascinated researchers as far back as the eighteenth century. People in that day were intrigued with the notion that human processes might be duplicated mechanically, and they knew that speech is uniquely human. Today we are interested in artificial speech not only out of scientific curiosity, but for many reasons—to create reading machines for the blind and voice answer-back by computer over telephone circuits, for example.

To make artificial speech, we must duplicate some of the functions of the human vocal tract, for it is within the vocal tract that the acoustic wave we hear as speech is generated. It begins with the lungs which are the primary source of energy for speech. In speaking normally, air is forced from the lungs and the resulting air stream carries this energy. This energy of flow is converted to sound by the vocal cords or by turbulence at a constriction formed in the vocal tract, for example at the teeth when making an "s" sound.

Actually, the sound produced by the vocal cords or by turbulence is easily duplicated mechanically. The vocal cord sound is merely a buzz, much like a "Bronx cheer" or other rude sounds. Many people who have lost their vocal cords through surgery use a transistorized artificial larynx to produce a buzzing sound for speaking.

This buzz does not sound much like speech—something more is needed. That something is provided by the remainder of the vocal tract formed by the tongue, palate, teeth, and lips. Together these form a tube through which the sound from the vocal cords passes, eventually to be heard by the listening ear. The vocal tract tube has resonances much as a bell or an organ pipe does, so that sound energy at some frequencies is emphasized with respect to energy at other frequencies. Thus, the vocal cord energy emerges from the lips not as an undifferentiated buzzing sound, but as a speech sound. If you hold an artificial larynx against the side of your throat and allow its sound to pass through your vocal tract, you can form vowel sounds in the usual way. That is to say, different vowels are produced by moving your tongue, teeth, and lips to give different vocal tract shapes. To produce an "ee" (heed) sound, for instance, my tongue is humped in the back. The sound "ah" (hod) is made by opening the tract without much of a hump anywhere. The vocal tract too can be duplicated mechanically by merely constructing a tube of the right shape.

All of the sounds of speech are made essentially in the same way. For those sounds such as "s" and "sh" where the energy is provided by a hisslike turbulence, the source is not at the larynx but at the point of constriction in the vocal tract—for both "s" and "sh," the constriction is at the teeth. In the case of "sh," the cavity formed by the lips and teeth is larger and so its resonance is lower in frequency than that for the "s" sound. Sounds made using the vocal cords are called "voiced" sounds, those using turbulence are "fricative" sounds. Some sounds use both sources; for example, the "zh" sound in "azure."

These basic facts about the individual sounds of speech have long been understood, at least in a qualitative way. For example, the German, Christian Gottlieb Kratzenstein, in 1779 won a prize from the Imperial Academy of St. Petersburg for explaining how different vowel sounds are made in the mouth. He also constructed mechanical models for reproducing these sounds. His vowel makers each consisted of a shaped resonant tube excited by a reed which carried out the functions of the vocal tract and vocal cords. The Hungarian Wolfgang von Kempelen, also in the late eighteenth century, went further and investigated the physics of drinking water, swallowing, and kissing. In more modern times, the 1920s, the Englishman Sir Richard Paget was able to demonstrate not only the vowel sounds but a large number of English consonants as well by using shaped tubes and air flow. Not too long after that, vowel sounds were produced with electrical equipment using an electronic buzz source and electrical resonant circuits tuned to the proper frequencies for making vowels. Today there are kits available for high school students to build such vowel makers from simple parts.

The most vital aspect of speech, however, is not the isolated speech sounds themselves but the dynamics of speech whereby the individual sounds are fused together into a smooth succession of words, phrases, and sentences. In the vocal tract, this dynamic aspect corresponds to continuous movements of the tongue, teeth, lips, and jaw, so the vocal tract resonances, and also the sources of sound energy, change continually. The basic energy is still supplied from the lungs. This energy is converted into sound by the vocal cords and turbulence. Finally, the phonetic content or the information in speech is superimposed on the sound energy by the resonances and gestures of the vocal tract.

The dynamic aspects of speech production are much more difficult to duplicate than the steady-state aspects. Von Kempelen recognized this fact; he endeavored to build a talking machine in which dynamic variations were supplied by a human operator. His machine, which was described in detail in his book published in 1791, is not a replica of the vocal tract, but its parts can be identified with the human anatomy. A bellows pumping a wind box takes the place of the lungs. Sound is produced by air flowing through various holes in the wind box. Some contain a reed to mime the vocal cords, others are merely constrictions to generate turbulent sound. The sounds of speech are produced by resonators and tubes of various sorts placed over the openings from the wind box. To make the device talk, the operator pumped the bellows with his forearm, placing his hand selectively over various tubes and resonators to vary their characteristics. There were special keys and valves for making certain sounds. I have seen a copy of this machine in the Victoria and Albert Museum in London and it must have taken an octopus to operate it. However, people who have heard demonstrations of this machine by Sir Richard Paget say it can produce sound that is somewhat speechlike.

Paget himself produced a unique talking machine with the

exclusive use of his hands. He cupped them together so that the only opening was between his thumbs. Three fingers of one hand were inside the hollow and could be moved about more or less as the tongue can. He excited this rudimentary talking machine with a reed. He said jokingly he used this talking machine when his real vocal tract was immobilized in the dentist's chair. His favorite utterance made in this way was, "Careful there, you're on the nerve."

The first dynamic talking machine of which we have a recording was the so-called Voder which was demonstrated at the 1939 New York World's Fair by the Bell Telephone Laboratories. Here the dynamic variations were provided by operators who played a keyboard with their fingers, pressed pedals with their feet, and operated switches attached to their wrists. Again, the sources of sound were electronic and these were modified by resonators under the control of the keyboard. Some special dynamic effects for sounds such as "p," "t," and "k" were produced with other keys. A wrist-operated switch invoked either buzz or hiss sound sources, while the foot pedal controlled the voice pitch when the buzz was on. It took between three and six months to train the operators to produce speech on the Voder.

During actual demonstrations the audience listened first to a human announcer pronouncing a sentence; the Voder then endeavored to speak the same sentence. People were able to understand these sentences in spite of the quality of the recording, which illustrates the fact that speech does not have to be pronounced very clearly for a listener to believe that he has heard what he expects to hear. Even a suggestion of the words to be spoken is sufficient to render garbled speech intelligible. Through suggestion, namely, the announced sentence preceding each artificial sentence, the Voder was able to make a deep impression on audiences who had never heard an artificial talking machine before.

It was soon realized, however, that hand-driven talking machines tend to be tongue-tied. Somehow, the hands and fingers are not as nimble as the tongue, jaw, and lips. So the next step in improving artificial speech was to drive the talking machine, not by hand, but from a prepared script. This script takes the form of a complete specification of the vocal tract resonances and their dynamics. This specification, in effect, carries out the control that the human operator provided for von Kempelen's machine and the Voder. This way of controlling a talking machine is much more effective than a human operator. The first machine of this sort to be used widely was constructed at the Haskins Laboratories in New York City in the late 1940s. The machine was used for experiments in speech perception, for it could provide the identical utterances over and over again, each time with a controlled modification; thereby scientific experiments were possible.

Because of the method of reading the control instructions and producing the sounds, the speech uttered by this machine seemed monotonous and somewhat lifeless. That was because its voice pitch did not vary; the machine spoke in a monotone. In order to provide inflection to make lifelike speech, a different technique was needed. This was provided in a later device, also constructed by the Haskins Laboratories. This machine, known as the Voback, was able to reproduce not only the correct vocal tract resonances and dynamics, but also varied the voice pitch and thereby gave inflection to the artificial speech. Sentences recorded from the Voback could usually be understood without presuggestion.

In the early phases of this work, the control script for artificial talkers was compiled by tedious measurement and analysis of human speech. More recently, rules have been worked out whereby these instructions can be prepared without reference to samples of real speech. These rules permit a person to translate a sequence of written symbols representing the desired utterance into a set of continuous instructions for the artificial talking machine. In doing so, the person paints a mask which is read photo-electrically to drive the machine. However, even with these rules, human ingenuity and, indeed, artistry play a role. Unless the human being can be removed entirely from the process, artificial speech cannot be used with the flexibility and versatility that is needed in many practical applications.

The final step in making true artificial speech began with the coming of the high-speed electronic digital computer. Modern computers can generate control instructions for driving an artificial talking machine without human intervention, provided that this process can be stated in rules that are as definite as a computer program. The first work toward this goal was done by J. L. Kelly, Jr., and L. J. Gerstman of the Bell Telephone Laboratories. Many people have worked on the problem since and considerable progress has been made.

The input to the computer is a sequence of symbols specifying what is to be said. This sequence is much like a written or printed script using English letters. In the Kelly and Gerstman experiments, there also had to be information about the duration of each speech sound and its pitch. Pitch and duration correspond in human speech to what we call intonation and stress. It turns out that these are extremely important, not only for intelligibility and expressiveness, but for meaning as well. For example, the two sentences, "Why did *you* do that?" and "Why did you do *that?*" mean different things to a listener and may draw quite different reactions.

By examining particular samples of human speech for duration and pitch, it was possible to make this machine talk with an appropriate stress and inflection pattern.

It turns out that specifying pitch and duration for the appropriate intonation and stress is even more difficult than merely creating the correct succession of speech sounds. But there is one case in which duration and pitch are quite well specified, namely, in singing. Musical scores provide this information, so it was much easier to make the Kelly-Gerstman machine sing than talk. It could even accompany itself on the piano!

However, even Kelly and Gerstman had to introduce the human factor in order to generate pleasing artificial speech. Since the Kelly-Gerstman work, strenuous efforts have been devoted to finding rules to give pleasing stress and intonation automatically. These rules depend not only on the sounds to be uttered, but also upon the grammatical and syntactical structure of the sentences. And, of course, as we noted, some reference to the meaning of the speech is needed. However, researchers do not yet understand how to include this latter factor, except in stereotyped situations, such as answering questions about some standard subject. Nevertheless, real progress has been made in this quest for naturalness in artificial speech. This progress has come through the study of the pitch and duration of sounds in real speech. For example, it has been long known that in English the voice pitch is raised at the end of a "yes-no" question and falls at the end of a statement. Much more complete rules are needed for generating artificial speech, however, and these rules must be quantitative. Also, rules are different in different languages. This whole area involving language and its relation to speech is still a fertile field for research. At the present time we are able to generate artificial speech automatically with intonation and stress patterns that at least are acceptable, if not completely natural.

Thus, artificial speech can be generated today more successfully than ever before. We can confidently expect further improvements, but what about the uses of artificial speech?

There are many uses. As was mentioned earlier, the artificial larynx is very useful to anyone who has lost his larynx and vocal cords through surgery. It enables him to speak again almost immediately after the operation. Later, such people can learn to speak by generating sound in the esophagus; but the artificial larynx provides an important supplement for those who cannot learn esophageal speech and for many laryngectomees during the early stages of their convalescence.

There are also important potential uses of artificial speech in voice answer-back by computer over telephone lines, and in reading machines for the blind. Actually, I know of no case in which artificial speech is used today in practical devices. Rather, almost all automated announcing systems today use prerecorded words and phrases. The recordings suffice if there are only a few messages to be spoken. Where a larger number of messages are involved, prerecorded words and phrases can be assembled into sentences. This technique is simple and feasible because both recording media and the control needed to juxtapose the necessary words are available. However, it lacks the flexibility that artificial speech can provide. Assembled utterances do not sound natural, and where complicated sentences and ideas are involved, can make comprehension difficult.

As an alternative to recording speech and playing it back, it is quite feasible to store instructions for an artificial talker. Several machines of this sort have been proposed and demonstrated, so it will not be too long until artificial speech will begin to replace recordings for voice answer-back systems, the advantages being more pleasant speech and less expensive storage requirements.

Another use for artificial speech is in speech communication systems. Ordinarily, on telephone circuits the speech signal from the microphone is transmitted directly to the destination point and there reproduced as sound by some form of earphone or loudspeaker. An alternative is to transmit, instead of the speech wave itself, instructions for an artificial talker to speak the message. At the transmitter an analyzer is required to examine the incoming speech as it is spoken and to derive instructions automatically for the artificial talker at the receiver.

Such a speech-analysis–artificial-talker system is known by the generic term "vocoder," which stands for voice-coder. The advantage of the vocoder is that many speech channels can be sent over a line that ordinarily handles only one. This is possible because instructions for an artificial talker can be less complex than the speech itself. Another important advantage is that instructions for artificial talkers inherently give a degree of privacy, since an eavesdropper cannot merely tap the line to listen in. Speech communication systems of this kind are coming into use where economy of circuits and privacy are important.

Although artificial speech is not yet as natural or intelligible as the real thing, great progress has been made, particularly since digital computers have become an experimental tool in this work. We can confidently expect that in the not too distant future acceptable artificial speech will be generated from literal forms and from other specifications that are closer to the acoustic form. The amount of equipment needed to implement artificial talkers is not forbiddingly large, and there will be economical applications in both person-to-person and computer-to-man communication. Indeed, artificial speech is leading to new dimensions in communicating.

14 LANGUAGE AND PERCEPTION

Thomas G. Bever

Many characteristics of every language are due to political and social accidents. For example, the names in different languages for animals are not systematically related to any particular property of the animals; the words "dog, chien, hund . . ." all refer to the same animal even though their sounds differ greatly. This variability of languages makes it appear that children come into the world with uncommitted minds about many of the specific aspects of the particular language that their parents speak. Previous chapters have described the kinds of abstract rules that describe biologically arbitrary, but socially important, differences in specific sounds, words, and meanings in different languages. In this chapter, I shall discuss some built-in habits of perception that are common to the mental life of all human beings, and I will show some of the consequences for language structure of these perceptual habits. I want to convince you that many aspects of linguistic structure are *not* arbitrary at all, nor merely due to social and political accidents, but rather that many conventional linguistic rules exist to help the language accommodate to the peculiarities of our habits of perception.

One outstanding characteristic of human perception is that we tend to organize our conscious perception of the world in terms of the highest available level of organization. For example, when you look at your radio you do not identify it as a particular combination of tubes, transistors, and wires in a box, but as a radio. When a truck drives past you don't perceive two tons of brightly colored noisy metal, you perceive a truck. Of course, you can *try* to perceive the world as a series of elementary sensations and consciously avoid the more general perceptions. However, not only is such behavior unnatural, in certain cases it is impossible.

Consider, for example, a classic case used by psychologists to show that it is impossible to account for the perception of a whole object simply by adding together the perception of its individual parts. Any three dots that are close together and not in a line can be perceived as forming a triangle; but you still have the conscious choice of whether you think you are looking at a triangle or at a group of three dots that are unrelated to each other. If the dots are connected by lines, it is almost impossible to perceive anything except a triangle, although the description of the drawing could be that it is three lines, each connected at both ends with one of the other lines. This description is technically accurate, but perceptually irrelevant. The perception of the whole triangle dominates the consciously separate perception of the straight lines as pieces of the triangle. It is in this sense that some psychologists argue that "the whole is greater than the sum of its parts."

Now let me turn to the relation between parts and wholes in sentence perception. The most general level of sentence organization is its meaning, whereas the most particular is the series of acoustic vibrations that move your eardrum back and forth. Somehow we intuitively and unconsciously translate the vibrations of our eardrums into meaningful sentences. The first step in understanding a sentence would appear to be to analyze the acoustic sequence into a series of individual speech sounds (see Chapter 12). For example, the word "dog" is made up of a "d" sound, an "o," and a "g." But how do we isolate these segments when we listen? Do we perceptually analyze short acoustic fragments to discover what sounds they contain? A machine might be able to do this, but we cannot. For example, if you heard one-tenth-second segments of a spoken word, in which each segment you heard was separated from the next by a half second of silence, it would sound like a string of unintelligible noises. It is almost impossible to understand bits and pieces of speech that do not correspond to the basic speech units. It is as though you got a glimpse of very small pieces of a triangle one at a time, and were asked what geometric figure you were looking at.

But what are the "basic speech units"? Suppose we assume that the first step in sentence perception is to isolate the individual sounds, rather than chopping the sequence of acoustic vibrations of your eardrum into segments of arbitrary length. Some of the sounds would be very short like "d" and some relatively long like "o." If each consonant and vowel sound were separated out from a sentence, it would be easier to understand than when the acoustic units were a constant 1⁄10 second in length, but even so it would be quite difficult. Intermittent speech is very difficult to understand even when the speech is presented sound by sound. Similarly, it might be hard to recognize a triangle if you saw the three lines in sequence, one at a time.

So the basic acoustic unit of speech analysis is not some small fixed time sample, and it is not the individual speech sound. Rather, it is some larger acoustic unit: some have argued that it is the syllable. If a spoken sentence is divided up between successive syllables, it sounds a little odd, but it is perfectly understandable when whole syllables are presented one by one.

The fact that the syllable is the first acoustic level of analysis in speech perception of which we are conscious is demonstrable in other ways. People can be asked to listen to a sequence of meaningless syllables and to raise their hands as soon as they hear the first syllable that begins in "b." For comparison, we can tell them ahead of time that the entire syllable to listen for is "boog." Most people respond almost a tenth of a second faster when they are told the whole syllable ahead of time than when they are told only its first sound, even though all the hand-raising responses are started well before the syllable is over. That is to say, it takes extra time, after you have recognized the whole syllable, to realize consciously that the first sound in "boog" is "b." Which shows that we are aware of the whole syllable *before* we are aware of its separate parts.

We listen to speech in terms of syllables. The conventional rules of linguistics, however, usually govern relations between individual sounds rather than whole syllables. For example, in

English there are certain restrictions on the kinds of consonant sequences that can occur at the end of a word. English speakers can say a harsh consonant like a *"ch"* or *"s"* followed by any consonant that comes to a full stop, like "p" or "t": "list," "lisp," "flask," "latched." Other languages, like Russian, can have sequences of more than one harsh consonant at the end of words. Thus, English has a conventional restriction against words with more than one harsh sound in a row, but Russian does not.

We can see that these conventional linguistic rules which differ from language to language are expressed in terms of restrictions on individual consonant and vowel sounds rather than restrictions on whole syllables. Thus the English rule that describes how to turn singular nouns into plural nouns is a statement to add the specific sound "s" to the end of the singular form, rather than a statement about changing the whole syllable at the end of the singular form. Perhaps some examples will make this formal distinction clear. Consider the following corresponding singular and plural words and try to find a rule for changing singular words into plural ones: "one pit," "two pits"; "one trap," "two traps"; "one sack," two sacks."

The first rule is this: *Add the sound "s" to the singular form to make the plural form.* This rule would ignore any specific properties of the singular form—just add "s." But, as we saw in Chapter 2, this rule is not quite right.

Consider the plural form of words that end in a voiced sound, a sound that you make while making the vocal cords in your throat vibrate: "one lad," "two lads"; "one hub," "two hubs"; "one bag," "two bags"; "one boy," "two boys." The plural of these words is made by adding the sound "z," rather than "s."

Thus the rule for how to change singular into plural in English must be a little more complicated: *Add the sound "s" if the singular form ends in an unvoiced sound, add the sound "z" if it ends in a voiced sound.*

Notice that this rule is dependent on the quality of the consonant or vowel sound at the end of the singular form, rather than being dependent on the whole syllable. Suppose we tried to change the rule to refer to whole syllables rather than particular pieces of syllables. Such a rule would have to list separately all the syllables that end in voiced and unvoiced sounds. Since there are about two thousand syllables of each type it will be quite a long rule. For example: "After the syllables pit, pat, kit, kat, kut, lip, lap, loop, lope, rupe, rope . . . sit, sat, sick, sip, and soup, add the sound 's.' After fed, fad, food, sad, sob, sill . . . rib, rub, robe, sky and skid, add the sound 'z.'" Obviously, the rule is a lot more complicated when we have to refer to entire syllables rather than being able to refer to small pieces of syllables. Not only is it more complicated to describe sound laws in terms of syllables, but such a rule would also fail to express the simple regularity in English that whether the plural sound is "s" or "z" is determined by the pieces of sound just at the end of the previous syllable. For reasons of this sort, linguists describe the conventions governing sound sequences in each language in terms of consonants and vowels, not in terms of unanalyzed whole syllables.

But now recall our discussion of speech perception. We said that the basic acoustic unit of listening is the whole syllable; the individual consonant and vowel sounds are consciously perceived only after the whole syllable is perceived. Thus, the basic unit of the sound-sequence conventions, which differ from one language to another, is the individual sound, but the basic unit of conscious perception is the whole syllable.

We might expect, then, that certain conventional rules governing the sequences of individual sounds in a language are themselves influenced by the syllabic properties of that language, even though the syllable itself is never referred to explicitly by the conventional rules. For example, we noted that it is a conventional rule of English that two harsh consonant sounds like "s" or "ch" may not occur in a row at the end of a syllable, even though many other languages allow such sequences. This rule complicates the conventional rule for plural formation of English. As we stated the rule for plurals above, it worked perfectly for the particular words we talked about, but what about a singular word that itself ends in a harsh sound? How do we add a harsh "s" or "z" sound to these words to form their plural? For example: "one bus," "one buzz," "one church," "one edge," "one bush." If we used the general rule we found before, we would produce the following incorrect plurals: "two buss," "two buzzz," "two churchs," "two edgz," "two bushs." These plurals follow the rule of adding "s" or "z" to the singular form, but sound incorrect just because they violate the general constraint on English syllables that two harsh sounds may not occur in a row. For example, the plural formation rule as we stated it takes a word like "one church" which ends in the harsh sound, "ch," and adds "s" to it to produce "two churchsss," which is wrong. Or the rule taking "one bush" to yield the plural "bushsss." This is wrong too. We must modify our original rule so that a vowel is placed between the two harsh sounds that otherwise would be placed next to each other. That is, the correct plural of "church" is not "churchsss" but "churchez"; the plural of "bush" is not "bushsss" but "bushez," and so on. The reformulated plural rule is: *Add the sound "s" if the last sound of the singular form is unvoiced; add the sound "z" if it is voiced; and add the sound "uhz" if the singular ends in a harsh sound.*

Basically, we can view plural formation in English as a rule for adding "s" or its voiced counterpart "z"; but we have also seen that the syllable is a basic unit of *perception,* of linguistic conventions. Thus the perceptual constraint that arises from our natural tendency to listen to syllables modifies the form of conventional linguistic rules that govern sequences of individual sounds; and thus there must be added a rule exception which takes care of the plural forms that would otherwise violate the constraints on English *syllables* that there cannot be two harsh sounds in a row.

How does this happen? How does the perceptual system, which emphasizes the primacy of the syllable, have an effect on the form of the conventional rules of a language, which emphasize the primacy of the individual sound? The answer appears to be quite straightforward. The two behavioral systems, speech perception on the one hand and linguistic convention on the other hand, are being learned at the same time by the very young child. In this way a young child can incorporate certain regularities about syllables as part of his perceptual system. For example, a child learning English may learn that two harsh sounds cannot occur together at the end of a syllable, and that rule becomes a useful part of his perceptual system; he knows that whenever he hears two harsh sounds in a row like the "ch" and "s" as in "branchstone" then the first harsh sound is the end of one syllable and the second harsh sound is the beginning of the next syllable. It is not until about age four or five that the conventional plural rule is fully mastered; thus as he is learning this conventional rule the child intuitively requires of the rule that it not produce plural forms that violate the perceptual generalizations about syllables that he has already discovered. So he intuitively requires a conventional plural rule that separates the plural ending—"s"—from preceding harsh sounds. The conventional way in which the harsh sounds are separated is by the introduction of the neutral vowel, "uh." Introducing this colorless vowel to maintain syllable structure is typical of many languages.

This discussion has illustrated the way in which the nature of speech perception can influence the system of conventional rules governing relations between sounds. Over the centuries that it takes for a language to change, rules that are hard for our perceptual system to manage will tend to be filtered out of the language. To put this another way, through the ages children are reluctant to learn conventional sound systems that are hard for them to understand.

Of course, another set of conventional rules and perceptual habits has to do with a much higher level of organization than syllables and sounds—with the level of words and sentences. You might think that words are the basic units we hear and that sentences are composed out of groups of words. But remember the principle that we tend to organize stimuli at the highest available level. Perhaps what we do in listening is to perceive the sentence first as a whole unit just like the triangle or the syllable. This question is the subject of a great deal of research today.

There are many ways to demonstrate the perceptual power of the sentence. For example, if isolated words are distorted or heard in a background of static you may not be able to recognize them, but if the same words with the same amount of static are in a sentence, then you may have no trouble identifying them.

Of course, most sentences are complicated and have many sentence-clauses within them, like this: "Because the price of gold has been rising the international monetary fund will be under pressure again although this time there should be no serious crisis." This sentence has three sentence clauses in it: the price of gold has been rising; the international monetary fund will be under pressure again; and this time there should be no serious crisis. Such clauses form larger perceptual units that are part of the whole sentence. As we hear sentential clauses we isolate each clause as separate from the others.

The perceptual power of this segregation can be shown by a simple experiment. If you play a sentence with a short tone in it, you can ask people to listen to the sentence and write it down after they hear it, with a mark where the tone occurred. If the tone occurs anywhere near a clause boundary, most people will think that the tone came between the first sentence clause and the second. For example, if you play "although it probably won't snow, don't forget your overcoat" and put the tone *in* the word "snow," most people will hear the tone as if it came after the word "snow." We have found that everybody tends to think that tones come between sentential clauses rather than in them, regardless of their real location. We think that this is because the pieces of each sentential clause stick together and "repel" the interrupting tone toward the boundary between clauses.

To show that sentences may be consciously perceived before the words in them are, we have asked people to respond to a particular sentence or word in a list, in the same manner that we asked them to respond to syllables or phonemes. Suppose I asked you to respond by raising your hand as soon as you heard the first sentence beginning in the word "boys" in a series of short sentences. If I told you instead that the entire sentence was "boys like girls," your responses would be slightly faster. That is to say, you can respond a little faster to the beginning of a sentence when you are thinking of it *as* a sentence rather than as a single word.

Of course, words play an important part in the description of the conventional rules of syntax. For example, in English there is a rule that allows speakers to omit relative pronouns from relative clauses. Consider these two sentences: "The cat that I patted meowed nicely"; "The cat I patted meowed nicely."

The second is the same as the first except the word "that" is omitted. Another pair: "I patted the cat that I like"; "I patted the cat I like."

Thus, English has the following rule of syntax: *The relative pronoun "that" may be deleted.* Some languages, like German, don't have such a rule, so this is an example of a conventional syntax rule that is unique to a particular language. Of course, stating the rule in terms of omitting the word "that" is a great deal simpler than listing all the pairs of sentences like the ones given above. So the conventional grammar must be organized in terms of rules about words, rather than rules about whole sentences.

But our rule is not quite right, for it will also predict certain sequences that are not good English. Consider these sentence pairs; in the second one of each pair, "that" is omitted and the sentence is ungrammatical: "The cat that meowed is nice," "The cat meowed is nice"; "The boy that fed the cat is happy," "The boy fed the cat is happy"; "The dog that barked is hungry," "The dog barked is hungry." In these cases the relative pronoun is the subject of the relative clause. In the earlier examples, in which one may omit the relative pronoun, the relative pronoun is the object of the relative clause. So we must change the omission rule: *The relative pronoun "that" may be deleted unless it is the subject of its own clause.*

The reason for this restriction clearly has to do with the misleading form of a sentence if "that" is deleted. The perceptual importance of the sentence makes us hear sentence clauses whenever we can. Consider an ungrammatical sentence with "that" omitted: "The boy fed the cat is happy." Without the "that," the first five words form an independent sentence clause, rather than a relative clause. Thus the restriction on relative clause pronoun omission is motivated by our overwhelming tendency to perceive speech in terms of sentences. The presence of the word "that" blocks this perceptual habit in relative clauses; in this way the conventional grammatical rules accommodate to our perceptual system by making sure that the relative pronoun is present whenever it helps to stop us from misgrouping and misunderstanding the sequence.

To summarize. The structures inherent to language behavior

are described by the conventional grammatical rules of each language. These rules are stated as restrictions on possible sequences of sounds and words. As a child learns these rules, the sequences that they allow interact with his perceptual system, which operates initially in terms of syllables and sentences. In some cases the child's perceptual system modifies his conventional sound system, and in others, the conventional system does not accommodate, since obviously as the rules of a language evolve in history they cannot change to allow every sentence that is difficult for a child to understand. Thus the child's perceptual system is a constant watchdog that rules out some evolutionary changes and allows others.

Language behavior is the joint product of many aspects of our mental capacities, our capacity for thought, our perceptual habits, our ability to move our mouths, and so on. When we consider the complexity of the interactions between these different systems we realize that there is no single evolutionary development in any one of these systems that can account for all the complexity of language. Rather than looking for an isolated evolutionary development that allows us to talk, we must examine how the instinct to communicate has integrated the many different aspects of our behavior into what we call "language."

15 LANGUAGE AND MEMORY

James J. Jenkins

There is a striking difference between the notion of memory that most of us have and the notion of language as it has been described in this book. Most of us think of memory as a lower mental function, a sort of simple machine we have in our heads that copies parts of the world and stores those copies to be found again later. On the other hand, most of us now think of language as a complicated, productive system of great power, a system that can produce new products appropriate to any situation in which we find ourselves, a system that is often compared to thought itself in terms of depth and complexity.

Language as a many-leveled, hierarchical system can be related to memory as a process. A human being is a very flexible psychological machine: he is capable of being either a very simple machine or a very complex one. I assume that a person learns a great deal about the world and the demands that it makes on him in particular situations. He then sets himself to act as a machine of appropriate nature for each situation, as he sees it. What he remembers depends on what kind of machine he is at the time.

The best and simplest way to illustrate this thesis is through the example of language. We agree that language is complexly and hierarchically structured, but memory functions change with the level of language used and with the demands of the situation.

Let us begin with the work of the first great scientific student of memory, Hermann Ebbinghaus. For over five years, Ebbinghaus worked on a vast set of experiments studying his own memory. As he investigated his memory of prose, he found that prior learning—things he already knew—played an important role. In order to get a better study of "pure" memory, he invented materials that were languagelike but carried no meaning. These were simple combinations of consonant-vowel-consonant that made syllables but were not real words. (In English, for example, the sequence M-I-B, "mib," is a nonsense syllable. One can pronounce it and spell it, but it doesn't mean anything.) Using materials like this to minimize the effect of past experience, Ebbinghaus studied his recall of lists of different lengths, over different periods of time, with different numbers of rehearsals, and so on.

Ebbinghaus's major achievement is often called "*the* curve of forgetting." This implies, of course, that there is only one pattern of forgetting—and if you think of memory as a simple copying device, that seems to be a reasonable belief. The curve of forgetting shows that you begin to forget each thing you learn almost immediately after learning it. The losses from memory are very great at first and then slowly level out. Thus, in the first day after learning a list, Ebbinghaus found that he lost between 75 and 80 percent of what he had learned. This picture of rapid loss from memory has been faithfully passed down through generations of psychologists and the general form of the curve has been confirmed in many experiments.

In spite of this great agreement, every psychologist who does learning experiments knows that one does not find great losses like these on other kinds of materials—such as stories—and (even more puzzling) that you do not find losses like these when you use naïve, inexperienced subjects in your experiments! As a matter of fact, the first list of nonsense syllables a subject learns is likely to be recalled quite well after twenty-four hours. The losses we usually find in our laboratory are more like 20 percent than Ebbinghaus's 80 percent! What does that mean?

We thought at first that the subjects remembered their first list so well because they took so long to learn it. When they learned later lists, they learned them faster. As they became fast learners, they recalled less and less of what they had learned the next day. It occurred to us that learning time alone might be a sufficient explanation. When we tested this idea, however, we found that learning time had no effect on recall twenty-four hours later. We had our subjects learn one list after another on successive days and, though they mastered the material in only half the time as they got to be better learners, we kept them at the task each day until they had had as many learning trials as they took on the first day. To our surprise, in spite of all this over-learning, their recall scores got worse and worse each day until they looked like Ebbinghaus's curve of forgetting. That is, the learners were recalling only about 20 to 25 percent of what they had learned the day before.

It is customary to talk about effects such as these as due to "interference" from the lists learned on preceding days. Yet there is little evidence for actual interference; the subjects do not recall materials from other lists in place of the list they are supposed to recall. Instead, we think that the subjects are learning to behave like very simple learning machines that accomplish the immediate task in such a way that they have little long-term memory. For the first list he learns, a subject can usually tell us all sorts of irrelevant things. He knows how many items there were; he knows what the syllables reminded him of; he knows what he was thinking about as he tried to relate the syllables to each other. Notice that none of this activity is particularly useful to the subject in the experiment: he is *overpowering* the task, and he recalls it very well twenty-four hours later. Now ask this subject about the fifteenth or twentieth list that he learns. The contrast is quite clear. He knows very little about the last list. He knows how to perform in the right way on the learning task, but he is not learning all the other "rich" details about this list that he learned about the early lists. He can't describe the nonsense syllables in any detail; he doesn't report any associations or images; he doesn't attach any meanings to the terms, and so on. In brief, the subject has learned to behave as a much less complicated machine in this task. He has lowered the power he is using but increased his efficiency on the immediate job. He does learn faster each day. But his long-term recall has been greatly reduced. We might conclude that the machine that learns this nonsense task effectively is a poor machine for storing materials over a longer period of time like a day.

At this point you may object that the preceding argument is purely speculative. You could invent a dozen other explanations that would be just as good. What one needs is more direct experimental evidence. Fortunately, there are many forms of evidence of the same kind of thing—once one starts to look for examples.

Take, for example, a set of studies that Thomas Hyde and I have been doing. We make a tape recording of a list of real English words such as "table, man, bird, salt," and so forth. Our subjects are asked to listen to each of these words and perform some task with respect to each one. One group of subjects is asked, for example, to make a check on a list if the word is spelled with the letter "e." Another group of subjects is asked to check on a list if the word is "pleasant" or "unpleasant." After all of the subjects have heard the tape, they are asked to write down all the words they can remember. Of course, the subjects have heard exactly the same tape recording; the same sounds have entered their ears. What is different is what the subjects did with those sounds. One group analyzed the words in the sense of spelling out the words (to themselves) and asking if there was a particular letter in the word; the other group thought about the meaning of the word and asked themselves if it was pleasant or unpleasant. The difference in recall between the groups is quite impressive. The group that was checking for letters recalled few of the words and showed no grouping or meaningful organization of the words of the sort that one usually finds in recall. The group checking for "pleasant-unpleasant" recalled the list very well. In fact, they were as good as a group that was only instructed to recall and had no incidental task to perform.

In exploring the effect of many different incidental tasks we have discovered that instructions that focus the subject on the form of a word (its spelling, sound, length, and so on) are very destructive to recall, while instructions that focus on the meaning (rating for pleasantness, judging how often people would use the word, giving an adjective or noun that can be used with the word, and so on) give excellent recall. In other words, this experiment demonstrates that recall is not just a function of what the outside world presents to you but also is a function of what you do with the events as you experience them. When you behave in one way, you remember very little about the word; when you behave in another way, you remember it very well. Thus, this experiment (and many others like it) supports the view that there are a variety of mental functions and that memory is differentially affected by the way the mental machinery is used. Notice that there is no suggestion here that the memory function is just a copy of the events that have occurred; it is rather a function of the mental operations performed on the material furnished by the world.

Now, perhaps, the problem is getting clearer. Can we show that memory is systematically affected by the different mental functions performed by our subjects at many different levels of language?

Let us consider the question of recalling verbal strings that are different statistical approximations to English (see Chapter 17). We usually consider a "zero-order" approximation to be merely a random sample of words of the dictionary—such a list is very hard to retain because it is usually made up of rare words like: *provinciality, energy, ralliform, talon, unceremoniously,* and so forth. Although such a string is made up of real words, it is very hard to recall.

A "first-order" list is one that is weighted for frequency of occurrence. This makes a list where words are represented many times if they are common words and only rarely if they are rare words. The word string will tend to be made up of words that we know quite well like: *until, he, do, grows, the, but, his, in,* and so forth. A list like this is easier to recall than the first, of course.

A "second-order" list is made up of words that could follow the preceding word in a sentence. That is, one starts with a word like *boy* and asks someone for a word that could follow *boy* in a sentence. Suppose he says something like *is.* Then we ask someone else for a word that can follow *is* in a sentence. We keep on in this manner until we have a string of words like: *boy, is, going, home, is, to, make, that, this,* and so forth. This string, in turn, is easier to recall than the first-order approximation. We can continue in this fashion, building higher-order approximations and finding that they get easier and easier to remember as they come to resemble English more and more. (We should notice, however, that approximations do not get to be as easy to remember as English sentences. Sentences are apparently something more than statistical strings of words.)

What these experiments tell us is that the memory processes can make use of transitional probabilities to aid in the remembering (or perhaps we should say reconstruction) of the material that the subject is trying to remember. This suggests again that the memory is not a copying device but a sort of construction process that uses what it already knows—like transitional probabilities—to construct the material that it is supposed to remember.

Can we now show that memory is sensitive to the truly linguistic structures of language—that is, can we show that memory can make use of the information contained in syntax in some systematic and reasonable way? Fortunately for our purposes, Dr. Neal Johnson has run the kind of experiment we need to examine at this point. Johnson used a memory task in which the subjects were to learn eight sentences—each sentence in response to a particular number. For example, the first sentence might be: *The tall boy saved the old woman.* And the second sentence might be: *The house across the street burned down.* And so on. Every sentence had the same number of words (seven) but the sentences showed two different kinds of structure. In the first type, the sentence has a major division between the third and fourth words. For example, *the tall boy* is a noun phrase that is the subject of the sentence and *saved the old woman* is the predicate. Thus, we suppose there is a major boundary between *boy* and *saved* and a minor boundary between *saved* and *the old woman.* Johnson predicted that most errors of recall would occur at the grammatical boundaries —that is, the subject would recall *the tall boy* even early in learning but would not remember what the tall boy was doing, so there would be many errors between *boy* and *saved.* This turned out to be true.

The second sentence was constructed so that it would have different boundaries. *The house* has a phrase attached to it that tells which house—it is the one *across the street*—and then finally we learn what happened to the house—it *burned down.* In this sentence Johnson predicted that there would be errors between *house* and *across* and another set of errors between *street* and *burned.* That is, he predicted that the memory would make use of the functional syntactic units of the sentence. He assumed that words would be tightly knit together within a syntactic unit but connections would be weak from one unit to another. Again, the results were as he predicted. Syntactic groups *were* functional memory groups.

But one does not need to stop here with the investigation of syntax and memory; one can go on to the comparison of types of sentences that are remembered. George Miller once advanced the hypothesis that sentences are not stored as copies but are reduced to some abstract general form with a set of "tags" or "markers" stored with them that specify the syntactic form of the sentence. For example, the question *Did the boy hit the ball?* might be stored in memory as "The boy hit the ball— Question" or something similar. He assumed that if the syntactic information got lost or forgotten, the sentence recalled would tend to be the simple declarative sentence, *The boy hit the ball,* as the most direct representative of the semantic content of the original sentence. Thus, he predicted that if the sentence were heard as a passive, *The ball was hit by the boy,* it might be recalled as an active sentence, *The boy hit the ball.* Miller and his colleagues showed there were numerous experimental settings where such effects occurred.

Although the hypothesis of memory-tagging in just this form is not being strongly pursued at the present time, there is abundant evidence that memory confusions between sentences that are related by syntactic transformations are very common. In English, it is hard to remember whether one heard a sentence in active or in passive form. Since *The boy hit the ball* and *The ball was hit by the boy* have the same meaning, there is little point in storing the forms of such sentences. There is a great tendency to confuse such sentences in memory, in recognition, and in discrimination experiments, and the sentences confused are just those that the subjects rate as being "most similar" when they are asked to study sets of such related sentences. The "similar" sentences turn out to be those that are most closely related by syntactic transformations.

An even better demonstration of the primacy of semantic relations over syntactic information in memory is found in the experiments of Jacqueline Sachs. Sachs had subjects listen to a story being read to them. At some point she would stop the story and ask the subject about a sentence that occurred earlier in the story. The question was whether after a short delay the subject remembered the form or the content of a sentence embedded in a story. When the delay was very short—that is, when she tested subjects by presenting the last sentence that they had heard—their memory was excellent, of course. Any violation of form or content was easily detected. With a slight delay, however, the specific form of the sentence seemed to disappear. Subjects seemed quite willing to accept an altered sentence (as long as it was a paraphrase of the same facts) but quite unwilling to accept a sentence in the same form that introduced different content.

Sachs's study suggested that the *information* in the sentence had been stored in memory but that the specific sentence itself had not been. Only its abstract representation was available and the form in which that content was presented was of little importance. This study, like the previous ones, suggests the general superiority in memory of semantic or meaningful encoding over the encoding of form or syntax or particular instances. General and abstract memory functions seem to be more adequate and more resistant to forgetting than specifics and particulars.

Recently two young men in my laboratory, John Bransford and Jeffery Franks, decided to take the notion of the efficiency of abstract memory as seriously as possible; they designed an experiment to demonstrate how powerful such abstraction can be. As the basic material to be remembered they took complex ideas like those represented by such sentences as:

> The rock that rolled down the mountain crushed the tiny hut at the edge of the woods.

and

The tall tree in the front yard shaded the man who was smoking his pipe.

Each of these ideas has four major relations in it. For example, in the first sentence we can say:

The rock rolled down the mountain.
The rock crushed the hut.
The hut was tiny.
The hut was at the edge of the woods.

For purposes of discussing the experiment, we will call such sentences "Ones," signifying that they express one relation.

It is easy to see that we can combine some of the information and make sentences that express two of the relations at a time. These we will, of course, call "Twos." These sentences are:

The rock that rolled down the mountain crushed the hut.
The rock crushed the tiny hut.
The tiny hut was at the edge of the woods.
The rock crushed the hut at the edge of the woods.

Similarly, there will be sentences that express three of the relations at once. These "Threes" will be:

The rock that rolled down the mountain crushed the tiny hut.
The rock that rolled down the mountain crushed the hut at the edge of the woods.
The rock crushed the tiny hut at the edge of the woods.

The complete complex sentences we will call "Fours" to signify that they contain all four relations.

Now Bransford and Franks did not just present the complex sentences to the subjects to recall. They devised a short-term memory task that kept the subjects busy while they heard some of the Ones, Twos, and Threes. A task that seemed especially suitable was a questioning task—that is, the subjects had to answer a question about each sentence just after they heard it. Thus, a sentence would be read to the subjects such as: *The rock crushed the tiny hut.* After a brief delay, the subjects were asked a question such as "What did?" and the subjects wrote down their answers, "The rock did." Then a sentence from another complex set was presented such as: *The tree was in the front yard.* Then a question was asked about *it.* This procedure continued over four sets of complex sentences with the subjects getting a few Ones and a few Twos and a few Threes from each set. No subject ever heard the full complex sentences.

At the end of this procedure, the subjects were told that they were going to be given a recognition test and that they should indicate for a list of sentences *which* were sentences from the original list. If they were sure that they had heard a sentence before, they were to give it a "plus five" rating; if they were fairly sure they had heard it before, they were to give it a "plus four"; and so on down to "plus one" which was to mean that they were nearly guessing but they thought they might have heard it. Then for the sentences that they thought they had not heard they had a similar scale: "minus five" meant that they were sure they had not heard the sentence, "minus four" meant that they were fairly sure they hadn't heard the sentence, and so on to "minus one" which meant that they were not sure but they thought that they had not heard the sentence. Thus, the subjects had a chance to indicate how sure they were that they had earlier heard or not heard each sentence on the test list.

The test list contained the rest of the sentences from the complex sets including the full sentences with all four relations in them. In addition, they had some control sentences that crossed over the relationships of the sentences, for example: *The tall tree in the front yard shaded the tiny hut at the edge of the woods.* This sentence was, of course, made from the elements of sentences that they had heard but it says something different as to general relations.

The results of the recognition test were very surprising to anyone who holds the copy theory of memory. The subjects gave top recognition scores to the full, complex sentences that they had actually never heard before—the Fours. They gave next highest ratings to the Threes, next highest to the Twos, and generally low ratings to the Ones. Whether they had actually heard the sentences before or not made no real difference. Their ratings were apparently governed almost wholly by whether the sentence on the test list matched the complex notion that they had abstracted from the sentences on the original question task.

Also important is the fact that the "cross-over" sentences got very, very low ratings (approximately, minus four). Thus, the subjects were telling us that in spite of the fact that all of the elements of these sentences are familiar, the sentences are clearly recognized as being new and different from the original sentences because they do not correspond to the overall complex ideas.

Now, there are several important aspects to this experiment that I want to stress:

First, the material that was evaluated in recognition was learned by the subjects *incidentally* while they were performing a short-term memory task. That is, it was an automatic form of learning. The subject was not instructed to learn nor was he trying to learn the material for future use.

Second, the materials were integrated over separated instances. That is, the subjects were collecting material from different points on the original task and putting these materials together in one complex idea. The materials for a given idea were not together in the list, but scattered through it. Thus, the mind was actively identifying content as "related" and putting the materials together into related wholes.

Third, the results of the recognition trials show that recognition here consists of estimating the goodness of matching of the complex idea and the sentence being tested. The better the match between the idea and the sentence, the more certain the subject is that he has heard the sentence before, even though it may be presented for the first time on the test list.

Finally, I would like to stress the fact that the whole process was spontaneous and "natural." In a sense the experiment is closer to daily life than most experiments.

I am very impressed with these experiments and the light they shed on the complex structural processes we can now see so clearly in memory. While many psychologists have been telling us for years about the contributions of *schemata* and "organizing principles," I do not think any body of data is more impressive than the changing memory effects that we can see when we ascend the language hierarchy in our choice of materials.

Many of us will continue to press forward with this line of work. I wish that the full story were available to give you now, but in its absence I will permit myself the liberty of a few speculations or conjectures concerning what we will find and what we will believe when all the facts are gathered.

I think we will eventually conclude that the mind remembers what the mind *does,* not what the world does. That is, experience is the mind at work, not the active world impinging on a passive organism—and experience is what will be remembered.

Second, I believe that we will find that some activities of the mind are better recorded and recalled than others. This may be because some activities are more rewarded than others, or more important than others, or more economical or efficient than others. In general, we will find that specific details, superficial structure, and elements of form are discarded and more abstract activities are retained. Notice that this is not to say that we *cannot* store such details—obviously we can—but it *is* to say that the storage of such details is not the normal rule nor is it the prototype of language.

Third, we will find that some representations may be used to generate certain other representations when we need them, but not others. Thus, if I remember an abstract idea, I may be able to generate a host of specific behaviors, ranging from talking about it all the way through acting on it. But I may not be able to remember the particular form in which I first learned it. On the other hand I may be able to recall something as a specific copy (like a memorized equation in physics) and not know how to use it or even know what it means. Understanding a subject matter presumably involves both kinds of memory and a comprehension of their relationships.

Finally, I expect that we will find that memory, like language, is hierarchically organized—whether it is verbal memory, or memory for motor skills, or even subject matter knowledge. Just as we see in language the relation of hierarchical governance from ideas to sentences, from sentences to phrases, from phrases to words, from words to sounds—with great evidence of system and interrelation everywhere—so we will someday see that human skills and human knowledge are similarly organized.

In this sense language may be a key to open the mysteries of the higher mental processes and to provide new understanding of the mind and its functions.

16 LANGUAGE AND THOUGHT

Janellen Huttenlocher

Thinking, by all definitions, is a covert activity, witnessed only by the person engaged in it. The experience of thinking has been variously described as talking to oneself, hearing voices speaking, seeing mental pictures, manipulating mental images. By virtue of our ability to think, we are able to consider objects and events that are absent, and can sometimes solve problems without actually trying out alternative courses of action. I want to consider here what role language may play in these thought processes.

First, however, we should consider some of the difficulties that psychologists have had in gathering information about thinking, and, in fact, in thinking about thinking. The empirical investigation of thought processes began, quite naturally, with an examination of people's introspective accounts of their conscious experiences. A person would be asked to think about some problem and then to describe everything that passed through his mind while he was thinking. Psychologists often found consistencies among different people's reports, especially when they had trained people in the technique of introspecting. Hopes for this method, however, proved overly optimistic.

A major difficulty with the introspective method is that it provides no objective way to check the accuracy of one's impressions. People generally can think of many alternative ways to explain various things that happen to them. So it should not be surprising if there are also alternative ways to analyze one's own conscious experiences while thinking. The only data of introspection are people's accounts of their private experiences.

If two people describe their experiences differently—for example, if one man claims to think in images while another claims to think in words—a psychologist has no basis for judging one of them to be wrong. Moreover, there were other limitations to the introspective method. For example, certain processes proved to be inaccessible to conscious experience; people might answer a question without any awareness of how that answer had been obtained.

If thinking need not be conscious, and if there are alternative ways to describe one's conscious experiences, one begins to wonder whether it is possible to base a real science on such phenomena. Perhaps the study of thinking must remain speculative, not amenable to the kind of self-correction that is possible in real sciences. Other questions arise about a science of conscious experience as well. What, for example, would be the relation between a science of the mind and the science of the brain? Might conscious experience be inappropriate for separate study because it is a mere reflection of the brain's activity?

Investigators who examined such questions concluded that the subject matter of psychology had to be redefined. To many, psychology became the science of behavior rather than the science of mind. Its data were the observed relations between overt behavior and the events preceding it. The purpose, according to some, was to predict future behavior. It was commonly believed that the relations between observable behavior and preceding events would prove to be describable by fairly simple mathematical functions.

In order to avoid speculating, many psychologists concerned themselves with problems that did not seem to require any consideration of internal processes. They tended to study animals rather than humans, and to consider such problems as how the speed of learning was related to amount of reward or punishment. However, psychologists cannot ignore the nature of human beings for very long. People's observable behavior clearly depends on complex operations of perceiving, recognizing, carrying out logical operations, and so on. One would therefore guess that a psychologist *must* take account of such processes in order to predict what people will do. The chief reason for attempting to explain the nature and operation of the human intellect, however, is simply the desire to understand it better.

Psychologists today still take as their basic data people's overt behavior and its relation to preceding events, much as the early behaviorists argued they should. This use of behavioral evidence does not preclude the study of thinking, however. Rather, people's behavior provides clues about the mental operations involved in producing it. The aim of such behavioral investigation is to give a logical description of the perceptual and cognitive functions of the human being. One approach is to chart the processing of stimuli from the moment of sensory activation until a response is made, as if one were describing the program of a computer which recognizes an input, carries out logical operations, and plans and produces an output.

Computer programs describe a sequence of operations performed on input without considering the physical materials that make up the machine. A computer program need not, of course, worry about any conscious experiences of the machine. Psychological descriptions of information processing based on people's behavior are analogous to computer programs in that they describe mental operations without considering the anatomy or neural activity of the brain, yet these descriptions need not incorporate people's conscious experiences. That is to say, the evidence about thinking, perceiving, and so on, is based on people's behavior and is arrived at independently of conscious experiences. Thus it is possible to ask how operations identified in this way compare with people's conscious experience of internal processes. Further, one can investigate how the operations identified in psychological studies are physically realized in the nervous system.

We are concerned here only with those mental operations that are involved in reasoning and problem solving. Consider, by way of example, the choice of moves by a chess player. The player does not automatically make a particular move whenever he encounters a particular arrangement of pieces, nor is he at a loss if he encounters some new arrangement of pieces that he has never seen before. Each of his moves is based on an evaluation of the long-range consequences of various alternatives. He need not touch the pieces to make his choices, and, in fact, the chess men and board need not even be present. In such circumstances, people apparently carry out internal operations that serve in the place of overt actions with real objects. Their thought accomplishes what might have been accomplished with real actions; the outcome of the thought process is directly applicable to their situation. Clearly, their thought is systematically linked to the situation they are thinking about.

One might at first see nothing mysterious about such cases of successful thought. One could say that a person tries out the alternatives "covertly" in his imagination, but the issue is not as simple as that. A person does not literally absorb the objects he thinks about, nor has he an actual hand or pencil to move about in his head. Thought does not duplicate reality, but rather represents it.

Insofar as thinking involves mental representations of the situations people encounter, it can be likened to people's many observable representational activities. The use of symbols to represent the elements of operations in one domain with those in another is characteristic of human beings. For example, certain aspects of people's experience are represented in natural language by means of a complex scheme of sounds and rules for combining them. Spoken language is itself represented in writing systems involving arrays of letters or pictographs which are mapped systematically onto temporal sequences of sounds or words. Quantities and the operations of adding, dividing up, and so on, are represented in the symbols of mathematics. Certain spatial characteristics of objects are represented in maps and pictures. Certain aspects of events are represented formally in scientific models and theories, and the theory's adequacy is tested by gathering its predictions and comparing them with the situation the theory was designed to represent. Small children at play also represent certain objects and operations with others, as when they pretend that sea shells are tea cups, that sticks are guns, and so on.

In order for the elements or operations of a symbol scheme to represent the elements or operations in another domain, the former must be systematically mapped onto the latter. There need be no resemblance between the elements or operations in the two domains as long as there are systematic relations among them. The sounds of the words of natural language do not resemble what the words connote, nor do the different arabic numerals resemble different quantities. Certain obvious restrictions are placed on a symbol scheme in order for it to represent particular information from the original domain, and no doubt, there are many other restrictions that are not so obvious. If, for example, ten different objects or events are to be represented, one must have a symbol scheme that can designate elements in ten different ways, and so on. Not only must a scheme be rich enough to represent a situation, but one must also establish how it is mapped onto various aspects of that situation.

These considerations about the representation of information are as applicable to mental representations as to those that are physically realized in spoken language, in diagrams, and so forth. A mental representation of a problem situation will work in problem solving only if the mental scheme is sufficiently rich, and if the correspondence between the situation and the scheme is established. If these conditions are met, a person can apply solutions achieved in thought to problem situations by replacing the elements and operations in his mental representation with the corresponding elements and operations in the external situation.

The notion that language is the medium for thought has appealed to a variety of investigators. Certain philosophers claim that men over the ages have concerned themselves with many vacuous questions because their natural language was so poorly formulated that it tricked them into generating pseudo-problems. The argument suggests that natural language is so centrally implicated in the thought process that people may end up thinking about nothing at all if their language permits it.

From a different vantage point, cultural anthropologists have also suggested that language exerts a molding and constraining influence on thought. They have proposed that the variations in the way different languages represent people's experience is closely tied to the variations in social customs and world view in different societies. Since language is learned early in life and certainly provides one means by which people communicate their world views to their children it seemed a possible factor in maintaining a society's particular world view. It has even been proposed that since people think in their natural language, they cannot escape the bounds it imposes on their view of the world around them. The notion that natural language is the medium of thought has also had many proponents among behaviorist psychologists. The great Russian physiologist Pavlov regarded language as a "second signaling system." Whereas the behavior of animals could be conditioned directly to preceding stimuli, that of human beings depended also on internal signals they could generate in the form of implicit speech. The notion that the overt speech of children becomes internalized as thought in mature humans and mediates between stimuli and responses has appealed to many investigators because inner speech seemed to them a clearly specifiable internal process.

Thus language has been assigned an important role in thought on the basis of very general considerations, rather than on the basis of any direct empirical demonstration of the linguistic mechanisms involved in thinking.

In any case, language is central to people's lives. Because the sounds of language are systematically mapped onto the world of events, and because the different members of a speech community share this linguistic code, people can use verbal messages to communicate information with one another. By listening to others talk, people learn about events that have occurred far from them in space and time, and they learn also about other people's explanations of events and about their attitudes and feelings.

Thoughts are communicated in words. If I ask someone what he was thinking, he *tells* me. Even if his thoughts were not in linguistic form at the time I asked him, he would give them linguistic form in order to meet the requirements of communicating. Given that he is going to talk about his experiences, he might plan such verbal messsages even before a listener is at hand. Some philosophers claim that knowledge, as opposed to skill or know-how, is propositional; that is to say, knowledge can be verbally formulated. Such considerations lead them to identify thought with language without providing any convincing reasons to enable one to conclude that natural language is the only form of mental representation used in thinking. I noted earlier certain criteria for mental representations to function in problem solving. On preliminary examination, at least, natural language seems to meet these criteria since it is a scheme that can preserve such a rich variety of information about events. But is it really adequate? And, if so, is it the only possible form of representation?

There is some scattered evidence about the types of mental representations people use in thinking, but there has not been much systematic empirical investigation. What evidence there is strikingly supports people's introspective experiences in solving problems. I would like to examine people's introspections about how they solve simple problems, and then consider what behavioral evidence might be relevant to their impressions.

The first type of problem is one that requires a person to reexamine familiar material stored in his memory in order to extract new information from it. Consider a set of several intersecting streets with which you are familiar. On each of a series of problems you are assigned a particular starting point and a particular destination in this geographic area. The task is to report the sequence of left and right turns along the shortest path from the one to the other. People generally claim that on the early trials they imagine themselves traversing the streets, announcing the turns as they go. After a few trials, they claim that they construct a map which they consult in determining the appropriate sequence of turns.

Consider next another type of problem, which requires a person to find the appropriate procedure to obtain an answer to meet certain criteria set forth in the problem. The following example is like many to be found in puzzle books. "Where on the earth can you walk first one mile south, then one mile east, then one mile north, and finish the walk at the point where it began?" One answer to this problem is to start at the North Pole. Another answer, which people are less likely to obtain, is to start near the South Pole, one mile north of where the circumference of the earth is exactly one mile. You would then begin by first walking south one mile, next go east one mile around the earth's circumference, and finally back north over the same path you took to the south. People claim to imagine a globe in solving this problem. They describe their attempts to find a path in one of several ways: some claim that they imagine tracing a path with their finger, some that they simply see a line appear, and some that they see a figure traversing a path. First, they find that various arbitrary starting points on the globe are inappropriate. The answer often occurs to people long after they have given up trying to find it; some say that a path "constructs itself" at an appropriate place.

Finally, consider a third type of problem where information given in one form must be changed into another as in deductive reasoning. For example, take the following problem, called an "ordering syllogism," which describes the relative heights of three people. The information is presented in two comparative sentences which are followed by a question about one of the items; for example, "Sue is taller than Ann. Sue is shorter than Jane. Who is shortest?" To solve such problems, people say that they imagine the three items described to be material objects which they must arrange in space. First they imagine arranging the two items described in the first premise, and then they imagine placing the third item with respect to the first two according to the information given in the second premise. Then they consult this spatial array in order to obtain the answer.

People's introspections about how they solve these problems are remarkably consistent. They claim to convert the information from each of these verbally presented problems to visual modes of representation. Not everyone describes his solution process, however. Some people say they do not know how they obtained the answers. But in no case do they regard their mental operations in obtaining an answer as involving natural language in any essential way.

People claim that they have to look at an imaginary something to solve these problems, although most of them say that what they see is not like a picture in the ordinary sense. If there should be some objective evidence for this claim of imaginary looking in addition to the phenomenal experience, it would substantiate one aspect of people's introspections about their problem-solving strategy. Consider an obvious fact about looking at real visual events. While a person looks at a real visual scene, he cannot examine *another* visual scene without having to look away from the first. If people looked at imaginary representations as if they were real stimuli, one might expect to find parallel effects. That is to say, if people have to look at real visual stimuli, this should prevent them from continuing to examine their imaginary visual representation.

One investigator sought such parallels between imaginary and real visual events in the following way. People were given problems like those described above where one had to find the sequence of left and right turns to get from one place to another. (Brooks, 1967, 1968.) The purpose of the study was to find objective evidence about whether people looked at imaginary maps to solve such problems. The test was to determine whether they would find it more difficult to look at a sheet of paper to check off their answers than to report the answers aloud when they were imagining visual events. They did. Conversely, when people imagined auditory events—for example, on tasks where they reported the parts of speech of successive words from a memorized passage—they found it more difficult to say the answers than to check them off on paper. Thus there is behavioral evidence to support one general feature of people's introspections: that to imagine looking at or hearing something makes it difficult to actually look at or to say something else.

Of course, these experiments do not provide any detailed information about the mental representations people use in problem solving. Since they show that imaginary visual events are in certain ways analogous to real visual events, these experiments do, however, lend support to people's introspective reports that they use visual modes of representation.

Behavioral evidence in support of people's introspections provides more detailed information about how they solve the ordering syllogisms. (Huttenlocher, 1968.) These problems involve two premises. The first describes the relation between two items, and the second describes the relation between a third item and one of the two mentioned in the first premise. A particular relation among three items can be described in eight different ways, as there are eight different forms in which a problem can be posed. These different forms of the problem differ markedly in difficulty.

In order to solve these problems people claim that they imagine themselves to be arranging the described items spatially, as if the premises were instructions about how material objects should be arranged. They claim that the first premise indicates to them how to arrange the first two items, and the second premise indicates to them how the third item fits in among the first two. People's introspections about their strategy are supported by the fact that the difficulty of solving different forms of these syllogisms parallels the difficulty of arranging real objects according to comparable instructions.

When people make actual spatial arrangements of real items, the difficulty of placing a new item with respect to the items that were placed earlier depends on how the information about its relative position is described in the instructions. When the new item is described as the grammatical subject in a sentence like "The red block is higher than the green block," it is easier to place than when it is described as the grammatical object. Similarly, when a new item is the described actor in an active or passive sentence like "John follows Harry" or "Harry is followed by John," it is easier to place than when it is described as the recipient of action. What is interesting about this from our point of view is the correspondence between those cases where it is easier to place a *real* new item according to a particular instruction and those cases where it is easier to place an *imaginary* new item in a syllogism. If the new item in the second premise of a syllogism is analogous to a real new item to be placed with respect to other real items, a syllogism would be easier when that premise describes a new item as the grammatical subject in a comparative sentence or the actor in a sentence with a transitive verb. These predictions were tested experimentally and were accurate in each case, lending support to people's claims that they build imaginary spatial arrays in the process of solving syllogistic reasoning problems.

The studies we have cited are very simple investigations of the mental representations people use in thinking. They do, however, suggest that people's introspections about how they solve certain kinds of problems capture something of their actual mental operations, and that their observable behavior reflects these mental operations in demonstrable ways. No doubt people's introspections provide only partial insight into their mental processes. One example of the incompleteness of introspective evidence is found with ordering syllogisms. Although people claim to reason by arranging imaginary items, they are *not* aware that the difficulty of a syllogism depends on how information about the third item is introduced in the second premise.

Given that people's introspections really are useful, let us examine them even more closely. Many people are quite adamant in claiming that while their representations of these problems are visual they don't involve pictorial images. An examination of people's claims about their representations shows them to differ in critical ways from realistic pictures of events. For example, the map people use in the problem where they must "read out the turns" is a very odd map. The turns are represented, but the lines connecting the turns, according to many, are of no particular length. Similarly, the globe used in the path problem involves a curved surface but not an entire globe; only a part of it is imagined at all, and even *that* has no particular color. The spatial arrays in the syllogistic tasks are similarly schematic. People don't actually see properties of these items but rather see letters, words, or just three points in space whose names they try to remember; nor are these spatial arrays embedded on any particular surface. Clearly, these representations are unlike ordinary pictures. They are ghostly diagrams that include only those aspects of the problem situation that are considered to be relevant. Such representations differ from any physically realized model. One could not make a real map where the turns connected without making the connecting lines of some particular length; one could not make a globe without its being of some particular material and color. In fact, it is a shortcoming of many physically realized models that they must include characteristics that are irrelevant to the situation they were intended to represent.

These mental schemes involve only those elements and operations that the person takes to be relevant, and there seems little question that they are symbolic and unlike percepts of particular events. Several interesting questions would arise if people's introspections were to prove accurate.

First, one wonders whether these consciously experienced representations have any real function in thought, or whether they are only the product of some deeper underlying processes. After all, the representations a person uses reflect only what he knows of a situation. In this way, they seem less a condition for successful thought than a product of it. It is difficult to evaluate this argument, but there seems no more reason to question the function of such mental representations than to question the function of physically realized representations like maps, diagrams, models of molecules, and so on.

After all, it is not clear that alternative symbolic schemes have equal potential for representing various aspects of events. This whole issue has not yet been systematically explored. Linguists stress the fact that a person who knows a language can formulate and understand an infinite number of new verbal messages. While this is certainly true, it does not follow that it is useful, or even possible, to represent all aspects of human experience in natural language.

For example, certain information clearly is not easily described in words. A map can represent the shape of the east coast of the United States accurately and to scale. Not only would a verbal description of this coastline take many pages, but it is not obvious that it could, in principle, provide all the information that the map does.

Questions also arise when one tries to analyze how natural language might function in the solving of problems. We suggested that for a symbolic scheme to be useful in problem solving it should be able to represent the initial problem situation; it also should provide operations that can transform that initial representation to yield a solution when reapplied to the actual situation. According to this analysis, the operations in the symbol scheme represent the actual operations appropriate to the problem situation. The operations of natural language do not seem to provide an appropriate scheme for problems like those we described; for example, problems that require representation of the effects or rearranging objects in space.

Although one can *describe* spatial rearrangements *in* language, the rules of language do not themselves represent operations of this type. But to consider this issue gets us far beyond what is known, and raises difficult problems which I will not pursue here.

In sum, we have explored the role of natural language in one area of cognitive functioning. We have considered the nature of those thought processes that can serve in place of overt actions, permitting people to solve problems in the world of events through the use of mental operations. There is little empirical evidence about the form of such mental operations, but such evidence can be obtained, and what there is suggests that symbolic schemes other than natural language are sometimes involved.

17 LANGUAGE AND PROBABILITY

Herbert Rubenstein

If everyone knew in advance exactly what a person was going to say, he wouldn't need to say it. Communication occurs only when his message is, at least to some degree, unpredictable. When we talk about communication, therefore, we are talking about unpredictable events. The way we talk about more or less predictable events, of course, is to use the theory of probability. And that is how the theory of probability gets involved in our theories of communication.

This chapter discusses some of the probabilistic aspects of linguistic communication. In particular, it reviews some of the psychological research on language that was stimulated during the 1950s by the realization that linguistic communication really is a probabilistic affair. I will point out some of the reasons people became dissatisfied with this line of research. And I will suggest another way to look at the relation between language and probability—a way that fits better with what we now know about how people produce and interpret linguistic messages.

Much of the psychological research on language during the 1950s was stimulated by the ideas of a man who was neither a psychologist nor a linguist, but a communications engineer—Claude Shannon. In his famous monograph, *A Mathematical Theory of Communication*, which appeared in 1948, Shannon advanced several significant ideas. Language, at least in its written form, consists of strings of letters or strings of words. These strings of symbols can be considered as being generated by a kind of device called a Markov process. In a Markov process, the probability of a particular event changes depending on the events that have just preceded it. As applied to language, this would mean that what symbol is selected next will depend on what symbols have just been selected; that is to say, how the message can continue is determined to some extent by the preceding context.

Another important notion of Shannon's was that, on the average, the more preceding context you know, the more predictable the next symbol will be. Taken together, these two notions suggest that messages in a language like English could be generated by a Markov process if only the Markov process could take into account enough of the preceding context. Exactly how much preceding context a Markov process would need is an open question, of course, so various ways were considered to get some kind of estimate.

One way to estimate how much preceding context is needed is to construct what are called statistical approximations to English. The lowest-order approximation to English results when all symbols can occur with equal probability. A first-order approximation is a little better; the symbols occur with the same probability in the text as in English as a whole, but the occurrence of any symbol is still independent of its preceding context. Here is an example of a first-order approximation where the symbols strung together by the Markov process are English words: *hens of at lax films were that and the she.*

A second-order approximation is produced by selecting each successive symbol according to its probability of following the symbol that immediately preceded it. In order to construct second-order approximations correctly, we would have to know the probabilities of all word pairs in English. Since no one has undertaken the enormous task of counting how often all possible word pairs occur, we have to use native speakers of English to help us construct the strings we want. For example, we can generate a second-order approximation to English as follows: We arbitrarily select some word—*gift*, say—and ask somebody to use it in a sentence. He answers, "He bought a gift for John." We take the word following *gift,* namely *for,* as the first word of our text. We then ask another person to use *for* in a sentence and we obtain "They did it for me." Then we take *me* as the next word of our text and ask another person to include *me* in a sentence, and so on. We might obtain a text like this: *for me please leave when you do it may not for their lips that time was he said.*

In a third-order approximation each word is dependent on the two preceding words—for example, *from the boat moves through still calm lake and stream where all boys have looked.* Note that it is difficult to read such a sequence of words with a normal sentence intonation.

A sixth-order approximation begins to sound something like English, *it has been a long time since they heard from him he said when we learn how to live.* The more preceding context we use, the better it seems to get, but even a tenth-order approximation, where each word is selected in the context of the preceding nine words, is a long way from good English: *while the guards fought the flames in the dead of night when she threw the whole mess out of the door and gave chase to the old man.*

One of the most stimulating notions that Shannon presented was his definition of a measure of uncertainty—often confusingly called a measure of information. Suppose we have received a string of symbols and we wish to measure how much uncertainty there is about the next symbol. Shannon's measure has the following characteristics: if only one symbol can occur after a certain context, the measure shows the uncertainty to be zero. For example, in English words, after the letter q only the letter u may occur; thus the uncertainty after q is zero—we know automatically what will follow. The measure also shows the uncertainty to be greater as the number of alternative symbols that may occur after the given context is greater. Finally, the measure shows a less obvious characteristic of uncertainty: Suppose any one of five symbols can occur after a given context. Suppose each of them occurs equally often, that is, each symbol occurs in 20 percent of the instances in which the context occurs. Shannon's measure shows that there is greater uncertainty involved here than in the case where there are again five alternatives, but they are unequal in their frequency of occurrence—say one of them occurs 90 percent of the time and each of the other four only 2.5 percent of the time. The unit of uncertainty is the *bit,* a term derived from the expression *binary digit.* The binary notion comes about from the fact that a decision that reduces alternatives by half is the most efficient way of identifying the symbol that actually occurs in a given context. One bit may be thought of as the uncertainty produced by two equally probable alternatives; 2 bits, the uncertainty produced by four equally probable alternatives; 3 bits, the uncertainty produced by eight equally probable alternatives; and so on.

Obviously Shannon's measure could be applied to studies of the statistical properties of language. Shannon himself did so in 1951. He was able to show one of the major properties of uncertainty; namely, that the longer the context affecting the choice of a particular symbol, the lower the average uncertainty of that symbol. Shannon measured the uncertainty of a letter as a function of the number of letters preceding it. He found the average uncertainty of the first letter in a string of words to be 4.1 bits. For the second letter it decreased to 3.6 bits, and for the third letter to 3.3 bits. For these positions he was able to use statistical information based on actual counts of the frequencies of single letters, of letter pairs, and of letter triplets in English. Since this kind of statistical information was not available for longer strings, Shannon estimated their relative frequencies by having people try to guess each letter until they were successful. He found that the uncertainty per letter went from 4.1 bits for the first letter to 1.3 bits for the one-hundredth letter in a string. This is equivalent to going from a choice among eighteen equally probable letters to a choice among two or three equally probable letters.

Shannon's ideas were quickly adopted by scientists interested in the psychology of language. The measure of uncertainty was especially exciting, since it seemed to be a direct measure of the amount of cognitive work a person had to do in order to identify a linguistic message correctly.

Psychological experimenters were able to use the measure in various ways to construct materials for their experiments in perceiving and remembering English messages (see Chapter 15). They designed nonsense languages into which they built predetermined probabilities. Or using natural language, they had people guess at words or letters appropriate to the context presented and then used the frequencies of the guesses as an approximation to the probability distribution of alternatives in that context. Another way they obtained stimulus materials that differed systematically in uncertainty was to compose texts corresponding to different orders of approximation to English.

Almost all aspects of language processing—recognition, learning, copying, comprehension, production—were investigated in these experiments. It was found that in general all these processes are facilitated when the uncertainty is reduced. Let me cite some of the experimental results. In *visual recognition* it was found that the higher the order of approximation to English letter strings, the more letters a person can recognize correctly when he sees them in a single brief flash. The increase in letters recognized is inversely proportional to the uncertainty, so that while the number of letters recognized varies, the total uncertainty resolved by recognition is constant over all orders of approximation to English. In *auditory recognition* a very regular relation was found, namely, that the probability of recognizing a word heard in noise is a simple function of the probability of occurrence of that word in that particular context. In studies of *short-term memory* it was found that the processing time per word in typing, copying, or reading aloud decreased as the order of approximation to English increased. The number of times a person has to look at the text in order to copy it decreases as the uncertainty of the text decreases. In the *rote memorization* of strings of letters, nonsense syllables, or English words, the lower the uncertainty per symbol, the more symbols are recalled. But no constancy in terms of uncertainty is obtained as is obtained in the case of visual recognition. That is, more symbols are learned in a passage where the average uncertainty is 1 bit per symbol than in a passage where the average uncertainty is 4 bits per symbol, but *not* four times as many. And in *comprehension,* too, lower uncertainty—that is, higher probability—is a facilitating factor. The comprehension of English texts is correlated with their predictability. The so-called *Cloze* procedure, which consists of deleting a certain proportion of words in a text, replacing them by blanks, and requiring people to fill in the blanks is now widely used as a language comprehension test (see Chapter 23).

Lastly, there were a few experiments in language *production* that related the behavior of the speaker to the probability of the words in his sentences. For example, the words before which a speaker pauses tend to have a low dependence on what has gone before, as measured by their predictability. Moreover, a speaker tends to pronounce a word more clearly when it is less predictable in the context in which it occurs.

In spite of these encouraging results, however, the interest in message probabilities diminished greatly toward the end of the 1950s. There were several reasons. For one, the mathematical model underlying these probability investigations was shown by Chomsky to be inadequate to describe human language. The model is the Markov process, according to which the probability of a symbol depends on the context preceding the symbol. A moment's reflection makes it obvious that there is really no limit to the amount of preceding context that might affect the selection of a symbol. Consider the sentence *The old man died.* The word *died* is clearly dependent on *old man,* and follows it directly. But there are many sentences in which there is equal dependence but the words are widely separated, for example, *The old man we used to meet at those concerts you enjoyed so much died.* Theoretically, there is no limit to the distance between a word and its relevant context. This means that the order of approximation that will produce any and all English sentences cannot be specified.

Another objection to the Markov model that has more obvious psychological relevance is that the time required to learn a language as a set of probability chains would far exceed the duration of childhood, even if a child learned a new set of probabilities every second.

Finally, and possibly most important—for the direction of

research does not change for negative reasons alone—Chomsky's transformational grammar came along in 1957 to capture the interest of psychologists as well as linguists. For the first time a method of describing syntactic relations was available that could be used to characterize much more subtle aspects of language behavior. The work stimulated by this grammatical theory has been described by other contributors to this volume.

For one reason or another, therefore, the interest in verbal probabilities declined sharply in the 1960s. Indeed, the pendulum may have swung too far in the opposite direction: probability differences are dismissed as merely the effect of the application of different linguistic rules. This cannot be true. It is just as absurd to make such a claim as it is to maintain that sentences are structured only in terms of the associative strength between each word and its context.

It seems perfectly obvious that a language must have a deterministic structure, and that the things we say are not generated by a probability machine. Not even in the heyday of the probabilistic theory of communication would anyone have seriously maintained that each particular speech act was randomly generated. The view of language as a stochastic process was held only for a whole corpus of utterances, and the measures of probability and uncertainty were viewed as useful for describing certain average aspects of the language corpus, but not for individual items in that corpus.

When I say that the pendulum may have swung too far, I am expressing my own view that probability really does play a role in communication. Even if we grant, as we surely must, that language has a deterministic structure, I would still argue that probability plays an *active* role in the way language is used and understood.

Most American psychologists who are interested in language have now accepted the doctrine that language is rule-governed behavior. The cognitive equipment of the language user is now considered to consist of his repertoire of phonemes and the rules for their combination, of a fund of knowledge about the words of the language (which for convenience I shall call the "internal lexicon"), and of the set of syntactic and semantic rules that govern the construction and interpretation of sentences.

However, all this equipment is not adequate to explain one of the most striking features of language behavior, namely, that understanding a spoken sentence is a real-time process; that is to say, it is simultaneous with its hearing. It is not the usual case that one hears a sentence and understands it a minute later. On the contrary, understanding is generally complete by the time the sentence ends. Indeed, we have all had the experience of understanding a sentence even before we had heard it all. This real-time understanding must depend on our ability to order the results of applying the grammatical and lexical rules in terms of their probability of occurrence in the given context.

Now when I refer to probability here, I am not talking about the probability of occurrence of letters or words in terms of their actual order of occurrence in sentences. I am talking about the probability of the co-occurrence of concepts contained in the deep structure of the sentence. Let's go back to the sentence used as an example above: *The old man we used to meet at the concerts you enjoyed so much died.* The deep structure of this sentence is approximated by these simpler sentences: *The man died. The man was old. We used to meet the man at concerts. You enjoyed the concerts very much.* The concepts found in the first two—*The man died* and *The man was old*—occur together often in our experience, and in a certain cause-and-effect relationship: "The man was old and so he died." If we gave our sentence minus the last word to a number of people, *The old man we used to meet at the concerts you enjoyed so much—*, and asked them to complete it, it is a reasonable guess that many of their completions would contain the word *died*. In the course of reading the sentence our readers would discover the syntactic relations and decide that *old man* must have a predicate. They would see that the clause *we used to meet at the concerts you enjoyed so much* is irrelevant, and so they would select such predicates as *retired, was ill, died,* and so forth, on the basis of their general knowledge about what old men do.

But how does this kind of probability relation facilitate a listener's task? First, it accelerates the recognition of words as they are spoken. The listener is a predictor. The results of applying syntactic and semantic rules to the part of the sentence he has already heard serve as a conceptual input into his internal lexicon. This input delimits the set of concepts that may follow and assigns probabilities to them. The recognition of the word the listener is presently hearing is facilitated by the fact that even as the acoustic signal is being segmented and the segments assigned to phonemes, these strings of phonemes are being compared against the lexical entries that have already been delimited by the context *in the order of the probabilities previously assigned to the lexical entries.* This procedure also facilitates recognition when—due to noise or inattention—there is uncertainty regarding the precise phonemic form of what was heard.

Secondly, probability ordering simplifies the listener's treatment of ambiguities. Ambiguity, which is usually resolved later on in the sentence, is a very frequent phenomenon in language. If a listener even unconsciously considered all the interpretations of every ambiguous expression and treated them all as equally likely, he would also, in keeping with his practice of predicting, have to work out and store all the predictions following from each of his interpretations. Such a necessity would hardly make for efficient processing. It seems more reasonable to believe that, if more than one interpretation is made, only the most likely of these interpretations is selected as the basis for prediction.

For example, in the ambiguous expression, *The lamb was ready to eat,* the more probable deep-structure interpretation would be that *lamb* is the object of *eat,* so the listener would make ready predictions like *(The lamb was ready to eat) so we sat down to dinner.* He would not prepare himself for the unlikely completion *(The lamb was ready to eat) so I fed it.* Another example: hearing the clause *We would have taken the plane to Washington,* a listener predicting only on the basis of the most probable interpretation would expect something like *but all the seats were taken.* He would not normally prepare predictions for the three other possible interpretations of *We would have taken the plane to Washington,* predictions like *but it was too heavy,* or *but the carpenter was using it,* or *but Washington didn't want it.*

Nothing has been said about the speaker's use of probabilities. In general we know very little about the processes underlying the speaker's performance. I would guess, however, that probability does not play a very significant role for the speaker. His performance is largely determined by what he wants his utterance to convey—not by what is more probable. It is true that when he is anxious to be understood, he may select the more expected over the less expected way of saying something. And we do know that a speaker tends to pronounce words of lower probability more carefully. However, this indicates an interpersonal adjustment to the listener, rather than a use of probability to facilitate his short-range task of composing an utterance. It is the listener who is uncertain about what is being said, and it is the listener who relies most on probabilities.

Now to summarize: the probability of a symbol, given the preceding context, was used in several kinds of measures to calibrate verbal materials used in psychological experiments. Many experiments were run during the 1950s and early 1960s that showed that higher probability facilitated all kinds of language processing tasks: in visual and auditory recognition, in learning, and in comprehension. These experiments produced trustworthy, clear, and useful results, but after a decade of interest in such problems, research diminished. There were several reasons. The most important were these two: first, the Markov process, which underlay the use of dependent probability, was shown to be inappropriate for language. And, second, a new model of language appeared, transformational grammar, which provided a whole new set of paths for psycholinguistic research.

Nevertheless, verbal probabilities are still relevant to today's interest in the performance of the language user. Not all effects of probability can be explained away by deterministic applications of language rules. The only way that the real-time character of understanding can be explained is on the assumption that we are able to order the likelihood of the outputs of linguistic rules and lexical look-up on the basis of our knowledge of the likelihood of the co-occurrence of concepts—a knowledge that is derived from our general experience with the concepts expressed by the deep structure of the sentence.

18 COMMUNICATION AND COMPUTERS

J. C. R. Licklider

When people communicate, they usually communicate to other people. Sometimes they talk to themselves, and sometimes they talk to their pets. Until very recently, however, they almost never tried to hold conversations with a machine. They might curse at their car when it did not start, but they did not really expect the car to answer back.

Today, however, things are changing. More and more people are now spending more and more time communicating to machines, and receiving communications back. I do not mean that they are just talking *through* a machine, the way a voice goes through a microphone. I mean they are interacting with the machine much as they would with a real conversational partner.

The machines I have in mind, of course, are the modern, high-speed computers. If you know how to speak their language, you can get these machines to help you solve many different kinds of problems. It can be rewarding to communicate with a computing machine, because the computer can serve as an aid in your thinking process. So more and more people are learning to do it.

In order to develop computers as aids to thinking, one needs to analyze the process of thinking and determine to what parts of that process computers can contribute. The first step of the analysis is simple: most problems require two stages of activity for their solution—formulation of a procedure and execution of the procedure. People—at least some people—are good at formulating procedures, but people are not good—as "good" is measured in this computer era—at executing procedures. Computers, on the other hand, although not yet able to do much formulating on their own, are very good—very fast, very accurate—at executing procedures. Ergo: let people formulate, and let computers execute, and there will be good work over-all.

That simple idea, while not by any means the final concept, is so important that it will be worth our while to spend a few minutes on it. Let us consider an example.

Suppose you plan to drive to eight points of interest during your vacation; you have a list of the distances of each point of interest from your home and of each from each other; and to save gasoline you want to make the total trip as short as possible.

Unless you are a profound thinker, the formulation of a procedure for solving that problem is easy: just arrange the eight points of interest in all possible sequences with your home at the beginning and end of each sequence, determine the total distance for each sequence, select the shortest total distance, and adopt the route that corresponds to it. That will solve the problem.

With that formulation, however, the execution is formidable. There are more than 40,000 different sequences to consider: Home to A to B to C and so on, Home to B to A to C and so on, Home to C to A to B and so on, and so on, and so on. In all, 40,320 different sequences. If you used a desk calculator, you might be able to calculate one total distance per minute. If your vacation were four weeks long, you might be ready to select your route on the last day of it, but too tired to start driving. On the other hand, if you had a small, modern digital computer, you might in an hour or two prepare a program that could carry out the calculation of one total distance in about 20 millionths of a second—and with it determine the 40,000 totals (and, in the process, also select the shortest) in less than one second.

That example illustrates in an oversimple way the idea of dividing a problem-solving activity into two parts, one (formulation) easy and natural for a person, the other (execution) easy and natural for a computer. It may even lead one to imagine a computerized vacation-planning service. Tell it where you live and eight places you want to go, and a second later it prints out the best route. But the example can illustrate some other things, also. For instance, consider what would happen if we magnified the problem a little.

Suppose that you want to visit not eight but twelve points of interest. Twelve are actually not so very many for a four-week trip. Then there are 11,880 times 40,320, or almost 500 million, different routes to consider, and the same computer that evaluated the eight-point problem in one second now requires thirty-three hours. Obviously, great speed in executing instructions is not by itself enough to provide a practical way of finding solutions to all problems of this kind. It is necessary to improve the formulation.

Indeed, the formulative part is the key part of problem solving. It is so much so that one can say, correctly for most practically significant problems, that without a good formulation no computer can carry out the execution by brute force. Obviously, then, we ought to focus our attention on formulation.

A closer look at the formulative part of thinking suggests that it involves frequent alternation between a part that employs heuristic (intuitive) methods to build up and experimentally modify some kind of a structured procedure and a part that overtly or covertly carries out the various versions of the procedure thus created. Research workers who study thinking use various sets of terms and images—none wholly satisfactory—to describe what they suppose goes on in thinking. For example: one builds a model in his mind; the model operates; he compares its behavior with what he sees happening in the real world, or with what he wants to have happen; he alters the model, hoping to improve the degree of correspondence; he rejects versions of the model that do not behave as they should and holds onto versions that do; if no version performs well, he drastically changes the model and experiments further with it; a model that behaves as it should is the solution to a problem or a plan for action.

If formulative thinking involves—as I have suggested it does— a large amount of procedure execution, how can the procedure-executing capabilities of computers be exploited in formulative thinking? Essentially, the idea is to change one key phrase in the foregoing description of thinking as model building: change "one builds a model in his mind" to "one builds a model in his computer." Let me try to explain what I mean by that.

Instead of thinking of a computer program as a procedure for solving a problem, we can think of it as a description of a process—as a description of how some system works. The system may be simple or complex, actual or merely imagined. In a computer program, one can describe it precisely and definitely. Then, when the program is fed into a computer and the "start" button is pushed, the description turns into a working model or simulation. It "runs," and one can watch it operate, observe its behavior, and examine the implications as they unfold.

Note that even such a simple, solid thing as the scale model of an airplane, placed in a wind tunnel, can "behave" in the way I have suggested and reveal design flaws not foreseen by skilled aerodynamicists. I remember vividly a wind-tunnel model of a fast aircraft with thin, flexible wings. At a certain air speed, the wings of the model suddenly disintegrated. In fast-action movies, one could see vibration begin, build up, exceed elastic limits, and—whoosh—the wings were gone. Fortunately, the designers understood what to change to prevent the vibration; by experimenting with further wind-tunnel models they developed a design that flew stably through the critical speed.

The aerodynamics of an airplane can be modeled in the form of computer programs, and the computer-program plane can be "flown" via simulation. Indeed, if the design is faulty, the computer-programmed wings may "vibrate" and "disintegrate." But the computer-modeling approach can be pressed much deeper. One can represent the structure of the aircraft in greater detail than is feasible in a scale model. He can incorporate functional characteristics, such as thrust and fuel consumption, as well as structural characteristics. He can simulate an entire flight, with takeoff and landing. He can change even the most basic dimensions of the aircraft without having to rebuild the entire model. And, most significantly, he can deal with a much wider variety of kinds of systems than could ever be represented by models made of wood or plastic or metal.

Now it should be obvious—as perhaps it was all along—that

the procedure for solving a problem typically involves devising and testing a whole complex of procedures, that it involves constructing models, operating them, observing their behavior, modifying them, and trying them out again until one has something that works the way he wants it to work—or at least works in a satisfactory way or a promising way. Moreover, because most of the things we think about depend upon uncertain conditions, there must necessarily be a large admixture of probability and statistics in the modeling.

If your concept of a digital computer is based on what have thus far been the main applications of digital computers, you are probably thinking that I have in mind something quite different from the computing machines that live behind glass walls, that are fed nothing but punched cards, that whirr their tapes and flash their lights and spew out great piles of paper covered with numbers and capital letters. That is partly right. Such computers, so employed, are most unlikely to be helpful in formulative thinking. But change the machines a little and the way of using them a lot, and I think we have the basis for the greatest advance in thinking since the invention of pencil and paper. Let us therefore turn briefly to what has been going on in the computer world. Let us look at a way of using computers in which people interact directly with computers—in which men and computers function in close partnership or teamwork.

Most digital computers have been used, and most still are used, in a way that separates formulation from execution. In payroll and inventory work, in finding numerical solutions to sets of equations, and even in guiding Apollo to the moon, what computers do—essentially—is merely to execute long sequences of instructions laid out for them in advance, painstakingly, by human programmers. The astronauts fed in a few numbers from time to time, it is true, but all the formulative thinking that went into the guidance process was done by people before the spaceship left the earth. And, of course, the execution was done by the computers afterward.

By and large, man-computer communication has been carried on through an awkward kind of correspondence—sending decks of punched cards to the computing center one day and getting back great stacks of "print out" the next. However, about seven years ago, significant numbers of people began to carry on what might be called (and in fact were called) "conversations" with computers.

At first man-computer conversation consisted only in the man's and the computer's typing back and forth to each other on a typewriter connected to the computer's input-output channel, and at first the computer could respond meaningfully only to statements made in a programming language—and therefore could communicate only with computer programmers versed in such a language. However, conversation with programmers was precisely what computers needed, and conversation with computers was precisely what programmers needed. Working directly with the computers took so many of the trials and tribulations out of programming that it became great fun to prepare computer programs, even very long and complex ones. In fact, computer programming quickly became a kind of addiction. Computer scientists worked all night at computer consoles, too engrossed in their efforts to keep track of the time and so eager to perfect and demonstrate their programs that they could not stop until all the "glitches" and "bugs" (as major and minor programming errors are called) had been eliminated.

Among the computers with which computer scientists engaged in conversational interaction were machines large and powerful for their time. The first such "interactive" machines were a pair of specially augmented IBM 7094 computers at the Massachusetts Institute of Technology in Cambridge, Massachusetts, and a giant computer called the AN/FSQ-32 at the System Development Corporation in Santa Monica, California. Those computers were augmented with typewriterlike consoles and televisionlike display devices to permit direct communication with users, and they were equipped with programs that let them skip quickly from one user's work to another's and carry on separate conversations with as many as thirty people at a time. Since a typical conversational work session lasted a couple of hours, and since interactive computing enthusiasts were willing to work at any time of the day or night, one big computer could serve a community of two hundred or three hundred people. Most of their typewriters were connected to the computers through telephone lines and switchboards, and most of the people worked in the convenience of their offices or homes. Thus was born "time sharing" or "multiaccess computing," which in a relatively short span of time grew into an industry with more than one hundred companies offering interactive information services through communication common carriers to some tens of thousands of subscribers in business, government, research, education, and other fields.

As I mentioned above, one of the significant things about interactive computing—working directly with the computer in the way that I have described—is that it greatly facilitates the preparation of computer programs. That facilitation is augmented by the fact that the large multiaccess computer systems permit users to keep their information files permanently in the systems' central storage units, ready for reference or execution at any time, and by the fact that in some systems there are large "public" libraries of already prepared procedures and data. With such facilities at his fingertips, a modern programmer can construct a large, complex program mainly out of parts already prepared by others and can increase his productivity by a factor of perhaps ten. Thus serious programming becomes an undertaking not for an individual but for a community. There are now several communities, most of them in universities, that have developed extensive programs in more or less the way suggested. Many of the programs are quite different from the ones, mentioned earlier, that dealt with payroll, inventory, and specific sets of equations.

Some of the new programs exploit the idea that a computer can aid a human thinker by relieving him of what would for him be the time-consuming and disconcerting bother of extensive clerical work. Such programs may be called interactive "intellectual-assistant" programs. A program called TROLL, for example, helps one analyze economic time series; MAP helps find numerical solutions to systems of mathematical equations; ADMINS helps process the results of surveys and opinion polls; TYPSET helps prepare and edit letters and reports; OPS helps prepare simulation models; and DDT helps test and correct ("debug," to use the jargon term) computer programs. Each of these aids is helpful in doing a particular kind of work. None "knows" very much about what it is doing and therefore none is truly an intellectual partner of the user, but each one makes an important contribution by carrying out quickly and accurately some of the procedure-execution parts of the thinking process that would otherwise cause delay or introduce error.

The companies that offer interactive computing services commercially have begun to provide thinking aids of the intellectual-assistant kind. One can now be led through the process of filling out his income-tax forms—and have all the calculations performed instantly—by handing over $25 and sitting down at a typewriter console. Programs are available for specialized book-keeping tasks, for optimizing investment portfolios, for scheduling job shops, for selecting advertising media, for designing building structures, and so on. If we identify separated formulation and execution as "phase zero," then the intellectual-assistant programs mark "phase one" of the development of computer aids to thinking, problem solving, and decision making.

Perhaps the most advanced example of computer augmentation of the intellect is Mathlab, a system of programs developed at M.I.T. by Drs. Martin, Moses, and Engelman and several colleagues. A lot of "knowledge" of calculus, algebra, trigonometry, and so on has been built into Mathlab. It can carry out the processes of symbolic differentiation and integration, for example, about as well as a good mathematician. Whatever it does, it does very accurately and quite rapidly. It is not bothered by formulae with hundreds of terms. It can always manipulate them and often simplify them. Thus far, however, it does not have all the creative mathematician's hunches about what to try out in hope of achieving a breakthrough in the solution of a complex and obstinate mathematical problem. The mathematician therefore guides the Mathlab program, suggesting mathematical stratagems and observing the results thereby achieved. He can experiment freely, trying out first this and then that, because Mathlab carries out in a few seconds the manipulations that could require months of work with pencil and paper. Thus, even though execution is scattered throughout the process of formulation, the computer helps the mathematician think. I would call Mathlab the first "phase two" program.

The near future of computer aids to thought will depend upon advances in incorporating knowledge into computer programs and upon advances in the languages and techniques through which people communicate with computers. Recent research has yielded programs that can solve arithmetic and calculus problems expressed in natural language, programs that can figure out the composition of chemical substances from data provided by mass spectroscopy, and programs that can store and retrieve complex patterns of semantic relations that one might call ideas. If further research is as productive, we can look forward to significant contributions from computers on a truly intellectual level.

But even without such advances, we can look forward to real assistance. A new generation of interactive multi-access computers is now emerging from five years of development, and advanced graphic displays are now available. In the new computer systems, it will be possible to unify the hitherto diverse "phase one" (intellectual-assistant) programs, and the ease with which they can be used—and their effectiveness—will be greatly increased.

In many fields of application, the factor of cost will continue to be inhibiting, but in the "cream" fields—such as planning in government and business and design of automobiles and aerospace vehicles—we shall be seeing a lot of computer-aided thinking.

In contrast, however, educational applications of computers have, on the whole, been disappointing. That fact is tragic because no field is in more dire need of the kind of breakthrough the computer tantalizingly promises—and in no field have efforts to apply computers been on the whole less apt. The field has been dominated too much by a restricted concept of computer-assisted instruction (CAI) which has been pressed too hard too early in the interest of commercial exploitation. To summarize the situation briefly:

1. The economic factor is especially restrictive in the neediest areas of education, and will continue to be so for at least several years.

2. Despite that fact, computer programs that merely provide drill and practice are not to be discounted. They, far more than others, meet economic criteria, and they do produce a measurable effect.

3. What is usually called computer-assisted instruction—that is, the full computer-programmed course of instruction—by and large has missed the boat. CAI has proven costly to create, costly to execute, and not very effective. At the root of the ineffectiveness is the fact that, even when equipped with a present-day course-long program, the computer cannot recognize or deal in any knowledgeable way with—cannot handle with any initiative of its own—misconceptions that arise in the student's mind, even though they are reflected in his responses. Unfortunately, CAI has been the main organized effort in educational application of computers.

4. Computer programs that incorporate the fundamental concepts and operations of a field of knowledge—in the way illustrated by Mathlab and by the Culler-Fried System at the University of California at Santa Barbara—have a great potential as aids to learning.

5. At the graduate-school, college, and even high-school levels, students can make excellent and highly educational use of computers, largely at their own initiative. Students should learn to program, and they should be given access to interactive multi-access computers. They can take it from there.

Human communication is not merely sending messages back and forth. It is a joint activity of two or more people—thinking together, solving problems together, making decisions together. More basically, it is modeling together—creating, exploring, comparing, modifying, adjusting, and evaluating models together. Just as modeling is the essential process in thinking, problem solving, and (although I did not go into it) decision making, modeling is the essential process in human communication.

The computer has not yet had much effect upon human communication, but I think that in a few years it will have a tremendous effect. I believe that people will communicate through networks of interactive multiaccess computers, making use of programs similar to those already described as aids to thinking—variants of those programs designed to interact simultaneously with two or more users. Such communication will of course employ speech and television pictures—which are not yet handled well by most digital computers—but it will make use also of handwriting, typewriting, sketching, diagramming, and all the other media now used in man-computer interaction.

Within the future context of computer networks, some communication will involve the communicators concurrently, as conversations and conferences do, and other communication will involve them sequentially, as written communication and printed communication do. Computer networks will make it possible, despite geographical separation, for people to work together with plans, charts, reports, and so on—all in the computer, of course. The ready availability of exact information pertinent to unanticipated questions will make a significant change in all kinds of meetings. Computer teleconferences will do away with a great amount of business travel.

At the same time, in some application areas, the computer will be replacing typescript and print. It will make no sense to mail a letter; most typing will go directly from the keys into a computer memory, from which it will be displayed to the originator for review and editing, and then it will go from the source computer memory to one or more destination computer memories. Instead of receiving a letter from John Smith, you will find a note in your console saying that you have correspondence in a computer file labeled "John Smith," which you may examine on your display screen at your convenience. Perhaps your abstracting program will have prepared a summary of it, and you may examine the abstract first—or instead —if you prefer. Technical papers will be published mainly through the computer network; once they are stored in a computer there will be little reason to print them on paper, for they will be more readily retrieved and examined, and their data more readily used, through the system of computers. Thus computers will take over some of the functions now served by libraries.

Following that line of thought takes us into the field of home information systems and into what will happen when computers become involved in the meld of television and coaxial cable.

Will digital information schemes replace newspapers and magazines? Will computer-generated "synthetics" replace live actors? Will everyone be an artist—and the computer program the universal medium of artistic expression? It could be so, perhaps even in a decade or two, but I am not very comfortable in long-term speculation.

19 COMMUNICATION IN SMALL GROUPS

Robert Freed Bales

For one reason or another, everyone spends a sizable fraction of his life interacting with other people in small groups. Whether for work or pleasure, such groups comprise a large part of our social lives, so it is not surprising that social scientists have been interested in understanding what goes on in such groups.

Our communication with each other in face-to-face situations is very subtle and complex. In addition to the meanings of the words used, there is a rich flow of contextual information by mutual eye contact. Bodily attitudes, gestures, and facial expressions play an important part. The obvious meaning of what is said in words is only a part, sometimes only a small part, of what is communicated, as we all know (see Chapter 21).

It has been found that a surprising amount of information is carried by the form of the interaction itself. For example, one can usually infer something about the relative dominance of members in a small group simply by counting the number of remarks each makes to the others. The number of remarks is roughly equivalent to the time consumed. In a small group, time is like money or property. It is not distributed equally among members, but in a gradient that has some relation to the social status of the members. Talking time in a group is not something that a member has with security—it is usually something for which he must compete. Some members take it almost by force, in that they take more than others are willing to give them. They exercise power in the taking of time, though they may not gain legitimate status. An increase in the amount of participation initiated by a given member may signal a bid for power.

Information about the positive or negative attitude of one group member toward another is also revealed by the formal characteristics of their communication. It is a relatively simple matter to count the number of acts of agreement versus disagreement group members give to each other. It is usually felt that one should not agree with another simply because one likes him, but in fact the rates of agreement and disagreement received by a man over a time period can reveal how well he is liked.

Formal characteristics of communication also give information as to where the individual member stands with regard to the work of the group. For this purpose it is useful to count the acts commonly called "giving opinion" and "giving suggestion." Persons give opinions and suggestions in the attempt to persuade each other. Attempts to persuade are central to the work of the group. A person who gives many opinions and suggestions is likely to be regarded as work-oriented by other members of the group. Joking and laughing, on the other hand, often show resistance to the work.

All of the kinds of activity I have mentioned can be recognized by characteristics that do not depend on what the group is talking about. In fact, the three dimensions I have mentioned (dominance versus submissiveness, friendliness versus unfriendliness, and work-acceptance versus work-resistance) could be distinguished reasonably well even if the observer did not understand the language spoken by the persons in the group. These dimensions formulate important and probably universal distinctions.

Methods of study that concentrate upon the type of interaction rather than upon the content of communication are called methods of *interaction process analysis*. *Process* analysis is similar to *content* analysis in that it provides information about the underlying attitudes and values of the communicator. But process analysis is unlike content analysis in that it concentrates on the action and reaction of individuals rather than on the content of their messages. Both owe something to *psychoanalysis*. The technique of psychoanalytic interpretation of dreams and free-associations has been a fertile source of insight into un-recognized or poorly controlled aspects of personality and group life. What the psychoanalyst does is not usually called content analysis, nor process analysis, but it is basically similar to both, in that it uses the surface characteristics of interpersonal communication to infer the underlying determinants. The inter-pretive techniques of psychoanalysis have made a tremendous contribution to our understanding of communication in small groups. It is by now quite commonly understood that highly animated chatter, entertaining conversations, gossip, unusually heated arguments, jokes, and other familiar phenomena of inter-personal interaction are basically quite similar to free associa-tion as known to the psychoanalyst. They are subject to inter-pretation in much the same way, and can be used as sources of insight by group members as to their underlying, unrecognized concerns.

People can be taught to utilize more effectively these partially hidden types of information about the attitudes and emotions of others. Groups called sensitivity training groups are increas-ingly being used for this kind of psychological education. Gains of knowledge and skill in this area are important across a broad front of practical applications—in sensitivity and leadership training for persons in business, government, community affairs, in education, and in clinical settings concerned with the assess-ment of personality and the treatment of individual and social problems. Face-to-face interaction of an intensive kind in small groups is being increasingly utilized, not only for group therapy, but for psychologically oriented education or attitude change of many specialized kinds. Alcoholics Anonymous is a classical example. Similar group methods are employed in the treatment of drug addiction, smoking, obesity, gambling, and in the chang-ing of attitudes underlying social problems such as prejudice, poor race relations, poor working relationships, delinquency, and criminality.

Skilled work in the conduct of such groups requires an ability to utilize to the utmost the clues about personality, attitudes, and beliefs that are presented naturally in spontaneous inter-action. In such groups members learn psychological skills in a practical form from their leaders or mentors, and then pass them on to new members or recruits. The clinical skills of the psychological professional are thus being rapidly democratized and passed on in the most relevant concrete form to individuals with problems. They learn to help themselves as they pass the skills on to still others, new recruits. The use of groups for psychological purposes, and the accompanying democratization of clinical skills has by now gathered tremendous momentum in the United States. Theoretical psychologists have much to learn from studying the successful instances of psychological group work. On the other hand, there is also an encouraging growth of technically based knowledge of natural communication in small groups; there is, indeed, more knowledge than has been put together and utilized.

Modes of participation in small groups are closely related to familiar types of neurotic problems and personality disorders. Fellow participants, though untrained in technical psychology, often agree surprising well in their characterization of an individual. If he is also a patient, or a prospective patient, these lay descriptions can be translated into a diagnosis that is about as reliable as one by trained clinical psychologists. The average group wisdom as to what such a person needs by way of interpersonal treatment is often surprisingly good.

The main dimensions of the distinctions group members make without technical training are essentially the same as those I described earlier: dominance versus submissiveness, friendliness versus unfriendliness, and work-acceptance versus work-resistance. The traits measured by many written personality tests are distributed in this same interpersonal space and may be inferred from observation of interpersonal communication. Even attitudes about political and economic affairs in the larger society, and values related to religious and philosophical beliefs appear to be related to these same interpersonal characteristics. A person who is very conservative in his political beliefs, for example, often also wants to be treated as a legitimate authority in the small group in which he participates. He is likely to be high on giving opinion or suggestion, and to be low on joking and laughing.

A theoretical model of a three-dimensional space can be used to summarize much of what is known about the relations of personality, attitudes, and values to interpersonal style of communication. As I describe each dimension in turn, it may help to visualize it as located in actual physical space.

The vertical dimension in the space, upward and downward, is related to dominance versus submissiveness as a personality trait. It is shown in interpersonal communication in the amount a person talks, and also in the amount of communication that is directed to him. A person lower in the dominance hierarchy tends to address his communications to a higher person in the hope that his ideas will be accepted and that he will thereby gain greater status in the group. The person in the higher position, however, is not so motivated to direct his communications to the lower, but rather to some other person still higher, or to the group as a whole. It turns out, then, that the lower person addresses a little more, generally, to the higher person than the higher person addresses to him. The higher person, especially if he is the highest in the group, is likely to address a large portion of his communication to the group as a whole.

Persons high in this hierarchy are likely to measure high on personality traits of dominance, extroversion, activity, adventuresomeness, and are likely to have values of material success and power. It is possible to be dominant, and also friendly, with a tendency to agree and ask others for their opinion. Such a person is likely to measure high on personality tests of sociability, and perhaps leadership. He tends to value social success and popularity. Dominance, on the other hand, may also be combined with unfriendliness and a tendency to disagree. These persons are likely to measure high on personality tests of domination, and may show some tendencies toward the more hostile and overactive personality disorders. They are likely to value a kind of tough-minded assertiveness in their dealings with others.

On the downward or submissive end of the vertical dimension are those who talk little, receive little, and seldom address the group as a whole. They are seen as introverted and perhaps depressed by their fellow group members, and measure so on written personality tests. They tend to confine themselves to giving information when they do talk, rather than giving opinion or suggestion, and they avoid joking or doing anything exhibitionistic or dramatic. In their attitudes and beliefs they tend to devalue themselves, and to wish there were a world in which desires and appetites did not exist, rather than one in which their desires are actively satisfied.

At right angles to the upward and downward dimension is another dimension one may think of as horizontal, extending from side to side, concerned with positive versus negative feelings. The positive end is marked by friendly behavior, asking others for their opinions, and agreeing with them. Persons on the far positive end of this dimension are likely to measure high on tests of calm, stable, and trustful feelings, and to have what some clinicians call "ego strength," that is, integrated control of their feelings and intellectual functions. Such persons tend to be liked by others, and to like and appreciate them in return. They tend to have an equalitarian and humanitarian set of values and attitudes. Persons on the negative end of this dimension tend to seem unfriendly in their behavior, alienated or isolated, and to disagree. Personality tests show them to have feelings of anxiety, suspicion, jealousy, fearfulness, doubt, indecision, and guilt. Neurotic personality problems of various kinds tend to put a person in this position. These persons are likely to value individual isolation and self-sufficiency.

Dislike is not the simple opposite of liking. Dislike in most groups does not center on the person simply at the negative end of the dimension, but on the one who is negative and at the same time dominating, and work-acceptant, that is, moralistic and dictatorial. This type of person is often called the authoritarian type, but probably should be called the dominating or autocratic authoritarian. There are also more submissive and positive authoritarians who tend to be more agreeable and are somewhat positively regarded by their fellow group members.

The work-acceptant versus work-resistant dimension is at right angles to both the preceding, and may be thought of as extending in the direction forward and backward from the intersection of the other two dimensions. Both types of authoritarians just mentioned are on the forward or work-acceptant end of the dimension. In groups that are concerned with the performance of tasks assigned to them by an external authority, the persons who are found far forward on the work-acceptant end of the dimension are themselves likely to accept authority, or to view themselves as legitimate representatives of authority. They are likely to be conventional or conservative in socioeconomic attitudes, and often in religious orientation as well. In interpersonal communication they are likely to be high in giving opinion, and in asking for and giving suggestions. The more submissive ones may seem somewhat overpersistent and dutiful. Those on the submissive *positive* side will seem altruistic and docile, those on the submissive *negative* side will seem somewhat self-punishing and complaining.

The acknowledged leader of the group, if there is one, is likely to be found somewhere on the work-acceptant end of this dimension. Usually he is also somewhat on the dominant side, and somewhat on the positive side in his behavior. A task leader who is simply dominant and work-acceptant, with no positive component in his behavior, is likely to encounter trouble. He is likely to be identified sooner or later as an authoritarian autocrat, and to suffer a revolt in which he is provoked into negative and dominating behavior.

Persons who make many jokes are found at the work-resistant end of the dimension, along with those who seem to have a preference for fantasy as the organizing process in their action. These persons often prefer to "act out" or dramatize their wishes rather than to analyze problems by logic and try to persuade others. There are both positive and negative varieties, and sometimes they seem quite different. Although the work-resistant type who is both dominant and negative is a rugged individualist, indeed a kind of outlaw, the dominant and positive work-resistant type is often an advocate of unconditional love, who tends to be emotionally supportive of those who cannot or will not conform, and seems warm and spontaneous to his fellows.

The submissive persons on the work-resistant end of the dimension tend to show various restless and inhibited signs of restraint and conflict that we may call showing tension. They tend to hold back from the task or from the suggestions or demands of authority. In their socioeconomic attitudes and beliefs, they are likely to be radical and heretical, rejecting authority, orthodoxy, conventionality, and established modes of social organization.

Personality differences among group members strongly affect their ability to work together. To see how this comes about in more detail, let us consider a group trying to come to a decision about a problem. The most frequently observed sequence in many groups is an act of giving opinion by one participant, followed by an act of agreement on the part of another. Both giving opinions and agreeing with them are frequent types of acts, and it is important for the success of the work that opinions should be produced that can command voluntary acceptance. But agreement on the basic facts underlying the problem is often also essential. Many decision-making groups start a problem-solving cycle with a review of facts. That sends the rate of giving information up for a while at the beginning. Only after they have essential agreement about the facts do they allow themselves to go on to an analysis and evaluation of the facts, and thus allow the rate of giving opinion to rise above that of giving information.

However, the needs of the dominant work-acceptant members may conflict, especially at the beginning, with the demands of such a task sequence. A work-acceptant person who likes to analyze and give his opinion is generally more active than one who is cautious and likes to confine his contributions, so far as possible, to giving information only. And the one who likes to give suggestions is more dominant still. Dominant members not only have a high total rate of participation, but they are likely to want to participate as early as possible in the meeting, and to get ahead with the action immediately. A quarrel among the most dominant and negative members is all too likely to begin early and to prevent an optimal approach to the task. Negative and unfriendly acts tend to lead to further negative and unfriendly acts. Once negativity starts in this circular fashion it has a tendency to build up and to spiral out of control.

One of the principal functions of the leader of such a group is to prevent such a negative buildup, or to bring it within control if it begins. A successful leader, if the group is fortunate enough to have one, is usually himself somewhat dominant, but not too much so. He must be able to cope with the most dominant and negative members, but he must not be too dominant or negative himself, or he will also alienate other group members. He usually needs the help of one or more other members on the positive side, who often form a kind of coalition with him. Acting as their agent, and with their help, the successful leader is able to control the negative elements.

The successful and acknowledged task leader is usually positive in his behavior rather than negative, and so is able to inspire enough liking and admiration to keep the coalition around him strong. He needs also to be work-acceptant in a task-oriented group, but should not be too impatiently so. It is usually due to him, if it happens at all, that the relevant persons, including the most submissive, are asked for information, and later for their opinion, and that the group is kept in an information reviewing phase for a sufficiently long time. The task leader is also often the principal receiver of their information, and provides as high a rate of agreement with them as he can, consistent with his feeling for the real demands of the task.

In many groups the problem of keeping the negative buildup from occurring is a constant one, and it is all the more difficult if the group contains many members with negative and dominant personalities. The composition of the group in terms of personalities may make it impossible to prevent negative buildups, but a skillful leader, especially one who is able to expose and analyze with insight the causes and operation of the negative feelings, can make a tremendous difference. The approach through group self-analysis however, assumes, or even requires, that the negative feelings be allowed to show themselves in sufficiently full play to be recognized and analyzed. The process of psychological self-analysis in training or therapy groups is often full of conflict. It may involve a hostile revolutionary attack on the leadership, and the uncovering of negative and psychologically primitive tendencies altogether too frightening for the inexperienced leader, and for some of the participants. It is in this area that the growth and diffusion of psychological knowledge and skill about group communication will probably contribute most to practical affairs. In any group there are personal and interpersonal problems to be solved in addition to those that are clearly related to the assigned task. Every group decision tends to put the whole group structure under strain—the delicate balance of power and status among the members, their liking and disliking of each other, and their modes of suppressing or expressing work-resistant tendencies.

The strains that accompany group problem solving and decision making may be held in check for a period, in order to get the job done, but they tend increasingly to break through the normal work facade as the effort continues. Eventually, often after the group has reached a decision, or even if there has been none, the group may break into a phase of joking and laughing, a circular interchange that tends to build up through some period of time while the tensions that have been held in check are dealt with. The atmosphere in this phase is quite different from that in the work-acceptant phase. Suppressed feelings or fantasies are expressed symbolically in the form of jokes, allusions, anecdotes, or spontaneous dramatization.

Activity of this kind is a natural form of therapy in most groups. It is generally recognized to have a legitimate time and place, even though it is work-resistant in direction. It is the result, in part, of work, and it is preliminary to more work. In groups where education or re-education is a part of the work goal, it is essential to have the level of tension lowered or the perception of new information will be impaired. The active part in the expression of fantasies and the lowering of tension is often taken by a joker or persons other than the usual task leader. If others are not available to take the lead in this direction, however, the task leader should optimally be able to switch from his work-acceptant orientation and take the lead in the direction of fantasy expression and spontaneous therapy.

In the most effectively operating groups, of whatever concrete kind, *leadership, therapy,* and *education* in some form *all* play a vital part. They are all three necessary and are normally present in the natural processes of interpersonal communication. We may hope that as knowledge and skills concerning these elementary necessities of group life are gained and diffused more widely, the quality of our attempts to solve special problems in many applied areas can be improved correspondingly. Research on communication in small groups promises many practical benefits.

20 MASS COMMUNICATION

Wilbur Schramm

If we think of the long history of life on earth as one day, ther mass communication has come into existence only in the last second before midnight.

Animals communicated with each other for millions of years before any of them developed language. Human animals spoke to each other in common languages for hundreds of thousands of years before any of them learned to write. Knowledge and ideas were shared and preserved in writing for thousands of years before there were mass media.

Thus, when we speak of mass communication we are really referring only to the five hundred years since it became possible to print from movable metal type in the fifteenth century. The rate of development has been truly extraordinary. From language to writing: hundreds of thousands of years. From writing to printing: thousands of years. From printing to films and broadcasting: four hundred years. From the first experiments with television to live television from the moon: forty years!

Technically, what has happened in the last five centuries is that man has developed some remarkable machines that can be inserted into the communication process to duplicate a message almost without limit, and to extend almost indefinitely a person's ability to see and hear and record, and thus to share, information. The communication process remains basically the same. The psychology of communication is basically the same as you have read about in other chapters of this book. But because man lives by information, this new ability to share it, and the extraordinary rate of development, has had a profound effect upon human life.

Each of the steps we have mentioned has made information more easily *portable*. When an animal growls, the message can be shared only as far as it can be heard, and its meaning can be fully known only by those able to see why or at what the creature is growling. Spoken language is meaningful away from the place where an event occurs, but the message can be heard only as far as the voice can carry. When man learned to write his language, he won a victory over both time and space, for now he could set down his history and preserve his records without having to depend on the oldest man to remember or the far traveler to repeat. But still he wrote in one copy, or had scribes make additional copies at enormous cost. For example, in the early fourteenth century it cost the equivalent of $5,000, in modern currency, to copy one thin volume as a birthday gift to a French princess.

Then someone inserted a printing press into the communication process. Perhaps the first man who did this was Gutenberg. Someone combined the discoveries of gifted men from many countries—ink, paper, the art of casting metal type, and an instrument developed from the wine press. And suddenly it was possible to duplicate writing in as many copies as one needed.

Whether the Renaissance stimulated the development of printing or printing stimulated the thoughts and ideas of the Renaissance is not a very important question. It is unnecessary, if not impossible, to specify cause and effect; rather, there were a series of interactions. The book and the newspaper moved hand in hand with the Enlightenment. The newspaper and the political tract were intimately involved in all the political movements and popular revolutions of the seventeenth and eighteenth centuries. The textbook made public education possible on a wide scale, at a time when there was a growing hunger for knowledge. The news sheet, first, and later the electronic media, made it possible for ordinary people to be informed about politics and to participate in government, at a time when there was widespread dissatisfaction with the locus of power. Without channels of mass communication, the Industrial Revolution of the nineteenth century could hardly have transformed our way of life as it did. This technical revolution, in turn, added new media to the channels available. The camera, the microphone, the tape and disc recorder, the transmitter, and the computer were developed and inserted into the communication process—all within little more than one hundred years.

It is no accident that we have used the word *revolution* in talking about these interactions of mass communication with society—the intellectual revolution, political revolution, industrial revolution, revolution in values. For history has taught us a basic precept: because communication is the fundamental social process, major change in human communication accompanies major social change.

The nature of this interaction we can see in miniature in some of the new countries just now emerging from an oral into a media culture. In these countries, five hundred years of communication development are being foreshortened to perhaps one-tenth that much, because the tools of communication are already available. In many cases, the order of development is changed, and the media tumble over one another as they grow, rather than following the historical pattern of print, picture, sound, motion, and electronics. For example, the electronic media often precede print, because they can leap the barriers of illiteracy. The media in new countries typically develop in the city and spread to the villages; therefore it is still possible in many countries to observe oral and media cultures side by side. And when we look at these premedia and postmedia areas, we find striking differences.

Life in the villages where the media have not yet penetrated tends to have a timeless, unhurried quality. Knowledge is power there, as elsewhere, but this power usually resides in the old men who are able to remember the sacred writings, the laws, customs, history, and genealogies. Much of communication is concerned with preserving and passing on ancient knowledge and ancient values. Time tends to be communicated by the sun, or by bodily needs, rather than by a clock. And even though life is often harsh and brief in these traditional villages, still when I see farmers in the morning stop to enjoy for a while the colors of a maple tree or the antics of a young animal, I think rather ruefully that at this hour, at home, I should be hurrying to work.

When radio and print enter a traditional village, the change is often spectacular. For one thing, the flow of communication is enormously increased. More important: it comes from farther away. Almost overnight, horizons are pushed back. Power passes from the men with long memories, because now the past and the precept can be written down. Written down, they become common property, subject to question. The people of the village learn how other people live. Very often they see something they want for themselves, and then communication is used to bring about change rather than to preserve changelessness. New concepts and images flow through the communication channels—crop rotation, insecticides, vaccination, elections, family planning. Power passes from the wise men who commanded private knowledge of old times to the informed men who command knowledge of faraway places and new methods of doing things. Thus the flow of communication comes to be centered less on time than on space, and to be used less for *ascription* (what one *should* do) than for *description* (what other people do, and what one *can* do). And the wheels of change are set in motion.

Without the profound changes that have taken place in communication, sixty new countries would not be in existence today. Without the mass media to support and extend education, and to help adults learn how to improve their level of living, the development plans and schedules of these new countries would be completely infeasible. I am not suggesting that the direction of change in these countries is in every case desirable; many observers regret the passing of some elements of the traditional culture. But given the currents of change, it is clear that the goals of these countries cannot be implemented without modern communication, and that without modern communication there would be no likelihood whatsoever of the ordinary people in such a country having any impact on the choice of goals and the decision as to what should be kept and what changed.

In the new countries, then, we can see the history of mass

communication foreshortened. In the economically advanced countries, we can see what has developed in five hundred years, and perhaps gain some idea of what the future will be like.

In Europe, North America, Japan, and other places where mass communication is well developed, the quality that would impress a visitor from another planet is the extraordinary *pervasiveness* of it. Radio is worldwide; only a few countries do not print a newspaper within their own borders; television is now in more than sixty countries. Where mass communication is readily available, as it ultimately will be everywhere, people typically spend three or more hours a day on it—more than they spend on any other daily activity except work and sleep. Many children spend as much time watching television alone, in their first twelve years of life, as they spend in school. Almost all news comes through the mass media—in fact, the concept of news was hardly known before the age of mass communication. A very high proportion of all entertainment comes through the mass media. Mass communication sells merchandise, provides education, carries the brunt of political campaigns, furnishes a flood of useful information—from prices to weather to schedules of events.

Peter Drucker says that the countries where mass communication is well developed are living in a "knowledge economy." He points out that as many books were published in the last twenty-five years as in the five hundred years before 1950; that perhaps 90 percent of all scientists and technologists who have ever lived are alive and working today; that workers engaged in providing knowledge to the public now outnumber farmers and industrial workers in the United States. Leading universities know that their libraries double about every fifteen years, and the amount of published science has been doubling about every twelve years.

In other words, there is good reason for calling the present time an Age of Information, when the possession of knowledge will become the chief resource of mankind, and the prime requisite of power. We can make some predictions about the direction that mass communication is likely to take in this age. When the mass media are young, the chief effort is to get information circulating farther, faster. In other words, the technology of mass communication has been developed primarily to assist the *sender,* and has given only secondary attention to the problems of the *receiver.* This trend has been relatively constant from the first printing press to the communication satellite. The satellite can carry thousands of messages at the same time, and deliver them to one-third of the earth. Within a few years we can expect to have wave guides that will carry tens of thousands of messages, and laser beams that will carry hundreds of thousands. But this pace of technological development has produced a paradoxical situation in which there is really *too much* information for any one individual, and at the same time it is extraordinarily difficult for that individual to get the information he badly *needs.* Thus, scientists have difficulty in keeping up with what other scientists are doing. Readers are deluged by news but cannot find the particular news that is important to them. The frequency spectrum is full of radio and television, but many people cannot get what they want when it is available. Or consider the case of instructional television, which has two conflicting needs—for better programs, and for more control of these programs by the teacher. Solving one of these problems makes the other harder. Better programs cost more money, and to make the unit costs acceptable it is necessary to have central production, transmission, and scheduling. But this makes it harder for the teacher to schedule the programs when the class is ready for them, to change the order, to repeat a program, or to stop in the middle and talk about them. In other words, there is a fundamental conflict between the needs of the sender, for wide distribution, and those of the receiver, for local control.

It is predictable that the next stage in the technology of mass communication will be concerned with the needs of the receiver: to help him separate out what he needs from the flow of information, call or recall it for use when he needs it, and establish special channels to and from other users with whom he needs to share. The computer will probably be the chief instrument in this coming Age of Information, but we shall also see new recording devices and vast data banks to be called upon when needed. We shall probably soon have "wired cities," "wired industries," "wired school systems" built around central information inputs and information storage. We can expect to see many activities that we now conduct face-to-face—conferences, business meetings, shopping—transferred in great part to wired television. We shall probably be able to specify the kind of news or instruction or entertainment we want delivered electronically to our homes. These new technologies will require us to develop new media organizations different from the newspaper, the television system, or the publishing house.

The emergence of these mass media organizations is a second aspect of our mass communication system that would certainly be noted by any visitor from another planet. A number of large organizations have grown up in the last few centuries to manage the flow of information. These are the book and magazine publishers, the newspapers, movie makers and distributors, radio and television stations and networks, and, among others, the advertising agencies. Some of these are extraordinarily complex; indeed, to an outsider, it seems like a little miracle that a daily newspaper or a day-long television schedule ever gets put together. They are powerful because they are gatekeepers of the flow of knowledge. They have the power to withhold, to add, or to interpret. Therefore, one of the most important considerations in the future of mass communication is who shall control these media organizations, and what should be expected of them.

In a number of countries of the world, an active program of mass communication research has been developed in the last few decades to study questions like the ones I have just mentioned. There is now a fairly large body of research on the nature and workings of the media, and the differences between mass media that are subordinate and are not subordinate to government; on the audiences of mass communication; on the content of the mass media channels; and on the uses and effects of mass communication. The chief question that scholars have been concerned with is the impact of mass communication—what does it do to us? I want to suggest a rewording of that question, but first let me mention briefly some of the things we now think we know about the effects of the mass media.

Perhaps I should begin by mentioning one thing we have become quite sure that mass communication is *not:* it is not an irresistible force that can overpower an audience. This was the concept of mass communication commonly held forty years ago, and it was the reason why World War I propaganda and, later, Nazi and Communist propaganda were so frightening to many people. At that time the audience was thought of as a helpless target. If a person could be reached by the insidious forces of propaganda carried by the mighty power of the mass media, he could be changed and converted and controlled. This might be called the Bullet Theory of communication: the audience was considered to be passive, waiting for mass communication to shoot a propaganda bullet into it. So research focused on the *content* of communication which was supposedly being *shot into* readers, and from this developed the method of content analysis under the leadership of scholars like Harold Lasswell.

But very soon it became apparent that the Bullet Theory did not square with the facts. The audience was obstinate. When hit by the bullet, it simply refused to fall over. Sometimes the bullet seemed not to penetrate. Sometimes it had an effect opposite to what was intended. Sometimes the audience seemed actually to enjoy being hit, and no change was perceptible. Trying to explain such phenomena, scholars looked for other variables that might be influential in the communication process. Paul Lazarsfeld and his pupils discovered that the social groups to which a person belonged, and his interpersonal relations, made an important difference in how he used and responded to mass communication. Carl Hovland and his associates found that a number of personal variables, and variations in the way the message was presented, had a great deal to do with the effect of the mass media. Other researchers found that it made a great difference whether the mass media were monopolized by one point of view or offered alternatives. And by 1960 the Bullet Theory was—if you will pardon the expression—shot full of holes.

The final touch in this process was given by Raymond Bauer and others, who were able to demonstrate dramatically that the audience was far from passive; that it actually went out seeking what it wanted from the mass media, interpreted what it found there to fit its own needs and predispositions, and seldom changed its mind as a result of mass persuasion. This development from the Bullet Theory to the study of an Obstinate Audience to the concept of an Active Audience is one of the interesting and important chapters in modern social science. For we have come very far from the concept of something flowing from a communicator into an audience. Rather, we think of the process as composed of two distinct acts: senders put out certain signs—print, pictures, sounds, whatever—and receivers choose among them, selecting some, rejecting some, making such use of them as they can and will.

The modern analogy, therefore, is not to a bullet shot into a target by the mass media, but rather to the way that an Indian friend of mine sells the cakes he gets up at dawn to bake every morning. He tries to bake the kind that people like. He tries to display them attractively. Then it is up to the patrons. The crowds move past. Some of them see the cakes; some do not. Some will be hungry, looking for food; some not. Some will be looking specifically for cakes; others not. Some have bought good cakes from this baker in the past, and will be more likely to buy from him than from others. Some will see the cakes, find their salivary juices are stimulated, and reach in their pockets for coins; and they may or may not find any. And if they buy, they may eat the cakes or give them to a friend.

I hardly need point out that this provides a new departure, not only for developing communication theory, but also for interpreting the effect of the mass media. It does not imply that the media have no effect, but that this effect is not automatic and irresistible. It leads us to think, not about "what mass communication does to us," but rather how parts of society use the media to talk to other parts. Therefore, when one studies the mass media he is not studying something acting on society, but rather studying society using its basic process. The effect of mass communication at any given time will depend on the condition, the needs, the goals of different parts of society. May I give one example? In 1963, four-fifths of all the American people engaged in an unprecedented act of national rededication, watching their television sets before and during the funeral of President John Kennedy. The mass media made this possible, of course; but the essential elements in whatever happened to the American people in late November of 1963 were the state of the society at that time, resulting from the assassination of a national leader.

We have spoken at some length of what mass communication does *not* do to us. Let us now mention some of the kinds of effect that it apparently has.

One of these is the effect that Marshall McLuhan and others have postulated. They believe that regardless of media content, there is an effect of receiving so much communication through the mass media, rather than interpersonally. McLuhan points out that when printing became widely available, it tended to *privatize* rather than socialize society, because reading is a private and individual act. It tended to remove readers from reality by translating life into a set of verbal signs that had to be received consecutively, in a line stretching across the page, rather than simultaneously, as one sees events in real life. McLuhan feels that television is a more healthful experience than print because it is closer to the experience of nonmediated communication.

Frankly, this is mostly speculation; there is little research at the moment to prove or disprove it. Yet, scholars have been intrigued for many years by the so-called Whorfian hypothesis that the way a person sees the world and reacts to it depends on his language. And it is likely that considerable effort will be devoted in the future to trying to discover the effect of filtering massive amounts of information through print as opposed to direct observation or audiovisual means.

McLuhan has stated this point of view in his often quoted sentence, "The medium is the message." However, the message is a great deal more than the medium, and one effect that most concerns us about mass communication is that any individual derives so much of his view of environment from the mass media. The media have the power to focus attention on some events, some ideas, rather than others. They have the power to interpret events, because no reporting can be completely objective, or objectively complete. They have the power to confer status on some persons, who have the ability to be interesting on radio or television, rather than on others. They have the power to fill in our knowledge of all parts of our environment that we do not experience directly.

This is an enormous power, and therefore, we have good reason to be concerned about how clear the lens of the mass media is. We have the right to be concerned about whether the leaders and candidates we see are "packaged" for television, and therefore whether we are seeing realistic or fictional persons. We have the right to be concerned about whether we are hearing all sides of an issue, whether the media are serving as a forum of ideas or showing us only one set of ideas. Considering human frailties, the safest thing is to have competing reports and competing ideas in our media. Therefore we must be concerned about monopoly control over the mass media.

Another power of mass communication is to provide models of behavior. All of us have seen children and young people imitate the people in movies or television. This is innocent enough when it encourages fads in clothing or popular music or language or play, but it is far from innocent if—for example—it presents models of violence as harmless or approved behavior. This is one thing that concerns us about the possible effects of mass media on young or impressionable people.

Perhaps the most evident effect of mass communication arises from the *massness* of it; so many people are seeing the same kind of entertainment, hearing the same ideas, seeing the same media personalities. This massness is not necessarily either good or bad; it may result in the vulgarizing of entertainment, or in bringing good music, drama, and literature to people who otherwise would never have experienced it; it may result in focusing attention on frivolities, or bringing realities of great importance to the attention of vastly wider audiences. As an example of the latter result, I think we can say with some confidence that hundreds of millions of people have now for the first time seen war in its harsh reality, through the medium of television, and as a result we can hope that attitudes toward war as national policy will be modified. We do not know how much the massness of mass communication will result in activity and change, as opposed to passivity. It can make political participation possible on a wider scale than ever before; it can bring people into an active society; it can offer advantages and opportunities to the disadvantaged people of the earth. Or, because of what it is used for, and the difficulty of feeding back reactions to the media, it may simply contribute to passivity and to maintaining the status quo of society.

It depends on how it is used! I said earlier that I wanted to reword the question, What does mass communication do to us? The way to ask that question is, What do *we do to ourselves* with mass communication? The mass media are potent tools. They put great power in our hands to do what we wish to our own society. They can help us destroy that society, or vastly improve it. They can help us elevate it or debase it. They can help us share education and useful information, or help us blunt the appetite for such improvement. But the media cannot do it themselves. They are essentially tools—duplicating machines, sensory extenders. We have it within our own power to use them as we think desirable. It behooves us, therefore, to think carefully, how and for what we are going to use them.

21 NONVERBAL COMMUNICATION

George A. Miller

When the German philosopher Nietzsche said that "success is the greatest liar," he meant that a successful person seems especially worthy to us even when his success is due to nothing more than good luck. But Nietzsche's observation can be interpreted more broadly.

People communicate in many different ways. One of the most important ways, of course, is through language. Moreover, when language is written it can be completely isolated from the context in which it occurs; it can be treated as if it were an independent and self-contained process. We have been so successful in using and describing and analyzing this special kind of communication that we sometimes act as if language were the *only* kind of communication that can occur between people. When we act that way, of course, we have been deceived by success, the greatest liar of them all.

Like all animals, people communicate by their actions as well as by the noises they make. It is a sort of biological anomaly of man—something like the giraffe's neck, or the pelican's beak—that our vocal noises have so far outgrown in importance and frequency all our other methods of signaling to one another. Language is obviously essential for human beings, but it is not the whole story of human communication. Not by a long shot.

Consider the following familiar fact. When leaders in one of the less well developed countries decide that they are ready to introduce some technology that is already highly advanced in another country, they do not simply buy all the books that have been written about that technology and have their students read them. The books may exist and they may be very good, but just reading about the technology is not enough. The students must be sent to study in a country where the technology is already flourishing, where they can see it first hand. Once they have been exposed to it in person and experienced it as part of their own lives, they are ready to understand and put to use the information that is in the books. But the verbal message, without the personal experience to back it up, is of little value.

Now what is it that the students learn by participating in a technology that they can not learn by just reading about it? It seems obvious that they are learning something important, and that whatever it is they are learning is something that we don't know how to put into our verbal descriptions. There is a kind of nonverbal communication that occurs when students are personally involved in the technology and when they interact with people who are using and developing it.

Pictures are one kind of nonverbal communication, of course, and moving pictures can communicate some of the information that is difficult to capture in words. Pictures also have many of the properties that make language so useful—they can be taken in one situation at one time and viewed in an entirely different situation at any later time. Now that we have television satellites, pictures can be transmitted instantaneously all over the world, just as our words can be transmitted by radio. Perhaps the students who are trying to learn how to create a new technology in their own country could supplement their reading by watching moving pictures of people at work in the developed industry. Certainly the pictures would be a help, but they would be very expensive. And we don't really know whether words and pictures together would capture everything the students would be able to learn by going to a more advanced country and participating directly in the technology.

Let me take another familiar example. There are many different cultures in the world, and in each of them the children must learn a great many things that are expected of everyone who participates effectively in that culture. These things are taken for granted by everyone who shares the culture. When I say they are taken for granted, I mean that nobody needs to describe them or write them down or try self-consciously to teach them to children. Indeed, the children begin to learn them before their linguistic skills are far enough developed to understand a verbal description of what they are learning. This kind of learning has sometimes been called "imitation," but that is much too simple an explanation for the complex processes that go on when a child learns what is normal and expected in his own community. Most of the norms are communicated to the child nonverbally, and he internalizes them as if no other possibilities existed. They are as much a part of him as his own body; he would no more question them than he would question the fact that he has two hands and two feet, but only one head.

These cultural norms can be described verbally, of course. Anthropologists who are interested in describing the differences among the many cultures of the world have developed a special sensitivity to cultural norms and have described them at length in their scholarly books. But if a child had to read those books in order to learn what was expected of him, he would never become an effective member of his own community.

What is an example of the sort of thing that children learn nonverbally? One of the simplest examples to observe and analyze and discuss is the way people use clothing and bodily ornamentation to communicate. At any particular time in any particular culture there is an accepted and normal way to dress and to arrange the hair and to paint the face and to wear one's jewelry. By adopting those conventions for dressing himself, a person communicates to the world that he wants to be treated according to the standards of the culture for which they are appropriate. When a black person in America rejects the normal American dress and puts on African clothing, he is communicating to the world that he wants to be treated as an Afro-American. When a white man lets his hair and beard grow, wears very informal clothing, and puts beads around his neck, he is communicating to the world that he rejects many of the traditional values of Western culture. On the surface, dressing up in unusual costumes would seem to be one of the more innocent forms of dissent that a person could express, but in fact it is deeply resented by many people who still feel bound by the traditional conventions of their culture and who become fearful or angry when those norms are violated. The nonverbal message that such a costume communicates is "I reject your culture and your values," and those who resent this message can be violent in their response.

The use of clothing as an avenue of communication is relatively obvious, of course. A somewhat subtler kind of communication occurs in the way people use their eyes. We are remarkably accurate in judging the direction of another person's gaze; psychologists have done experiments that have measured just how accurate such judgments are. From an observation of where a person is looking we can infer what he is looking at, and from knowing what he is looking at we can guess what he is interested in, and from what he is interested in and the general situation we can usually make a fairly good guess about what he is going to do. Thus eye movements can be a rich and important channel of nonverbal communication.

Most personal interaction is initiated by a short period during which two people look directly at one another. Direct eye contact is a signal that each has the other's attention, and that some further form of interaction can follow. In Western cultures, to look directly into another person's eyes is equivalent to saying, "I am open to you—let the action begin." Everyone knows how much lovers can communicate by their eyes, but aggressive eye contact can also be extremely informative.

In large cities, where people are crowded in together with others they neither know nor care about, many people develop a deliberate strategy of avoiding eye contacts. They want to mind their own business, they don't have time to interact with everyone they pass, and they communicate this fact by refusing to look at other people's faces. It is one of the things that make newcomers to the city feel that it is a hostile and unfriendly place.

Eye contact also has an important role in regulating conversational interactions. In America, a typical pattern is for the listener to signal that he is paying attention by looking at the talker's mouth or eyes. Since direct eye contact is often too intimate, the talker may let his eyes wander elsewhere. As the moment arrives for the talker to become a listener, and for his partner to begin talking, there will often be a preliminary eye signal. The talker will often look toward the listener, and the listener will signal that he is ready to talk by glancing away.

Such eye signals will vary, of course, depending on what the people are talking about and what the personal relation is between them. But whatever the pattern of eye signals that two people are using, they use them unconsciously. If you try to become aware of your own eye movements while you are talking to someone, you will find it extremely frustrating. As soon as you try to think self-consciously about your own eye movements, you do not know where you should be looking. If you want to study how the eyes communicate, therefore, you should do it by observing other people, not yourself. But if you watch other people too intently, of course, you may disturb them or make them angry. So be careful!

Even the pupils of your eyes communicate. When a person becomes excited or interested in something, the pupils of his eyes increase in size. In order to test whether we are sensitive to these changes in pupil size, a psychologist showed people two pictures of the face of a pretty girl. The two pictures were completely identical except that in one picture the girl's pupil was constricted, whereas in the other picture her pupil was dilated. The people were asked to say which picture they liked better, and they voted in favor of the picture with the large pupil. Many of the judges did not even realize consciously what the difference was, but apparently they were sensitive to the difference and preferred the eyes that communicated excitement and interest.

Eye communication seems to be particularly important for Americans. It is part of the American culture that people should be kept at a distance, and that contact with another person's body should be avoided in all but the most intimate situations. Because of this social convention of dealing with others at a distance, Americans have to place much reliance on their distance receptors, their eyes and ears, for personal communication. In other cultures, however, people normally come closer together and bodily contact between conversational partners is as normal as eye contact is in America. In the Eastern Mediterranean cultures, for example, both the touch and the smell of the other person are expected.

The anthropologist Edward T. Hall has studied the spatial relations that seem appropriate to various kinds of interactions. They vary with intimacy, they depend on the possibility of eye contact, and they are different in different cultures. In America, for example, two strangers will converse impersonally at a distance of about four feet. If one moves closer, the other will back away. In a waiting room, strangers will keep apart, but friends will sit together, and members of a family may actually touch one another.

Other cultures have different spatial norms. In Latin America, for example, impersonal discussion normally occurs at a distance of two or three feet, which is the distance that is appropriate for personal discussion in North America. Consequently, it is impossible for a North and a South American both to be comfortable when they talk to one another unless one can adopt the zones that are normal for the other. If the South American advances to a distance that is comfortable for him, it will be too close for the North American, and he will withdraw, and one can chase the other all around the room unless something intervenes to end the conversation. The North American seems aloof and unfriendly to the South American. The South American seems hostile or oversexed to the North American. Hall mentions that North Americans sometimes cope with this difference by barricading themselves behind desks or tables, and that South Americans have been known literally to climb over these barriers in order to attain a comfortable distance at which to talk.

Within one's own culture these spatial signals are perfectly understood. If two North Americans are talking at a distance of one foot or less, you know that what they are saying is highly confidential. At a distance of two to three feet it will be some personal subject matter. At four or five feet it is impersonal, and if they are conversing at a distance of seven or eight feet, we know that they expect others to be listening to what they are saying. When talking to a group, a distance of ten to twenty feet is normal, and at greater distances only greetings are exchanged. These conventions are unconscious but highly reliable. For example, if you are having a personal conversation with a North American at a distance of two feet, you can shift it to an impersonal conversation by the simple procedure of moving back to a distance of four or five feet. If he can't follow you, he will find it quite impossible to maintain a personal discussion at that distance.

These examples should be enough to convince you—if you needed convincing—that we communicate a great deal of information that is not expressed in the words we utter. And I have not even mentioned yet the interesting kind of communication that occurs by means of gestures. A gesture is an expressive motion or action, usually made with the hands and arms, but also with the head or even the whole body. Gestures can occur with or without speech. As a part of the speech act, they usually emphasize what the person is saying, but they may occur without any speech at all. Some gestures are spontaneous, some are highly ritualized and have very specific meanings. And they differ enormously from one culture to another.

Misunderstanding of nonverbal communication is one of the most distressing and unnecessary sources of international friction. For example, few Americans understand how much the Chinese hate to be touched, or slapped on the back, or even to shake hands. How easy it would be for an American to avoid giving offense simply by avoiding these particular gestures that, to him, signify intimacy and friendliness. Or, to take another example, when Khrushchev placed his hands together over his head and shook them, most Americans interpreted it as an arrogant gesture of triumph, the sort of gesture a victorious prize fighter would make, even though Khrushchev seems to have intended it as a friendly gesture of international brotherhood. Sticking out the tongue and quickly drawing it back can be a gesture of self-castigation in one culture, an admission of a social mistake, but someone from another culture might interpret it as a gesture of ridicule or contempt, and in the Eskimo culture it would not be a gesture at all, but the conventional way of directing a current of air when blowing out a candle. Just a little better communication on the nonverbal level might go a long way toward improving international relations.

Ritualized gestures—the bow, the shrug, the smile, the wink, the military salute, the pointed finger, the thumbed nose, sticking out the tongue, and so on—are not really nonverbal communication, because such gestures are just a substitute for the verbal meanings that are associated with them. There are, however, many spontaneous gestures and actions that are unconscious, but communicate a great deal. If you take a moving picture of someone who is deeply engrossed in a conversation, and later show it to him, he will be quite surprised to see many of the gestures he used and the subtle effects they produced. Sometimes what a person is saying unconsciously by his actions may directly contradict what he is saying consciously with his words. Anthropologists have tried to develop a way to write down a description of these nonverbal actions, something like the notation that choreographers use to record the movements of a ballet dancer, but it is difficult to know exactly what the significance of these actions really is, or what the important features are that should be recorded. We can record them photographically, of course, but we still are not agreed on how the photographic record should be analyzed.

Finally, there is a whole spectrum of communication that is vocal, but not really verbal. The most obvious examples are spontaneous gasps of surprise or cries of pain. I suspect this kind of vocal communication is very similar for both man and animal. But our use of vocal signals goes far beyond such grunts and groans. It is a commonplace observation that the way you say something is as important as what you say, and often more important for telling the listener what your real intentions are. Exactly the same words may convey directly opposite messages according to the way they are said. For example, I can say, "Oh, isn't that woNderful" so that I sound enthusiastic, or I can say, "Oh, isn't THAT wonderful" in a sarcastic tone so that you know I don't think it is wonderful at all. Because the actual words uttered are often misleading, lawyers and judges in the courtroom have learned that it is sometimes important to have an actual recording and not just a written transcript of what a person is supposed to have said.

Rapid and highly inflected speech usually communicates excitement, extremely distinct speech usually communicates anger, very loud speech usually communicates pomposity, and a slow monotone usually communicates boredom. The emotional clues that are provided by the way a person talks are extremely subtle, and accomplished actors must practice for many years to bring them under conscious control.

A person's pronunciation also tells a great deal about him. If he has a foreign accent, a sensitive listener can generally tell where he was born. If he speaks with a local dialect, we can often guess what his social origins were and how much education he has had. Often a person will have several different styles of speaking, and will use them to communicate which social role he happens to be playing at the moment. This is such a rich source of social and psychological information, in fact, that a whole new field has recently developed to study it, a field called "sociology of language." Since the sociology of language is discussed in Chapter 24, I will not say anything more about it here.

One of the most significant signals that is vocal but nonverbal is the ungrammatical pause. (See Chapter 23 for a more detailed analysis of pauses.) In careful speech most of our pauses are grammatical. That is to say, our pauses occur at the boundaries of grammatical segments, and serve as a kind of audible punctuation. By calling them "grammatical pauses" we imply that they are a normal part of the verbal message. An ungrammatical pause, however, is not a part of the verbal message. For example, when I . . . uh . . . pause within a . . . uh . . . grammatical unit, you cannot regard the pause as part of my verbal message. These ungrammatical pauses are better regarded as the places where the speaker is thinking, is searching for words, and is planning how to continue his utterance. For a linguist, of course, the grammatical pause is most interesting, since it reveals something about the structure of the verbal message. For a psychologist, however, the ungrammatical pause is more interesting, because it reveals something about the thought processes of the speaker.

When a skilled person reads a prepared text, there are few ungrammatical pauses. But spontaneous speech is a highly fragmented and discontinuous activity. Indeed, ungrammatical pausing is a reliable signal of spontaneity in speech. The pauses tend to occur at choice points in the message, and particularly

.efore words that are rare or unusual and words that are chosen with particular care. An actor who wanted to make his rehearsed speech sound spontaneous would deliberately introduce ungrammatical pauses at these critical points.

Verbal communication uses only one of the many kinds of signals that people can exchange; for a balanced view of the communication process we should always keep in mind the great variety of other signals that can reinforce or contradict the verbal message. These subtleties are especially important in psychotherapy, where a patient tries to communicate his emotional troubles to a doctor, but may find it difficult or impossible to express in words the real source of his distress. Under such circumstances, a good therapist learns to listen for more than words, and to rely on nonverbal signals to help him interpret the verbal signals. For this reason, many psychologists have been persistently interested in nonverbal communication, and have perhaps been less likely than linguists to fall into the mistaken belief that language is the only way we can communicate.

The price of opening up one's attention to this wider range of events, however, is a certain vagueness about the kind of communication that is occurring—about what it means and how to study it. We have no dictionaries or grammars to help us analyze nonverbal communication, and there is much work that will have to be done in many cultures before we can formulate and test any interesting scientific theories about nonverbal communication. Nevertheless, the obvious fact that so much communication does occur nonverbally should persuade us not to give up, and not to be misled by our success in analyzing verbal messages.

Recognizing the great variety of communication channels that are available is probably only the first step toward a broader conception of communication as a psychological process. Not only must we study what a person says and how he says it, but we must try to understand why he says it. If we concentrate primarily on the words that people say, we are likely to think that the only purpose of language is to exchange information. That is one of its purposes, of course, but certainly not the only one. People exchange many things. Not only do they exchange information, but they also exchange money, goods, services, love, and status. In any particular interaction, a person may give one of these social commodities in exchange for another. He may give information in exchange for money, or give services in exchange for status or love. Perhaps we should first characterize communication acts in terms of what people are trying to give and gain in their social interactions. Then, within that broader frame of reference, we might see better that verbal messages are more appropriate for some exchanges and nonverbal messages for others, and that both have their natural and complementary roles to play in the vast tapestry we call human society.

22 PERSUASION

William J. McGuire

People communicate for many reasons. They communicate in order to give information, to ask help, to give orders, to make promises, to provide amusement, to express their ideas (or, as Voltaire said, to hide them). The present discussion deals with another important function, persuasion. Much of the communicating that people do is intended to persuade someone to change his attitudes or the way he behaves. Because persuasion is both a very common and a very important reason for communicating, it has received a great deal of attention from psychologists interested in social interaction.

The study of persuasion is interesting both on scientific and on practical grounds. On the scientific side, it helps us to understand better why people behave the way they do, and why their behavior sometimes changes. On the practical side, an understanding of persuasive techniques would have obvious value to an advertiser, a politician, an educator—to anyone whose job it is to change what people think and do. It is probably not surprising, therefore, that the amount of research devoted each year to this topic has been growing even faster than the burgeoning rate of psychology as a whole. There have been literally hundreds of experiments on persuasive communication during each of the past decades.

As soon as we begin to think seriously about the process of persuasion, it is obvious that an enormous range of factors can contribute to its success or failure. In order to study persuasion analytically, we would like to vary each of these factors and see what effects they have. Each of these variable factors—or variables, as psychologists call them—must be identified, isolated, and measured. And the resulting mass of data must then be summarized in some kind of theory that will make it all meaningful and easier to grasp and use.

As a general strategy in approaching very complicated problems, psychologists have learned that it helps to classify the variables involved under two general headings. We call them the "independent variables" and the "dependent variables." In this case, the independent variables have to do with the communication process; these are the variables that we can manipulate in order to see what happens or to test whether a theoretically predicted effect is actually produced. The dependent variables have to do with what happens, with the changes that occur, with persuasion itself; these are the variables that we expect will change when we manipulate the independent variables. Taken together, the independent and dependent variables define what we might call the "communication-persuasion matrix."

The communication-persuasion matrix summarizes whatever factual data we have about the relations among the independent and dependent variables. In my own view, the independent variables should be thought of in terms of the numerous aspects of the communication, and the dependent variables in terms of the information processing that a person does when he receives a persuasive message. In terms of this "information processing approach," the following organization of independent and dependent variables has been found the most useful.

On the independent variable side, communication is a matter of "who says what to whom, via what channel, and with what effect." To keep up with the times, I label these classes of independent variables that make up any communication situation in terms of the jargon of communication engineering. In this terminology, any persuasive communication involves five classes of variables, namely, *source, message, channel, receiver,* and *destination.*

Turning to persuasion, or the dependent variable side of the communication-persuasion matrix, we can single out six separate steps that a person must go through when he is persuaded to take some new attitude or action. He must first of all have the persuasive communication *presented* to him. Second, given that the material is presented, it is necessary that the target person *attends* to it. And, given that he attends to it, he must also *comprehend* what is being argued; he must at least comprehend the conclusion being urged even if he does not comprehend the arguments being offered in its support. Fourth, besides comprehending the position being urged, the recipient must *yield* to it; he must adopt a new position, at least on the verbal level. Moreover, if we are interested in anything but the most immediate effects, a fifth step is necessary, that this yielding be *retained* until some subsequent time at which the effect is to be measured. A sixth and final step is required if we are interested in effects that go beyond the strictly verbal level, in that the person must not only retain the new attitude but must also *act* on it, whether by purchasing the product, voting for the candidate, getting the cancer checkup, or whatever is the target behavior at which the persuasion campaign is aimed.

This analysis helps us to organize our thinking about persuasion, whether we are trying to formulate or evaluate a campaign against atmospheric pollution, or a campaign urging young women to receive inoculations against rubella, or whatever. It is useful to analyze the campaign in terms of these dependent and independent variables. On the communication side, the campaign would be analyzed into variables belonging to each of the classes mentioned: the perceived source of the communication; the message style, contents, and organization; the characteristics of the channel through which it is transmitted; the traits and abilities of the target receivers; and the destination (or specific target behavior) at which it is aimed. Variables falling under each of these five headings in the communication campaign are introduced or evaluated in terms of their efficiency in producing each of the six steps in the dependent variable of persuasion. That is to say, each of the communication variables is evaluated in terms of its efficacy in increasing the probability that the communication will be presented to the target receivers, that it will be attended to, comprehended, yielded to, retained until the opportunity arises for the target behavior to be performed, and then acted upon.

This analysis of the communication-persuasion process can

give rise to very elegant theories with mathematically precise equations. Some beautiful work of this type has been done in psychological research on persuasive communication, work whose elegance and power have provided much creative pleasure to the researchers and esthetic pleasure to the observer who can grasp the outlines of the work. Those who are not psychologists may prefer to find their pleasure elsewhere, but even on the less formal level at which the nonspecialist may be interested in persuasion, this analysis of the communication-persuasion process has utility both for aiding comprehension and for being provocative of new ideas to an extent that probably justifies the effort involved in its use.

One value of the analysis is that it forces us to remember the importance of attention and comprehension in the persuasion process. In the absence of such an analytic system, people tend to stress the more dynamic step of overcoming the resistance to yielding. For example, when a person is asked to predict how a receiver variable like intelligence is related to persuasibility, he is likely to say that the more intelligent an individual is, the harder it will be to persuade him. If we push our respondent to explain his prediction, he mentions a number of factors. He says that the more intelligent the individual, the more information he tends to have to back up his own views, the greater his critical skill in detecting the weaknesses of the opposing arguments, the less gullible he is and the more willing to maintain a discrepancy between his own belief and that of others, and so on. This answer is reasonable as far as it goes, but it does not go far enough. It concentrates almost exclusively on the yielding variable in determining the relation between intelligence and persuasive impact. It completely disregards the role played by the earlier steps of attention and reception in affecting persuasive impact.

When we look at the obtained results on the relation between intelligence and persuasibility, we see that this overemphasis on yielding can be a serious source of error. Some studies by Carl Hovland and his associates during World War II provide an interesting illustration. The United States Army had a morale program that included a series of documentaries, the "Why We Fight" films, which attempted to demonstrate to American soldiers that the war had been started by the Axis powers, that their British, Soviet, and Chinese allies were doing their part or more in the total war effort, and so on. Hovland carried out a fairly large-scale study to assess the persuasive efficacy of these films and to pinpoint the critical variables that contributed to their effectiveness. The research indicated that over the whole range of opinion items measured, the effectiveness of the films increased with the educational levels of the soldiers. Or, if we can agree that education probably furnished a reasonable index of what we might call "intelligence," the more intelligent soldiers were more persuaded.

This finding that persuasibility increases with intelligence (or at least with years of education) suggests that it is important to consider also the attention and comprehension steps in the persuasion process. Although a more intelligent person is protected against being persuaded by his greater resistance to yielding, his increased attention to and comprehension of the message make him more vulnerable. It would appear that in the World War II persuasion campaign mentioned, the intelligent person's superior attention and comprehension were more important than his greater resistance to yielding.

The matrix analysis of the communication-persuasion process that I have described redirects our interest to the attention and comprehension steps. It thus emphasizes that persuasion is as much a problem of communicating information as it is a problem of overcoming resistance to yielding. Because of its emphasis on attention and comprehension, this approach has been called the information processing theory of persuasive communication. It has probably been the most productive approach to understanding persuasion during the past ten years, so I shall focus on it. But it is not the only approach that has provoked interesting research on persuasion; other formulations have also proved useful. First, however, I shall provide an example of the information-processing approach by applying it to an analysis of the role of fear in persuasive communications.

Appeals to fear do not arise in every persuasion campaign, since some use only positive appeals. It may be possible, for example, to urge people to buy chocolate bars solely on the basis of the pleasure they give. Likewise, it may be possible to win votes for a political candidate simply by telling all the good things that his election will bring to the voters. But the use of negative appeals, such as fear arousal, is sometimes compelled by the nature of the behavior or attitude that the campaign is designed to change. For example, in marketing a product like a deodorant, it is hard to think of an advertising campaign that would not to some extent be based on the arousal of fear; even political campaigns often stress the dangers of electing the opposing candidate as much as the benefits of electing the candidate being advocated. And there is one kind of persuasion campaign in which fear appeals are almost invariably used, namely, public health campaigns designed to induce the public to submit to some diagnostic procedure, or to take some preventative measure, or some healing treatment, in the interest of good health.

We might take as an example a campaign urging people to get inoculations against smallpox, tetanus, or rubella. We can hardly design such a campaign based on purely positive appeals, since it is difficult to claim that the inoculation procedure itself is intrinsically pleasant when it involves a certain amount of nuisance to obtain and is a mildly unpleasant treatment. The campaign necessarily involves the negative element of stimulating the person's anxiety about the disease that he might contract if he is not inoculated. Such positive element as there is in the campaign is in the reassurance he is then given that the urged inoculation can prevent the illness about which his fear has been aroused.

The role of fear arousal in such a campaign is to make a person sufficiently concerned about the illness that he will take the preventative measures being urged. On the basis of this analysis, the greater the fear arousal the more motivated the person should be to accept the recommendation and to get the preventive inoculation.

Although this analysis may be correct as far as it goes, a closer look at the nature of fear and our habitual human ways of coping with it suggests that its effects may be much more complex.

Machiavelli said that the Prince is better served by fear than love, but the persuader who utilizes fear is playing a dangerous game. Although fear may be a powerful human motivation, psychological theory suggests that it is something more than a motivator. Besides being a motivational state that energizes and drives the organism, fear has also a cue or directive quality that evokes habitual responses and channels behavior in certain ways. Thus, although fear as a motivator multiplies ongoing behavior (such as a tendency to agree with the communication), as a cue fear has directive properties, and leads to such responses as fight or flight, which can interfere with reception of the persuasive message.

Thus, anxiety-arousing communication has a double effect. On the one hand, it raises the person's fear about the likelihood of his contracting the illness or its dangerousness if he does, thus enhancing persuasive impact by increasing his motivation to take the preventative action. On the other hand, fear also cues off certain characteristic responses, most generally called flight and fight, which in the case of persuasive communication might take the form of hostility toward the communicator, or refusing, insofar as possible, to think about the illness. These latter responses evoked by fear in its cue aspects would interfere with the persuasive impact of the campaign by reducing attention, comprehension, or retention of the message.

To summarize, appeals to fear can affect both message reception (including attention and comprehension) and yielding to the arguments (insofar as they are effectively received). In its effect on reception, fear arousal tends to interfere with persuasion; the higher the fear, the greater the disturbance of attention, comprehension, and retention and, therefore, the less the persuasive impact. On the other hand, by motivating yielding, fear tends to increase the persuasive impact. Such dynamic situations, in which an independent variable like the appeal to fear is related in two opposite ways to a dependent variable like persuasive impact, are by no means rare and tend to have interesting implications when they occur.

In such situations it can be shown algebraically that under a wide set of initial conditions the value of the dependent variable will first increase and then decrease as the independent variable increases. That is to say, if we have an extremely low level of fear and if the message raises our fear somewhat, the message will be made more persuasive. Up to an intermediate level of fear, the more fear the message arouses, the more persuasive it will be. Beyond this intermediate level, however, further increase in fear will be counterproductive. The persuasive impact will fall off if fear is aroused beyond this intermediate level. Hence, the implications of the information-processing analysis of the communication-persuasion process, along with a two-factor theory of anxiety, lead to a prediction that the most powerful persuasive effect will occur when the person is aroused to an intermediate level of anxiety, neither very high nor very low.

A theory that predicts such curvilinear relations is extremely powerful in accounting for experimental observations, a power that is both its joy and its despair. It can account for a wide variety of obtained relationships, including outcomes in opposite directions to one another, by simply making some reasonable assumptions about the particular natures of the situations studied. Allowing ourselves a bit of freedom as regards initial assumptions, we can go a long way, even in opposite directions.

As a matter of fact, the outcomes require us to be fairly agile in moving in opposite directions. In one well-known study a negative relationship was found. Junior high school students were given a set of recommendations regarding dental hygiene, with either a low, a moderate, or a high level of fear arousal regarding possible diseases that could occur if the recommendations were not followed. Two weeks later, when the children were asked to report on the degree to which they had adopted the urged toothbrushing practices, compliance was reported by 36 percent in the low-fear condition, by 22 percent in the moderate-fear condition, and by only 8 percent in the high-fear condition. Under the conditions of this experiment, then, it would appear that the more the persuasive message aroused the person's anxiety about dental cavities and other diseases, the less likely he was to adopt the preventative toothbrushing practices that were being urged.

Other studies, of at least as high quality, have come out with the diametrically opposed relationship. For example, college students were urged to obtain inoculation against tetanus. The discussion of tetanus shots and the recommendation to get them were accompanied for different groups of students by either low, medium, or high fear arousal regarding the frequency and danger of tetanus. It was found that the higher the level of fear arousal, the stronger the intention these students reported of getting the inoculation. Moreover, when a follow-up study was done a month later at the university health center, it was found that only 6 percent of the students in the low-fear-arousing condition actually obtained the shots, while 13 percent in the medium-fear condition, and 22 percent of those in the high-fear condition obtained them.

Now the information-processing approach to persuasive communication, along with the two-factor theory of anxiety and certain assumptions about initial levels, can account for both of these opposite outcomes. It is fairly reasonable to assume that people are ordinarily not very anxious about tetanus, so that with this issue they start off at a fairly low level of anxiety and have to be frightened as much as possible before they will take preventive measures. On the other hand, dental decay is a constant problem and the notion of going to the dentist is generally terrifying; in this case further arousals of fear by the persuasive message leave the person at levels of anxiety that produce the opposite effect of interfering with persuasion.

This power of the theory in accounting for opposite outcomes is an embarrassment of riches. If a theory aspires to scientific status, there must be some outcomes that could disprove it. This theory seems so robust that it can survive opposite outcomes with no trouble. It sounds as if this Protean theory could be a refuge for scoundrels.

Actually, the situation is not so grim. The theory has other implications about factors that affect the relation between fear arousal and attitude change. For one thing, it has implications about how other aspects of the communication situation will interact with the level of fear arousal in affecting persuasive impact. For example, the analysis of the dental hygiene and tetanus inoculation situations that we gave a moment ago depended on the intrinsic anxiety-arousal capacity of the issues. This characteristic of the issues could be deliberately manipulated to provide a more stringent test. Similar implications can be made about the anxiety proneness of the audience at which the communications are urged. It would be predicted that for people who are chronically anxious or who have high feelings of physical vulnerability, low levels of fear arousal would be relatively more efficacious, while for those who feel relatively invulnerable and are not given to worry, high fear arousal would be more effective. Still other kinds of predictions deal with the complexity of the persuasive message and with the difficulty of obtaining the treatment. For example, it would be predicted that as the message complexity increased the level of fear arousal that would produce the most compliance would go down. Likewise, to the extent that obtaining the preventive treatment required a great deal of work or ingenuity, lower levels of fear appeal would be more efficacious. All of these interesting and useful hypotheses can be derived from the theory and subjected to empirical test.

One hypothesis that has already been tested focuses on the personality of the listener. According to the information-processing analysis, for those people who have a chronically high tendency to yield, increasing the fear arousal in the persuasive message would be detrimental to its persuasiveness; while for those who have a low tendency to yield, the persuasive impact would be increased by higher levels of fear arousal. There are a couple of studies in which initial tendency to yield is estimated by the person's level of self-esteem, it being assumed that the higher his self-esteem the less his tendency to yield to pressure. In these studies, people who are high in self-esteem are increasingly likely to take the urged health practices as the fear aroused by the message increases. For those who are quite low in self-esteem, on the other hand, increasing the level of fear aroused by the communication tends to reduce the likelihood of compliance.

Another hypothesis derivable from the theory (and one that has a somewhat paradoxical flavor to it) predicts that increasing the fear arousal should be particularly detrimental for those who are most vulnerable to the health danger. Some support for such a prediction is found in an experiment on discouraging cigarette smoking. In this study visitors to a county fair were shown a film portraying the dangers of cigarette smoking as the possible cause of lung cancer, with either low, medium, or high fear arousal for different groups of visitors. Those who saw the films were then urged to obtain a chest X-ray as a diagnostic precaution, and a mobile X-ray unit was available just outside the room in which the motion pictures were shown. The nonsmokers in the audience, the group for whom the message was least relevant and threatening, showed about the same level of reporting for the X-rays regardless of the threat level, about 45 percent of the nonsmokers taking the X-ray under each level of fear arousal. The smokers, on the other hand, were the people most vulnerable and presumably most needing the X-ray, but for them there was a negative relation. Under low fear arousal, slightly over 50 percent of the smokers obtained X-rays, while of those smokers who received the communication with high fear arousal only 5 percent obtained X-rays. Such observations have social implications worth pondering. Arousing fear may actually frighten away the audience most needful of taking the health precautions.

In summary, therefore, although the information-processing approach can hardly be said to have led us unerringly through the tangled network of practical wisdom and experimental results on this important issue, it has raised some useful suggestions and provided some indications for informed social action in the public health area. As mentioned earlier, however, the information-processing approach is only one of several that have been used in psychological research on persuasive communication. It is probably the most popular and successful approach. It happens also to be my own favorite, though it need not be less true on that account. In any case, I should at least mention briefly some of the other approaches to persuasive communication that have been tried. At least three others—which we might call the consistency-theory approach, the perceptual-theory approach, and the functional-theory approach—have been sufficiently productive so that it would be neglectful not to mention them.

The consistency-theory approach views the recipient of the persuasive communication, not as the information processor we have just discussed, but rather as an "honest broker" trying to strike some optimal compromise among many conflicting forces. He has to adopt beliefs that are the best possible compromise among such considerations as his own behavior, his knowledge of the facts, and the social pressures being put on him. He gravitates toward a solution that keeps his attitude from getting too far out of line with any of these factors. While the information-processing approach has stressed that one first changes attitudes in order to produce change in behavior, the consistency-theory approach has stressed that one can often proceed more efficiently in the reverse direction. If we first change behavior (for example, by legal constraints), we can expect an attitude change to follow. As Wesley said (and Pascal and St. Paul before him), one acts on faith in order to believe, rather than acts on faith because he believes. The consistency-theory approach has produced a rich body of results on how a person reacts with internalized attitude change after he has been forced to comply overtly with an action at variance from his initial belief. The findings here have frequently been counter-intuitive and even paradoxical, though making good sense in terms of the consistency-theory approach.

The perceptual approach to persuasive communication depicts man as a conceptualizing machine, busy imposing meaning on the stimuli that come to him. According to this view, a person sorts the stimuli into categories and changes his categorizing system when necessary. Perhaps it can be presented in starkest contrast to the information-processing approach by saying that while the latter approach assumes that a persuasive communication changes a person's attitude about some object of judgment, the perceptual theorists view it as changing his perception of what object he is giving his attitude about. For example, when the person is put into a conformity situation where he is told that his friends uniformly and strongly rate "politician" as a much more honorable and desirable profession than the person himself initially did, then the person typically upgrades his own rating of politician. The two approaches differ somewhat in their interpretation of what has happened. The information-processing approach says that the person has changed his attitudes regarding politicians; the perceptual approach says that the person has changed his perception of what he was giving his attitude about: at first he assumed that by politician was meant a backroom manipulator, but the information regarding the high rating given by his peers convinces him that the term was meant to refer to a statesman. Some quite interesting new insights into the persuasion process have emerged from this perceptual approach, though it has not given rise to quite as much research and theoretical advancement as have the information-processing and the consistency-theory approaches.

A final approach to the persuasive communication process that I shall mention is generally called the functional approach, though much of the work has derived from a particular type of function, namely, the function of defending one's own ego. The ego-defensive theory holds that attitudes serve to help a person live with himself and with the inadmissible needs that drive him on. For example, this approach has given rise to research on the so-called authoritarian personality. People who have authoritarian personalities tend to feel great hostility toward those who differ from themselves in nationality, profession, life style, skin color, religion, and so forth. According to the ego-defensive theory, these attitudes derive not so much from experience with the hated outgroup members, nor even from secondhand knowledge (correct or incorrect) about them, but rather from the person's own deep-seated needs that may have nothing to do with the target persons. The authoritarian personality structure is theorized to have developed from childhood difficulty in resolving the hostile aspect of the Oedipal complex. Circumstances at that time may have required the inarticulate child to repress rather traumatically the hostility he felt toward his father. Then to safeguard this difficult repression he would have tended to a reaction formation that idealized his father and by extension the other authority figures of his society, a resolution that is further bolstered by an extreme hostility toward the outgroups of that society. As a result, the authoritarian person tends to have extreme positive and negative feelings regarding others, idealizing the power figures of the society and detesting those who are on the fringes or different from the norm. According to the functional approach, such attitudes can be changed, not so much by providing this type of person with favorable information regarding the hated target groups, but rather by giving him insights into his own personality difficulties. Some empirical work has provided at least suggestive support for such an analysis.

The four different approaches to an understanding of the communication-persuasion process that I have discussed are best thought of, not as mutually exclusive or in conflict, but rather as supplementary. Each approach suggests aspects of the persuasion process that might have gone unnoticed on the basis of the other approaches; though once an insight is suggested by any of the approaches, it usually can be accommodated within the others. Advocates of each of these theories have, of course, often taken a rather competitive stance and made progress trying to disprove hypotheses yielded by other approaches. Nevertheless, we feel that in the long run a somewhat more permissive stance is usually the better course. Each of the approaches has on a number of occasions advanced our understanding of the persuasive process, both by making predictions that have been confirmed and by making predictions whose disconfirmations have been even more provocative. Research on persuasion is currently quite lively, and there is every reason to believe that it will remain an exciting area in which to work and will continue to progress rapidly for some years to come.

23 LANGUAGE AND PSYCHOPATHOLOGY

Brendan Maher

Pathology is the branch of medical science that studies the conditions associated with diseases or other abnormal functions. Psychopathology is the branch of pathology that is particularly concerned with psychological disorders. One of the most common symptoms in patients suffering from some form of psychological disorder is a difficulty or abnormality in linguistic communication.

It is natural, therefore, for students of psychopathology to be interested in language, and in recent years there has been a notable increase in the study of the relations between language and psychopathology. The reasons for this increase are certainly very complex, but some of the major factors involved can be identified.

The first of these is the general impact of the rapid growth of knowledge and theory about the psychology of language in general. We may approach the study of linguistic communication from the point of view of structural linguistics on the one hand, or from the more psychological point of view of associative learning on the other hand. In either case, however, the result is to emphasize the formal aspects of verbal behavior, rather than the semantic problems concerned with the meaning of verbal utterances.

A second development, facilitating the work of quantitative analysis in linguistics, is the increasing availability of high-speed computer techniques for language analysis. Many questions dealing with problems of sentence formation, syntactic style, and other measurable aspects of our verbal utterances would remain unanswered if it were necessary to perform all the tabulations and calculations by hand. This is no longer the case, however. The use of computers has not only speeded up processes that were already in use, but has made possible investigations that would have been completely impractical without their aid.

Third, we can observe that the study of the psychology of language has become increasingly well integrated with the study of other psychological processes, especially those involved in attention, short-term memory and information processing—a point of view that runs counter to some long-established psychoanalytic hypotheses regarding the role of unconscious motivational influences in generating language disorder in psychosis.

Finally, we might note the declining influence of psychoanalytic explanations of psychopathology in general and the concomitant interest in alternative approaches to all psychopathological phenomena.

Bearing these various influences in mind, it may now be of interest to examine recent empirical work in the United States and elsewhere that is relevant to the trends just described.

The development of interest in the concepts of information and redundancy (see Chapter 17) has led to an increasing use of the so-called *Cloze* technique for estimating redundancy in verbal utterances. It is a matter of common observation that normal utterances are redundant; that is to say, it is possible to eliminate parts of an utterance without impairing the ability of a listener to comprehend the message that the utterance was intended to convey. This redundancy rests, in turn, upon the fact that the probability that any given word will be followed by specific other words in normal speech is variable and for many words is higher than zero. Provided that we have the first few words of a sentence, then we can guess at the next word in the sequence with some real probability of being correct. The more probable it is that the next word will be a specific word, the more redundant its utterance at that point. Nearly forty years ago, Edgar Rubin, the Danish psychologist, pointed out that redundancy serves an important purpose in language, rendering comprehension easier by virtue of the repetition of the message that redundancy creates. The principle that redundancy corresponds to comprehensibility is the basis of the *Cloze* technique—a procedure whereby words are eliminated from a text at periodic intervals (every fifth word, for example). Readers are then asked to read the text and to guess the missing words. The higher the percentage of words that can be correctly guessed by a group of readers the more redundant is the text and hence the more comprehensible.

This procedure lets us study the effects of such conditions as schizophrenic psychosis or the effects of psychological drugs upon the comprehensibility of language utterance. A significant series of studies has been reported in which hallucinogenic drugs (psilocybin and LSD) and the tranquilizer chlorpromazine were given to normal subjects and the effects on their comprehensibility were recorded. In the case of all these drugs, after an initial improvement in comprehensibility (that is, increased redundancy) there was a marked reduction in comprehensibility lasting from three to four hours. On the other hand, treatment with epinephrine raised comprehensibility.

While this procedure shows promise in detecting gross differences in language utterances it does not permit a detailed examination of the different ways in which comprehensibility is impaired.

Several studies have reported that schizophrenic language is characterized by low redundancy. Although there are many possible explanations for this, one view is that the patient is, in effect, uninfluenced by his own prior utterances. When the normal person is presented with part of a language text it is possible for him to estimate what sequence of words might come next. His estimate is based, presumably, upon his monitoring of the preliminary text and his use of the information to determine what highly probable words might come next. If he does not monitor the first part of the utterance it is clearly unlikely that he will correctly estimate the subsequent part of the utterance. If such is the case, we should expect that the schizophrenic patient will be relatively uninfluenced by contextual cues in his perception of other people's language as well as in his own.

A systematic series of studies has investigated this problem, using a technique where words with two or more meanings—or "portmanteau" words, as they are sometimes called—are placed in sentences where the context calls for only one of the meanings of the word. An example in English might be "The farmer drove his cattle into the pen." Here we would expect that the word *pen* would be understood to mean *an enclosure for cattle* and not *a writing instrument*—the other English-language meaning of *pen*. Schizophrenic patients are deficient in the use of context cues to determine the meaning of ambiguous words. I have confirmed these findings in further studies with both English and Danish schizophrenic subjects. Similar findings have been reported by investigators studying the effect of prior lists of words on double-meaning words. If, to repeat the kind of example mentioned above, I present a person with the following list of words: *paper, ink, pen,* and then ask him to define the meaning of *pen,* I am likely to get a response referring to it as a writing implement. On the other hand, if I have given a list that runs: *cattle, barn, pen,* I will probably get a definition that refers to a place to confine cattle. At least, this is what is found when the task is given to normal subjects. When given to schizophrenic patients the effects of the context are, once again, minimal and a patient's response may be either of the two possible meanings.

These findings from research have obvious implications for the kinds of language characteristics that we see in clinical cases of schizophrenia. The common observation that the patient appears to have a sense of humor, frequently making puns and using plays on words, may be understood as an example of the fact that the patient finds it difficult to utilize the context of his own speech to control the meanings of words that he uses.

The extent to which patients are able to use the contextual organization of spoken passages to assist in remembering the passages some time later has also been studied. Earlier work had shown that the higher the degree of contextual organization, the better is the recall, in the case of normal subjects. In more recent work it has been found that in passages with little or no contextual organization, patients and normal controls are about equally good at recall. However, as the context improved in organization, normals were able to improve their recall—that is to say, normals were able to use the context to help them remember—but the schizophrenic patients were not able to do so, and hence did not improve.

This inability to use context has been nicely illustrated in interviews with patients. One such patient, referring to his own difficulties in understanding the speech of others, remarked:

> When people talk to me it's like a different kind of language. It's too much to hold at once. My head is overloaded and I can't understand what they say. It makes you forget what you've just heard because you can't get hearing it long enough. It's all in different bits which you have to put together again in your head.

Schizophrenic patients who show this kind of disability were also shown to be highly distractible on other kinds of tasks, suggesting that the poor linguistic performance of patients may be understood as a deficiency of attention. Indeed the hypothesis that the primary deficiency in schizophrenia is an inability to focus attention has gained wide support from many investigations of their perception and attention. This hypothesis can easily be extended to include an explanation of language pathology in schizophrenia.

Another example of language pathology in schizophrenia has been advanced by the Australian psychologist, Aubrey Yates, who attributes the patient's difficulties to a deficiency in short-term storage processes and recall. This deficiency is regarded as involving a slowing of the rate at which incoming information can be processed, with a consequent overload of information in short-term storage. This overload is such that information is lost and never registered in long-term storage, and so is unavailable for later use. The remarks by the patient just quoted are compatible with this view. At the present time, however, there is very little empirical data that would illuminate this hypothesis directly, although there is significant evidence that schizophrenic patients generally do poorly on tasks involving the processing of information unless it is presented slowly.

Several investigators have been concerned with the possible biological factors that might be found to relate to language disorder in schizophrenia. One approach has considered that the schizophrenic suffers from deficiencies in what has been called "autonomic arousal." The idea here is that the schizophrenic has something wrong with his autonomic nervous system, which controls the vital functions of the body. These deficiencies might produce the kinds of attentional malfunction that are believed to account for the disorders of language that I have described. Progress along these lines is very slow, in large part because the concept of arousal is, itself, complex and poorly defined and, in part, because the empirical findings so far suggest that our diagnostic classification of schizophrenia is too crude to define the various kinds of primary defect that fall under that heading. However, some suggestive data are being obtained. A relationship has been found between the reactivity of the autonomic nervous system and the tendency to be confused by portmanteau words. The relation between biological aspects of schizophrenia and linguistic symptoms may develop into one of the most intriguing areas of investigation of schizophrenic language.

Turning from the problems of attention and the formal aspects of language utterance, I would like to discuss next some of the work on the content of schizophrenic language. Tape recordings can be made of the speech of schizophrenic patients and classification schemes can be developed for categorizing the kinds of topics the speaker is talking about. These classifications can then be related to the severity of the schizophrenic state of the speaker as assessed clinically. With this information it has been possible to establish a numerical scoring system whereby the content of any language sample could be coded and quantified to measure the severity of the speaker's disturbance.

The complete set of categories that has been used is complex and lengthy, but some idea of its nature can be provided with a few examples. For instance, references to religious topics are found to be associated with severity of psychosis, as are the tendency to repeat phrases or clauses, expressions of hostility towards other people, or the belief that other people were avoiding the speaker. On the other hand, references to the weather, to other people as being helpful or friendly, and to personal feelings of well-being are indicative of milder psychotic states.

With student colleagues I myself have conducted investigations of the characteristics of schizophrenic language as revealed in the spontaneous writings of hospitalized patients. We compared the writing of individuals bearing a diagnosis of schizophrenia with other hospital patients whose diagnosis was of a psychiatric kind but was not schizophrenia. Using very large samples of written language we were able to compare the two kinds of writing with the aid of a computer employing a language-classifying program, the *General Inquirer*. From these comparisons emerged certain reliable differences, the chief of which were the tendencies of schizophrenic letter-writers to produce sequences of nouns at the end of a sentence, to make frequent references to religion and world politics, and to make less frequent use of words relating to cognitive processes.

These investigations go only a little way toward providing answers to our questions about the nature and origin of language disorder in schizophrenia. They can be regarded, at best, as preliminary surveys of gross differences in the language topics of psychotic and normal individuals. They do not provide data sufficient to justify any detailed hypotheses about the origin and nature of schizophrenic language disorganization.

An entirely different approach to the question of language content in psychosis has been developed by Julius Laffal. Laffal has pursued the hypothesis that the disordered language of the schizophrenic may be understood by an analysis of the associations that the patient uses to convey his feelings or beliefs about emotionally significant matters. The assumption is that the language of the schizophrenic, and indeed the language of a normal speaker, contains words that enter into the utterance because of their associations with other words in the utterance. This principle can then be used to understand what the psychological significance of a particular concept or word might be—let us say, for example, *mother*—by tabulating other words that tend to appear in the speaker's language whenever the text includes references to mother. Even though the associated words may not be obviously connected with the concept of mother, their appearance in the surrounding text suggests, according to Laffal, that there is an important association between them even though this may not be recognized by the speaker. In psychotic language this kind of associated intrusion is supposed to become more and more evident and more and more disruptive of the coherence of the utterance. To date, Laffal has applied his method mainly to the study of single cases. It has not yet been possible to arrive at any general conclusions about schizophrenic pathology on the basis of these observations alone.

Before turning from the discussion of language disorder in schizophrenia to the characteristics of language in other kinds of psychopathology, it may help to summarize the present state of investigation and to point up the directions in which further work seems to be heading. First, we might note that the general emphasis of recent findings is that schizophrenic language disorder can be seen as the consequence of a disorder of attention, and the effect of this disorder is to reduce the ability of the individual to use contextual features—such as redundancy, grammatical structure, and the like—to monitor and process what he hears, including what he hears of his own speech or even what he can utilize of what he has just written. In this sense, the disorder of language might be seen not as a reflection of a disorder of thinking but as a disorder of sensory processing.

A second major field of interest in the study of language and pathology has developed around the phenomena of speech timing and fluency. It is a matter of common observation that the fluency and continuity of speech may vary with different states of emotion and with different people, and may also vary with the complexity of the structure of the language sample that the speaker is uttering. These observations have given rise to investigations of the systematic relationship between speech patterns and the state of the speaker. One of the major characteristics that has been investigated is the matter of *pauses* or *hesitations* in speech. George Mahl, a psychologist at the Medical School of Yale University, has paid particular attention to the pauses and disruptions that occur in speech when the speaker is anxious. In his work he found it useful to recognize eight types of speech disruption: the intrusion of "ah," sentence correction, sentence incompletion, repetition of words, stutter, intruding incoherent sound, slips of the tongue, and omission of words or parts of words. Leaving aside the intrusion of "ah," Mahl found that the ratio of the number of disruptions to the total number of words spoken correlated positively with anxiety; hence, this ratio could be used as a measure of the speaker's state of anxiety.

Much the same kind of finding has been reported by Goldman-Eisler from London on the relationship between pauses and emotionality of the content of what is being discussed. In her work on language production, Goldman-Eisler has paid additional attention to the relation between the complexity of a sentence and the pattern of pauses and hesitations that occur. Of particular interest to students of psychopathology is her report that the drug chlorpromazine produced a decline in the complexity of sentence utterance, the effect being the same in both normal and schizophrenic patients.

Goldman-Eisler has also reported that the appearance of a pause in speech is related to the redundancy of the language utterance at that point, pauses generally occurring when redundancy is about to drop. The effects of chlorpromazine do not disrupt this relation because as the complexity of sentences diminished under chlorpromazine, so did the frequency of pauses. The implication of this finding is that chlorpromazine does not merely facilitate the action of speech itself but also influences the neural centers that control speech. Goldman-Eisler has placed special emphasis upon the pause as an indicator that cognitive activity is occurring, activity that will determine the subsequent content of the utterance. With pauses as a measure, it is possible to get some insight into the changes that occur in thinking, and not simply those that may be attributed to the motor activity of speaking itself.

The effects of drugs upon the emotional content of language samples has also been studied. Workers have been particularly interested in expressions of anxiety and hostility, two emotional states that are of great importance in psychopathology. The technique has involved the development of scales for coding or classifying the content of the utterances of a speaker and observing changes in this content under the influence of various drugs.

It has been reported that in a sample of delinquent adolescents the drug librium produces a significant decline in expressions of both hostility and anxiety. Similar results have been found for the drug perphenazine on a sample of adult patients. A reversal of these effects was seen in a small study using the drug impramine—a drug used to counteract depression. In the case of impramine, the effect was to produce increases in the anxiety and hostility scores. As the effects of chlorpromazine and impramine are generally opposed, this finding is not surprising. What is of interest is the demonstration that drug treatments can produce measureable changes in language content in this way.

Turning towards a different class of drug, we may take note of the work that has been done upon the effects of the hallucinogenic drug LSD upon language utterance. I noted earlier that LSD results in lowering the predictability of language. Other effects of LSD have also been investigated. Subjects under dosages of 50–100 milligrams of LSD, behaving in a group situation where other members were also under the influence of the drug, showed an increase in emotional expressions, both of a positive and of a negative kind—this latter including expressions of hostility or anxiety. There was a marked increase in laughter and joking, but a decrease in the amount of speech uttered in a given amount of time.

It has been reported that the speech of individuals under LSD contains more separate ideas for the number of words spoken than is found under normal conditions. There are also a greater number of unfinished statements and a greater difficulty in communicating ideas to other people. Although it would be hazardous to draw from these studies inferences about the nature of language and thought disorder in psychosis, the similarity of some LSD effects to psychosis makes it plausible to examine them with an eye to generating hypotheses about any underlying similarity of malfunction.

Finally we may turn to a third area in which work relating language to psychopathology is being pursued—that of verbal conditioning. Several leading psychologists engaged on this work have hypothesized that the improvement in psychotherapy that is reported for some patients may be understood as due to the patients having acquired new patterns of language interaction. These have been acquired, it is argued, as a consequence of the unintentional words of praise or punishment uttered by the therapist. Put another way, the process of psychotherapy may be viewed as a kind of verbal training in which the patient learns more suitable ways of communicating with other people. From this point of view, a patient who is unusually unresponsive to the social influence of others will also be unresponsive to the influence of the therapist—and hence less likely to show changes in psychotherapy. Two classes of patient have come in for special attention in this regard—the psychopath and the schizophrenic.

In view of the general belief that the psychopath is best understood as deficient in response to social disapproval, it is natural that investigations of verbal conditioning should be conducted with this group of patients. This kind of patient does not seem able to acquire verbal conditioned responses on the basis of social influence. It is possible to wonder whether or not this is simply a failure of conditioning that would have been found with any kind of conditioning, but this explanation seems improbable in the light of the evidence that psychopathic subjects do acquire other kinds of conditioned response. It seems more plausible to conclude that the psychopathic subject is specifically insensitive to social praise or blame from the experimenter.

In the case of verbal conditioning of schizophrenic subjects, the results are a little more complex. Schizophrenic patients seem to acquire verbal responses when they serve to avoid social punishment, but not to gain approval. Put more simply the patients seem to be sensitive to blame or censure, but insensitive to praise or approval from another person. We can see from this kind of investigation a rather interesting example of the way in which a laboratory technique like verbal learning can also shed light on the kinds of social motivation that are present or lacking in a patient population.

I have only sketched some of the central features of current work on problems of language and psychopathology. I have not touched on the many investigations of such special problems as language in aphasia, mental retardation, and other conditions. The picture I have presented is one of a rapidly growing field with many important problems yet to be approached and many others still at an elementary stage of investigation. There seems to be little doubt, however, that the scientific study of language and its psychological and biological bases holds enormous promise for a better understanding of the behavior of those suffering from psychological disorders.

24 THE SOCIOLOGY OF LANGUAGE

Joshua A. Fishman

"Sociology of language" is the name that has recently been given to the renewed scholarly interest in the social or societal aspects of language behavior.

Man is constantly using language—spoken language, written language, printed language—and man is constantly linked to others via shared norms of behavior. The sociology of language examines the interaction between these two aspects of human behavior: use of language and the social organization of behavior. Briefly put, the sociology of language focuses upon the entire gamut of topics related to the social organization of language behavior, including not only language usage per se but also language attitudes and overt behaviors toward language and toward language users.

Overt behavior toward language and toward language users is a concern shared by political and educational leaders in many parts of the world and is an aspect of the sociology of language that frequently makes headlines in the newspapers. Many French-Canadian university students oppose the continuation of public education in English in the Province of Quebec. Many

Flemings in Belgium protest vociferously against anything less than full equality—at the very least—for Dutch in the Brussels area. Some Welsh nationalists daub out English signs along the highways in Wales and many Irish revivalists seek stronger governmental support for the restoration of Irish than that made available during half a century of Irish independence. Jews throughout the world protest the Soviet government's extermination of Yiddish writers and the forced closing of Yiddish schools, theaters, and publications.

Swahili, Philippino, Indonesian, Malay, and the various provincial languages of India are all being consciously expanded in vocabulary and standardized in spelling and grammar so that they can increasingly function as the exclusive languages of government and of higher culture and technology. The successful revival and modernization of Hebrew has encouraged other smaller language communities—the Catalans, the Provencals, the Frisians, the Bretons—to strive to save *their* ethnic mother tongues (or their traditional cultural tongues) from oblivion. New and revised writing systems are being accepted—and, at times, rejected—in many parts of the world by communities that hitherto had little interest in literacy in general or in literacy in their mother tongues in particular.

Such examples of consciously organized behavior toward language and toward users of particular languages can be listed almost endlessly. The list becomes truly endless if we include examples from earlier periods of history, such as the displacement of Latin as the language of religion, culture, and government in Western Christendom and the successive cultivation of once lowly vernaculars—first in Western Europe, then in Central, Southern, and Eastern Europe, and, finally, in Africa and Asia as well. Instead of being viewed (as was formerly the case) as merely fit for folksy talk and for common folk the vernaculars have come to be viewed, used, and developed as *independent* languages, as languages suitable for *all* higher purposes, and as languages of state-*building* and state-*deserving* nationalities. All of these examples too feed into the sociology of language, providing it with historical breadth and depth in addition to its ongoing interest in current language issues throughout the world.

269

However, the subject matter of the sociology of language reaches far beyond interest in case studies and very far beyond cataloging and classifying the instances of language conflict and language planning reported in chronicles, old and new. The ultimate quest of the sociology of language is pursued diligently and in many universities throughout the United States and is very far from dealing directly with headlines or news reports. One part of this quest is concerned with describing the generally accepted social organization of language usage within a speech community (or, to be more exact, within speech-and-writing communities). This part of the sociology of language—*descriptive sociolinguistics*—seeks to answer the question, Who speaks (or writes) what language (or what language variety) to whom and when and to what end? Descriptive sociolinguistics tries to disclose the norms of language usage—that is to say, the generally accepted social patterns of language use and of behavior and attitudes toward language—for particular social networks and communities, both large and small.

Another part of the sociology of language—*dynamic sociolinguistics*—seeks to answer the question, What accounts for different rates of change in the social organization of language use and behavior toward language? Dynamic sociolinguistics tries to explain why and how the social organization of language use and behavior toward language can be selectively different in the *same* social networks or communities on two different occasions. It also seeks to explain why and how two once similar social networks or communities can arrive at quite different social organizations of language use and behavior toward language.

Let us look first at descriptive sociolinguistics, since that is the basic task of the sociology of language. Unless we can attain reliable and insightful description of *existing* patterns of social organization in language use and behavior toward language it will obviously be impossible to contribute very much that is sound toward the explanation of why or how these patterns change or remain stable. One of the basic insights of descriptive sociolinguistics is that members of social networks and communities do not always display either the same language usage or the same behavior toward language. Perhaps a few examples will help illustrate this crucial point.

Government officials in Brussels who are of Flemish origin do not always speak Dutch *to each other,* even when they all know Dutch very well and equally well. Not only are there occasions when they speak French to each other instead of Dutch, but there are some occasions when they speak standard Dutch and others when they use one or another regional variety of Dutch with each other. Indeed, some of them also use different varieties of French with each other as well, one variety being particularly loaded with official governmental terms, another corresponding to the nontechnical conversational French of well-educated and rather refined circles in Belgium, and still another being not only a more colloquial French but the colloquial French of those who are Flemings. All in all, these several varieties of Dutch and of French constitute what sociolinguists call the *linguistic repertoire* of certain social networks in Brussels. The task of descriptive sociolinguistics is to describe the general or normative patterns of language use within such a speech network or speech community so as to show the systematic nature of the alternations between one variety and another among individuals who share a repertoire of varieties.

However, not only bilingual or multilingual speech networks or communities utilize a repertoire of language varieties. Even in monolingual speech communities the linguistic repertoire of particular social networks may consist of several varieties. Different social classes, different regional groups and different occupational groups may speak different varieties of the *same language.* For example, monolingual, native-born New Yorkers speak differently to each other on different occasions—and these differences can be pinpointed phonologically (that is, in the way words are pronounced), lexically (that is, in the very words that are used), and grammatically (that is, in the systematic relations between words). The same young man who sometimes says "I sure hope yuz guys 'll shut the lights before leavin' '" is quite likely to say, or at least to write, "Kindly extinguish all illumination prior to vacating the premises." It's all a question of when to say the one and when the other, even though one may be interacting with individuals who could equally well understand both, but who could consider use of the one when the other is called for as a serious *faux pas*.

The description of societal patterns of language variety use— a variety being either a different language or a different social "dialect," or a different occupational "dialect" or a different regional "dialect"—whenever any two varieties are present in the linguistic repertoire of a social network—commonly utilizes the concept of *situation*. A situation is defined by the co-occurrence of two (or more) people related to each other in a particular way, communicating about a particular topic, in a particular setting. Thus, a social network or community may define a beer party between university people as a quite different situation from a lecture involving the same people. The topics of their talk in the two situations are likely to be different; their meeting places and meeting times are likely to be different; and the relationships of the people to each other are likely to be different. Any one of these differences may be important enough for these situations to be defined as *sufficiently* different by the members of the university community to require that a different language or language variety be utilized in each case. If that be so, then woe unto him who speaks at a beer party as if he were delivering a lecture, or who delivers a lecture as if he were at a beer party!

Members of social networks sharing a linguistic repertoire must (and do) know when to shift from one variety to another. One category of such shifts is that known as situational shifts. A shift in situation may require a shift in language variety. A shift in language variety may signal a shift in the relationship between co-members of a social network, or a shift in the topic and purpose of their interaction, or a recognized shift in the privacy or location of their interaction.

The careful reader will note that I have said "may require" and "may signal." Does that mean that a shift in situation does not always and invariably require a shift in language variety, or that a change in language variety does not always and invariably signal a change in situation? Yes, precisely. At times, members of the same speech network or community go from one situation to another *without* changing from one variety to another. Thus, interaction with one's friends and with one's siblings—two seemingly different role relations that may well transpire in generally different settings and involve at least somewhat different topics—may still be acceptably conducted in the very same variety. Thus, what is or is not a different situation with respect to language use is a matter of the internal social organization of particular speech networks or communities. Native members of such networks or communities slowly and unconsciously acquire *sociolinguistic communicative competence* with respect to appropriate language usage. They are not necessarily aware of norms that guide their sociolinguistic behavior, and probably would not be able to describe them to strangers. Newcomers to such networks or communities—including language researchers—must discover these norms for themselves, and must do so more rapidly, more painfully, and, therefore, more consciously than did the native members themselves.

One thing is clear: there are classes of occasions recognized by each speech network or community such that several seemingly different situations are classed as being of the same kind. No speech network has a linguistic repertoire that is as differentiated as the complete list of apparently different role relations, topics, and locales in which its members are involved. Just where the boundaries come that do differentiate between the class of situations generally requiring one variety and another class of situations generally requiring another variety must be empirically determined by the investigator, and constitutes one of the major tasks of descriptive sociolinguistics. Such classes of situations are referred to as *domains*. The various domains and the appropriate usage in each domain must be discovered from the data of numerous discrete situations and the shifting or nonshifting that they reveal. This is a central task of descriptive sociolinguistics, and it can only be accomplished by painstaking research—by participant observation, survey methods, experimental designs, and depth interviews.

The fact that members of the same speech networks or speech

communities also change from one variety to another without signaling any change in situation also reveals the kind of social categorizing that native members do so frequently and effortlessly. When one person switches and the others do not, the switch is commonly *metaphorical* in nature. By calling it metaphorical I mean that it is used for purposes of emphasis or contrast, rather than as an indication of a situational change. A switch to Cockney English where Received Pronunciation (and grammar) is called for may well elicit a brief raising of eyebrows or a pause in the conversation—until it is clear from the speaker's demeanor and from the fact that he has reverted to Received Pronunciation that no change in situation was intended. However, such metaphorical switching can be risky. Someone might feel that Cockney is in poor taste for the situation at hand. Metaphorical switching is a luxury that can be afforded only by those who comfortably share not only the same set of situational norms but also *the same views about their violation.* Since most of us are members of several speech networks, each with somewhat different sociolinguistic norms, the chances that situational shifting and metaphorical switching will be misunderstood—particularly where the language usage norms have few or insufficiently powerful guardians—are obviously great.

A speech community maintains its sociological pattern as long as the functional differentiation of the varieties in its linguistic repertoire is systematically and widely maintained. Let me illustrate what I mean by this.

A traveler in a foreign land once came to a five-sided clock tower. He walked around the tower and noticed that the clock on each side showed a different time. He stopped a native of the community and asked, "Why do you need all of those clocks; they don't even show the same time?" "That's exactly why we need them all," he was told; "If they all showed the *same* time, we could get along with just one!"

The same principle applies to the functional differentiation of any speech community's linguistic repertoire. As long as each variety is associated with a separate class of situations there is good reason, and established means, for retaining them all, each in its place, notwithstanding the modicum of metaphorical switching that may occur. However, if two or more varieties of language serve the same social functions, it becomes difficult to maintain them both and, in the end, one must either displace the other or a new functional differentiation must be arrived at between them. Let me describe briefly how such changes in linguistic repertoire or in functional allocation can occur.

At the very same time that a linguistic repertoire with its particular allocation of varieties exists in a particular speech community, certain of these same or very similar varieties may be found in other or neighboring speech communities in association with other functions. If the members of these two speech communities are brought into greater interaction with each other, or if their relative power to influence or control one another changes sufficiently, then the allocation of the linguistic repertoire of one or both communities is likely to undergo change. Thus, most immigrants to the United States have experienced sufficient interaction with English-speaking Americans, particularly in the work domain and in the education domain, to learn English. This has also long been true for French Canadians in large industrial centers such as Montreal. Yet, consider how differently these two processes of changing the linguistic repertoire have worked out. In the United States the immigrants largely lost their mother tongues within one, two, or, at most, three generations. In Montreal each new French Canadian generation starts off monolingual in French and then acquires English later in life without, however, handing on this second language to the next generation as its *initial* language. How can we best describe and account for this difference in outcome between two populations each of which was forced to acquire English for its educational and economic improvement? The difference seems to be related to the ability of one population to maintain a certain functional differentiation within its linguistic repertoire, whereas the other was unable to do so.

American immigrants needed English as a lingua franca or general language because they came from so many different speech communities. They also needed English as a passport to social and economic advancement. Because they had to abandon their "old country" rural or small-town ways (as a result of rapid exposure to American urban, industrial society) it quickly became impossible for them to maintain the original home and family *patterns upon which their only chance for domain separation* depended. Those whose English was better, progressed more rapidly on the American scene and became models *within* the immigrant home and *within* the immigrant organization and neighborhood. Thus, the home and much immigrant-to-immigrant interaction became domains of English—particularly under the onslaught of the American school and the Americanizing and amalgamating efforts of American churches. As a result, children of immigrants soon became bilingual even though they remained within immigrant families and neighborhoods. Since English was the only language of value *outside* of the immigrant home and the immigrant neighborhood, these people could have preserved their non-English mother tongue only if the home and neighborhood, at the very least, had been able to maintain themselves as separate, self-contained domains.

Immigrant speech networks could do this only in those few cases where immigrants of a single background clearly predominated (as they did for a long time in the case of German and Scandinavian language islands in the Midwest) or where their social mobility was sharply restricted (as was and is the case of Spanish-speakers in the Southwest). Almost everywhere else, economic advancement and the dislocation of the traditional immigrant home, neighborhood, and organizational practices went hand in hand. There was no domain in which the non-English immigrant mother tongue alone was required for "membership." As a result, there was no domain in which it was necessarily maintained. The non-English immigrant languages continued somewhat longer to serve fleeting metaphorical purposes, but there were soon no situational shifts in which they were required. As a result, children who had become bilingual in the very bosom of the family and in the immigrant neighborhood became increasingly monolingual English-speakers as they passed to and through their English-speaking schools, their English-speaking careers, and their own English-speaking neighborhoods. Such individuals raised their own children in English and these latter children no longer could use or follow metaphorical switching in the immigrant mother tongue of their parents and grandparents.

In Montreal the situation was and still is much different. French-speakers were initially exposed to English instruction and to English job success only slowly, over a long period of time. Their elementary schools long remained entirely French (as did their churches); even their secondary schools (in which English instruction was offered to those rather few who were fortunate enough to attend) were under French (and under Church) control. The result was that the monolingual French-speaking child remained such as long as his life was restricted to home, neighborhood, and church. He became increasingly bilingual as he passed through more advanced levels of the school and work domains, but he then reverted to increasing French monolingualism if his school and work careers were kept at lower levels or when he passed beyond their reach. As a result, the domains of English and the domains of French were kept functionally quite separate. Not only did the English domains reach proportionally fewer French Canadians and not only did they reach them more superficially, but both the early and late domains of the speech community's social networks were basically French-speaking (except for metaphorical purposes), thus assuring that the next generation would be French-speaking as well.

However, something new has recently been added to the Montreal picture. French-Canadian education expanded to the point that it produced more well-qualified or highly qualified individuals than could be assimilated into the various English-managed industrial, commercial, and cultural enterprises which traditionally reserved most of their leading positions for English Canadians. As a result, French-speaking elites have increasingly sought to control existing enterprises and to form their own enterprises in these domains. For them English has become increasingly superfluous in view of its lack of domain separation and situational need. In addition, of course, it has become symbolic of their not being masters in their own home, and, as such, is opposed both for general symbolic as well as for specifically functional reasons.

These two sociolinguistic patterns, the American immigrant and the French-Canadian nationalist, have been repeated many times in the past century. The increasing use of Russian alone by Soviet minorities—particularly the smaller ones—whether they be immigrants to large urban centers in other regions or outnumbered by Russians and various other immigrants to their own regions, has followed the same path as the increasing use of English alone by immigrants to the United States, the increasing use of Spanish alone by indigenous Indian populations moving to urban centers throughout Latin America, or the increasing use of Wolof alone by the diverse Senegalese populations that began to move to Dakar more than a generation ago. Similarly, the increasing use of the mother tongue in the domains of education, industry, and government (which had previously "belonged" to English, so to speak) that has increasingly typified French Canada is not at all unlike the growing displacement of English in Puerto Rico, Tanzania, India, Malaysia, and the Philippines.

The last four instances—Tanzania, India, Malaysia, and the Philippines—also exemplify the constantly recurring need to develop newly promoted indigenous national languages, so that they can be effectively and uniformly utilized in the new domains and situations that they have won or are winning for themselves. How this process of language planning is conducted, who accepts and who rejects the manufactured terminologies, orthographies, and grammars, whether their differential acceptance can be influenced by differing approaches to the implementation of language planning and language policy, these too are parts of the sociology of language—applied sociolinguistics to be sure —but their discussion will have to wait for another time. Here it will be enough to conclude that the sociology of language is not merely an interesting intellectual adventure, but that it also sheds light on many social and political conflicts that are occurring all over the world. The sociology of language will not resolve such conflicts, of course, but it is unlikely that we shall ever resolve them unless we can better describe and understand the social and linguistic facts and processes that underlie them. This, then, is what the sociology of language is especially fitted to help us do.

25 TRANSLATION AND BILINGUALISM

Paul A. Kolers

It would be a marvelous thing if we could persuade a machine to translate for us. Imagine giving a machine a document in a foreign language and having it returned to you in your own language, or having something you had written translated into any language you chose. A great many clever engineers have been trying to build machines that will do just these things. The details of human language are so complex, however, that the engineers have not yet been very successful. In contrast, people who know two languages find translating a very easy thing to do. But if ordinary language use is complex and difficult to understand, imagine how much more difficult it is to understand this phenomenon of bilingualism, the condition of people who know two languages.

Perhaps for this reason the study of bilingualism at the present time is little more than a small bump on the increasingly large body of psycholinguistics. Its smallness is in some ways unfortunate, for bilingualism offers us a distinctive way to study some of the mental activities underlying the way that people acquire and use information. Providing a bilingual person with information in one of his languages and testing him for it in the other enables us to study how the mind handles different kinds of information. It also enables us to separate skills in handling information from the content or information itself. Thereby we can learn something perhaps not otherwise directly accessible to study, and that is how certain kinds of information in a person's mind are tied directly to the language used in getting it there, while other kinds are not.

The study of bilingualism is, however, full of many complications and difficulties. Some of these are surely due to structural differences between languages and the way they organize words, which make the interpretation of data difficult. But most of the limitations are due to sparsity of knowledge. The greatest part of our current information about bilingualism comes from travelers to foreign lands who have recorded their linguistic experiences or who have interviewed other people about theirs. Some of it comes from translators who describe their problems in translating poetry or prose. Only a very small quantity comes from laboratory investigations. Hence a number of practical questions concerning bilingualism—such as the best way to become bilingual, the age at which the child of bilingual parents should be exposed to a second language, the effect of bilingualism on intelligence, on personality, and on political identity —cannot yet be reliably answered. It is just in these areas of practical concern that many opinions abound but little well-tested information exists. Despite this inadequacy the study of bilingualism does make some contribution to general questions in the use of language and the functioning of human minds.

Let us first consider why it has been impossible to devise a thoroughly satisfactory translating machine. One view of language that many people now realize is inadequate is that because languages seem to consist only of sets of words and rules for combining them, merely supplying a translator or a large computing machine with two dictionaries and two grammar books should suffice to yield translation. Holding this view, some engineers did achieve partial successes with computers, but their effort is also remembered for the humor it provided. A standard phrase in English such as "the spirit is willing but the flesh is weak" was translated by a machine as "the vodka is good but the meat is poor," according to one legend. One reason that a dictionary and a grammar book by themselves are not sufficient is that most words in a language, and many of its grammatical sequences, have more than one meaning; their interpretation depends in some measure upon the linguistic context within which they are used. The words "mutiny" and "revolution" are clearly synonyms in some contexts; yet in mathematics one can speak of a surface of revolution but not of a surface of mutiny. A leader may stand at the head of an army or at the head of an orchestra, and both conquerors and conductors are leaders of men. But while one could speak of Napoleon the great conqueror we would hardly speak of Napoleon the great conductor. Phrases such as "they are eating apples" can equally describe what people are eating or the kinds of apples people are talking about. And what shall we say of a phrase like "they are teaching machines"? These opportunities for multiple interpretation hinder the translator, and translators often lament their difficulties in finding equivalents. But actually the problem is deeper than this, and understanding it shows at once how much more is involved in translation than word-by-word equivalents. It also shows one of the great difficulties for machine translation.

Most matters of fact can be translated adequately. If I say in English "the dog bit the man," I can also say in German "der Hund biss den Mann," and in French "le chien mordait l'homme," and convey the same facts in all three cases. But consider another common word, say "lamp," which can probably be translated into almost any other language. What lamp are we speaking of? For an industrialized city dweller, a lamp is usually a device that is attached to a wall by an electric wire and that is lighted by moving a switch; for a rural Asian or African farmer, however, a lamp is likely to be a device that can be carried about and that is lighted by applying a flame to a wick. The same word "lamp" therefore may refer to two quite different objects, according to the social and cultural context in which it is used. Guidebooks, instructions, and many kinds of prose suffer no hardship because of these problems. But suppose one wanted to translate something a little richer. To be fair to the original, the translator must render not only its meaning, but its style of writing and its literary devices as well, even perhaps its punctuation. As the writer Isaac Babel once remarked, after all, "There is no iron that can enter the human heart with such stupefying effect as a period placed at just the right moment." The translator seeks to convey that force. But even there the problem does not end, for the translator is faced with an infinite number of characteristics in an original work; he cannot be faithful to them all in his translation.

In this respect natural languages are fundamentally different from some other kinds of human developments. If you write music in America, the conventions you use enable the score to be read by anyone else who knows them. The same is true of mathematics, and of certain other technical activities. The basis of the difference between music and mathematics on the one hand and natural languages on the other is that music and mathematics are written to accord with strict rules that govern the interpretation of terms. The Greek letter *pi* refers to the same ratio between the circumference of a circle and its diameter all over the world and everyone who uses the letter *pi* in a standard way uses it to express the same value. But the words of natural languages by and large lack this basic standardization in what they refer to.

Even the names of colors do not refer to precisely the same hues in different languages. Laboratory investigations have shown that the range of hues that in English are called "blue" and that are distinguished from "green" for example do not coincide with the range some other languages, such as Japanese or Navaho, designate with their words that translate blue or green. Thus two words may be given as dictionary equivalents, but that does not indicate that they really refer to the same thing. The city dweller and the poor peasant have different objects in mind and go through different sequences of action to light a lamp. The city dweller will move a switch that allows current to flow, but the peasant will reach for a match or a coal to light a wick. Thus different thoughts, attitudes, expectations, and assumptions develop in the minds of the two people in respect to lamps. Suppose then that we have a person who is fluent in English and in the dialect spoken by a remote desert tribe. If he were speaking the dialect with a colleague in the desert, the normally smooth coordination of behavior in lighting a lamp or even perhaps in talking about it could break down. The man might well reach for a match in America or look for a light switch in the desert tent, if he were momentarily distracted. Doing so, he would manifest a form of linguistic or cultural interference, as it is called.

Our words are commonly used in contexts, in situations that are defined both by their physical characteristics and by our habits, attitudes, dispositions, and intentions toward them. These cognitive and emotional conditions affect the way we interpret a word when we hear it or see it; they affect the meaning we give to the word. In turn, the meanings we give to words affect our beliefs about what to anticipate from our use of the words. If the activities are different, we must expect the meanings to be different, and the same is true for feelings, intentions, and the like. It is no surprise then that it is difficult to translate culturally distant languages, and that people fluent in two languages maintain that they have different experiences when they read a poem or a play in one or the other of them.

One could overemphasize the purely subjective basis for these differences; I stress them because usually they are underemphasized. Languages do have different characteristics; they differ in the richness of their vocabulary in one or another department of human experience, and in the way they can form new words or give expression to shades of meaning. The late Albert Schweitzer, who was Alsatian, grew up speaking German and French; he once remarked that when he wanted to be allusive and philosophical he wrote in German and when he wanted to be precise and direct he wrote in French. To be sure, we might expect this preference to be heavily affected by personal inclinations—one can be vague or direct in any language, probably—but his remark does have some objective support. To use a new word in French the speaker often has to define it explicitly, or use many qualifications; but in German he often can merely connect two nouns or a noun and a verb and the literate German will infer more or less what is intended. It is the more-or-lessness of the inference that sometimes gives German philosophical writing the aura that more is implied or intended than can actually be said or proved.

The subjective sense that one has different thoughts, feelings, and attitudes when he is using one or the other of his languages has been tested somewhat in the laboratory. There it has been found that bilingual people do indeed interpret in different ways words that are dictionary translations of each other. In general it has been found that words referring to objects that are used in very similar ways irrespective of language—words such as pencil, broom, desk, book, and the like

—tend to have quite similar meanings across languages. But words that refer to abstract political and ethical ideals or to emotional states—words like democracy, socialism, and government, or words like love, hope, anger, anxiety—tend to have quite different meanings. While love, hope, and anger are found all over the world, the way in which people relate to each other in expressing them often differs from culture to culture. How a man regards a woman—whether he holds a door for her or not, walks in front of her or by her side, or in general regards her as an equal or not—differs in different lands. The actions expected in return also differ. Words, then, are interpreted within their context; the bilingual person imaginatively supplies a context when he is using the words of a particular language. He often switches his perception of himself and his set of assumptions about the way of the world when he switches his language.

One psychologist investigated this kind of switching by requiring people to make up stories to account for the action in pictures they were shown. The people tested were native speakers of French who were living in the United States and who spoke English well. The pictures used were from a standard psychological test called the Thematic Apperception Test or TAT. Some stories people make up may have a great deal of aggressive content, others may suggest strong ambition by being success-oriented, and still others may concentrate upon domestic matters, say. The psychologist found that the kinds of stories people told, and the emotions expressed in them varied according to whether the story teller was using French or English. Of course, this is not a definitive experiment; certain desirable control tests were missing in the experimental situation; but it is a suggestive experiment directed at the very difficult problem of measuring changes in attitude and feelings that are associated with using different languages.

The switching has been measured in other ways. In one test I required people to read aloud sentences in which words appeared haphazardly in French or in English. An example will illustrate the matter. "His horse, followed de deux bassets, faisait la terre résonner under its even tread. Des gouttes de verglas stuck to his manteau. Une violente brise was blowing.

One side de l'horizon lighted up, and dans la blancheur of the early morning light, il aperçut rabbits hopping at the bord de leurs terriers. Tout de suite the two hounds rushed sur eux and, vivement throwing them back and forth, brisaient leur échines."

The participants in my test were generally fluent in both languages. The average amount of time they needed to read aloud passages wholly in English or wholly in French was always less than the time they needed to read mixed passages of the kind just illustrated. By dividing that difference in time by the number of changes from French to English in the mixed passage, it was possible to calculate that switching from French to English or from English to French took about one-third of a second. In other words, it took about one-third of a second longer, on the average, to read aloud "His horse, followed de deux bassets" than to read aloud "His horse followed by two hounds" or "Son cheval, suivi de deux bassets."

A large component of the switching in these tests is of mechanical origin. The jaw is held differently and the tongue lies lower in the mouth to make French sounds than English ones. Merely moving the tongue and jaw into their proper positions takes some time. Furthermore, it seems implausible that a whole mental set or attitude must be changed each time a speaker switches from French to English words or the reverse. Because of these limitations I asked people to speak freely in the manner of the mixed passages—for example, by giving us some autobiographical information. The speech they produced was as grammatical in the mixed language as it was when they spoke only French or only English, but they always took much longer to speak a mixed passage. Here is an example, produced by a native speaker of French. "Well, I have been ici for quatre ans maintenant and je m'y plais very well. I am going to retourner en France pour un length de je ne sais pas combien de temps but it is certain que je vais aller to this country because je m'y suis plus tremendously."

In speaking aloud, people take about one and one-third seconds to switch between languages, on the average. This does not mean that they pause for one and one-third seconds at every linguistic transition, for this is only an average figure. But even as averages, the pauses suggest something about the usual way we produce language. The fact is that when we speak in a single language we do not usually do so one word at a time; rather we speak in sequences of words and use a small number of grammatical constructions that become more or less automatic with long practice. This is shown by the following. When my test subjects read mixed passages aloud, they not only sometimes spoke American words with a French accent and French words with an American accent, they even unconsciously corrected syntactic sequences. In French an adjective usually follows a noun but in English it precedes, and other relations also differ. Reading a phrase like "une violente brise" native speakers of French sometimes automatically said "une brise violente;" and reading a phrase like "made resound the earth" native speakers of English sometimes automatically said "made the earth resound."

We tend to use a typical vocabulary and use it with a small number of grammatical structures when we use a language; these make up the style of our speech and writing. Interfering with a person's ability to call on these familiar and comfortable tools by requiring him to use mixed languages forces him to select his words from two vocabularies, and forces him to connect them with two different sets of grammatical rules. In normal language use, on the other hand, foreign phrases that are used frequently become regular residents in the person's normal vocabulary, and using them requires very little switching, of course. With sufficient use the foreign word takes on the local coloring and is conjugated or declined as a native word. These the linguist calls borrowings or loan words; their use is to be distinguished from that of less established or less familiar sequences of the kind illustrated in the mixed passages.

The fact that we can interfere with the smooth coordinated use of language raises some issues that are related to other kinds of mental skills. An old and persistent assertion in philosophy and psychology is that our minds are filled with some sort of insubstantial mental something or other that drives our hands or tongues. This something or other we usually call ideas or thoughts. An equally persistent question in philosophy and psychology asks what it is to know something. I have already noted that what a person knows about a simple thing like a lamp varies somewhat with the language he is using. Thus we may say that our knowledge of some things is not altogether a single and simple piece of information stuck away someplace in our minds that we make access to independently of the language we are using. In still other experiments we can find additional evidence that some things we know and know about are related to a specific language, and that in expressing our knowledge we make use of very specific skills.

In one experiment I asked bilingual subjects to say the alphabet backwards. They practiced this task until they could say the alphabet backwards as rapidly as they could forwards. Half of the subjects acquired this skill on the English alphabet; the other half acquired it on the alphabet of their native language, which was French, or German, or Arabic, or Korean. After practicing the task in one language, the subjects were tested in the other language. I was interested in measuring whether practice in one language helped performance in the second language. A naïve view of what it is to know something or to know how to do something would suggest that acquiring the skill in one language would enable the person to express it in the other; but as with so many views that we call naïve, this one too was not up to the facts. What we found was that a marked degree of facilitation characterized the native speakers of French and German, a lesser degree characterized the speakers of Arabic, and none whatever was found with the speakers of Korean. The names of the letters in French and German are very similar to their names in English; Arabic has a few letters, especially at the beginning and again in the middle, whose names are similar to those in English; and the Korean alphabet has almost none that are similar.

Therefore what we found is that knowing how to do something in one language does not necessarily permit one to do it in another. The skill, however trivial it is, of speaking an alphabet backwards does not float loose in the mind, but is tied closely to the actions that have to be performed; in this case the action is making certain sounds in a particular order. Arithmetic and typewriting are other examples of the linguistic limitation on mental activities. Bilingual people who have practiced typewriting in only one of their languages can typewrite the second, but far more poorly than the first. Again, people who learn their arithmetic in one language usually have to use that same language in their calculations, however fluent in a second language they may otherwise be. And we can extend these simple facts to more complicated topics. Bilingual engineers I have talked with tell me that when it has happened that their formal education in one branch of engineering or mathematics was acquired in one language and their education in another branch was acquired in a second language, they usually work on problems in the language in which they acquired their education in the subject. I have not tested this fact formally, but it does seem plausible.

They say still another thing. When a person leaves his native country at an early age—say younger than fourteen or fifteen—to finish his schooling and do his professional work in another whose language he masters, his skill with his native language often shows a stunted development. Unless he practices the complex structures and acquires the vocabulary of sophisticated conversation, his skill with his native language will lag considerably behind his skill with his second language. He will have thoughts and ideas that he can express in his second language but not in his native language! The opposite is of course the more familiar case. In the Middle East I once complimented a man whose native language is Hebrew, for his knowledge of English was good enough for him to make witty puns and jokes in English—something many people use as a rule-of-thumb criterion for assessing a person's language skill. "Ah, no," the man replied. "In English I say what I can, but in Hebrew I say what I want to." And so again we see, even anecdotally, that the expression of our thoughts and our knowledge is intimately tied—by vocabulary, by syntax, by jargon words, and by habits of mind—to the language in which we acquired the knowledge and mastered the particular skills.

What do these findings say about the use of language and the workings of mind? Some contemporary students of language believe that the workings of the mind can be expressed independently of the language it uses. Such an idea assumes that there exists some universal structure that we can call "the human mind"; others believe rather that there are structures that we may indeed call "human minds," but that the way they are organized to evaluate, store, and use information depends very heavily upon the contexts in which and the manner by which they were trained. Many rules may simultaneously characterize the information-handling operations of a man who lives on the desolate and barren Kalahari desert and you or me, they would say; but many other rules seem to be quite different. Some scientists prefer to consider similarities, others to consider differences. What it comes down to for a theory of language use is how important a difference is in respect to considering things as similar. The study of bilingualism should help to answer some of these questions just because it enables us to study similarities and differences in the same person.

SUGGESTIONS FOR
FURTHER READING

1. PSYCHOLOGY AND COMMUNICATION

Blumenthal, Arthur L. *Language and Psychology: Historical Aspects of Psycholinguistics.* New York: Wiley, 1970.

Deese, James. *Psycholinguistics.* Boston, Mass.: Allyn and Bacon, 1970.

Miller, George A. *Language and Communication.* New York: McGraw-Hill, 1951.

Miller, George A. *The Psychology of Communication: Seven Essays.* New York: Basic Books, 1967.

Schramm, Wilbur (ed.). *The Science of Human Communication.* New York: Basic Books, 1963.

Slobin, Dan I. *Psycholinguistics.* Glenview, Ill.: Scott, Foresman, 1971.

2. PSYCHOLOGY AND THE THEORY OF LANGUAGE

Chomsky, Noam. *Syntactic Structures.* The Hague: Mouton, 1957.

Halle, Morris, and Keyser, Samuel Jay. "What we do when we speak." In P. A. Kolers and M. Eden (eds.), *Recognizing Patterns: Studies in Living and Automatic Systems.* Cambridge, Mass.: MIT Press, 1968.

Lenneberg, E. H. (ed.). *New Directions in the Study of Language.* Cambridge, Mass.: MIT Press, 1964.

3. THE REALM OF SYNTAX

Chomsky, Noam. *Language and Mind.* New York: Harcourt, Brace, Jovanovich, 1968.

Langendoen, D. Terence. *The Study of Syntax.* New York: Holt, Rinehart and Winston, 1969.

Lyons, John. *Noam Chomsky.* New York: The Viking Press, 1970.

Reibel, David A., and Schane, Sanford A. *Modern Studies in English.* Englewood Cliffs, N.J.: Prentice-Hall, 1969.

4. THE REALM OF MEANING

Katz, J. J., and Fodor, J. A. "The structure of a semantic theory." *Language,* 39 (1963), 170–210.

Katz, J. J. "Semantic theory and the meaning of 'good.'" *The Journal of Philosophy,* 61 (1964), 739–766.

Katz, J. J. *The Philosophy of Language.* New York: Harper & Row, 1966.
Katz, J. J. *Semantic Theory.* New York: Harper & Row, 1971.

5. BIOLOGICAL ASPECTS OF LANGUAGE

Lenneberg, E. H. *Biological Foundations of Language.* New York: Wiley, 1967.
Lenneberg, E. H. "On explaining language." *Science,* 164 (1969), 635–643.
Lenneberg, E. H. "A word between us." In J. D. Roslansky (ed.), *Communication.* Amsterdam: North Holland, 1969.

6. THE BRAIN AND LANGUAGE

Geschwind, Norman. "The development of the brain and the evolution of language." *Monograph Series on Languages and Linguistics,* 17 (1964), 155–169.
Geschwind, Norman, and Levitsky, W. "Human brain: left-right asymmetries in temporal speech region." *Science,* 161 (1968), 186–188.
Geschwind, Norman. "The work and influence of Wernicke." *Boston Studies in the Philosophy of Science,* 4 (1969), 1–33.
Geschwind, Norman. "Anatomy and the higher functions of the brain." *Boston Studies in the Philosophy of Science,* 4 (1969), 98–136.

7. SPEECH DEVELOPMENT AND BIRD SONG: ARE THERE ANY PARALLELS?

Bellugi, Ursula, and Brown, R. (eds.). "The Acquisition of Language." *Monographs of the Society for Research in Child Development,* 29, No. 1 (1964).
Chomsky, Noam. "The formal nature of language." Appendix A in E. H. Lenneberg, *Biological Foundations of Language.* New York: Wiley, 1967.
Kellogg, W. N. "Communication and language in the home-raised chimpanzee." *Science,* 160 (1968), 423–427.
Konishi, M. "The role of auditory feedback in the control of vocalization in the white-crowned sparrow." *Zeitschrift für Tierpsychologie,* 22 (1965), 770–783.
Marler, P. "Characteristics of some animal calls." *Nature,* 176 (1955), 6–8.
Marler, P. "The voice of the chaffinch and its function as language." *Ibis,* 18 (1956), 231–261.
Marler, P. "A comparative approach to vocal learning: song develop-

ment in white-crowned sparrows." *Journal of Comparative and Physiological Psychology,* 71, No. 2, Part 2 (1970).

Marler, P., and Tamura, M. "Song dialects in three populations of white-crowned sparrow." *Condor,* 64 (1962), 368–377.

McNeill, D. "Developmental psycholinguistics." In F. Smith and G. A. Miller (eds.), *The Genesis of Language.* Cambridge, Mass.: MIT Press, 1966.

Nottebohm, F. "Ontogeny of bird song." *Science,* 167 (1970), 950–956.

8. PRIMATE COMMUNICATION

Altmann, S. A. *Social Communication among Primates.* Chicago, Ill.: University of Chicago Press, 1967.

Altmann, S. A. "Primates." In T. A. Sebeok (ed.), *Animal Communication: Techniques of Study and Results of Research.* Bloomington, Ind.: Indiana University Press, 1968.

Marler, P. "Communication in monkeys and apes." In I. DeVore (ed.), *Primate Behavior: Field Studies of Monkeys and Apes.* New York: Holt, Rinehart and Winston, 1965.

Marler, P. "Aggregation and dispersal: two functions of primate communication." In Phyllis C. Jay (ed.), *Primates: Studies in Adaptation and Variability.* New York: Holt, Rinehart and Winston, 1968.

9. TEACHING APES TO COMMUNICATE

Brown, Roger. "The first sentences of child and chimpanzee." In *Psycholinguistics: Selected Papers by Roger Brown.* New York: Free Press, 1970.

Gardner, R. A., and Gardner, Beatrice T. "Teaching sign language to a chimpanzee." *Science,* 165 (1969), 644–672.

Hayes, Catherine. *The Ape in Our House.* New York: Harper & Row, 1951.

Lancaster, Jane B. "Primate communication systems and the emergence of human language." In Phyllis C. Jay (ed.), *Primates: Studies in Adaptation and Variability.* New York: Holt, Rinehart and Winston, 1968.

Premack, D. "The education of S*A*R*A*H." *Psychology Today,* 4, No. 4 (1970).

10. THE DEVELOPMENT OF LANGUAGE IN CHILDREN

Berko, Jean. "The child's learning of English morphology." In S. Saporta and J. R. Bastian (eds.), *Psycholinguistics: A Book of Readings.* New York: Holt, Rinehart and Winston, 1961.

Bloom, Lois. *Language Development: Form and Function in Emerging Grammars.* Cambridge, Mass.: MIT Press, 1970.

Braine, M. D. S. "The ontogeny of English phrase structure: the first phrase." *Language,* 39 (1963), 1–14.

Brown, R. *Psycholinguistics: Selected Papers.* New York: Free Press, 1970.

Ervin, Susan M. "Imitation and structural change in children's language." In E. H. Lenneberg (ed.), *New Directions in the Study of Language.* Cambridge, Mass.: MIT Press, 1964.

Fodor, J. A. "How to learn to talk: some simple ways." In F. Smith and G. A. Miller (eds.), *The Genesis of Language.* Cambridge, Mass.: MIT Press, 1966.

McNeill, D. *The Acquisition of Language: The Study of Developmental Psycholinguistics.* New York: Harper & Row, 1970.

11. LEARNING TO READ

Carroll, J. B. "The nature of the reading process." In H. Singer and R. B. Ruddell (eds.), *Theoretical Models and Processes of Reading.* Newark, Del.: The International Reading Association, 1970. Also in NINDS Monograph No. 11, *Reading Forum,* 1970. Can be obtained from National Institute of Neurological Diseases and Stroke, Building 31, National Institutes of Health, Bethesda, Md. 20014.

Chall, Jeanne. *Learning to Read: The Great Debate.* New York: McGraw-Hill, 1967.

Chall, Jeanne, and Feldman, Shirley. "First grade reading: An analysis of the interactions of professed methods, teacher implementation, and child background." *The Reading Teacher,* 19 (1966), 569–575.

Dykstra, R. *Final Report of the Continuation of the Coordinating Center for First-Grade Reading Instruction Programs*—U. S. Office of Education Project 6–16151. Minneapolis, Minn.: University of Minnesota, 1967.

Dykstra, R. "The effect of code- and meaning-emphasis in beginning reading programs." *The Reading Teacher,* 22 (1968), 17–23.

Lorge, I., and Chall, Jeanne. "Estimating the size of vocabularies of children and adults; an analysis of methodological issues." *Journal of Experimental Education,* 32 (Winter 1963), 147–157.

12. THE SPEECH CODE

Kimura, Doreen. "Functional asymmetry of the brain in dichotic listening." *Cortex,* 3 (1967), 163–178.

Liberman, A. M., Cooper, F. S., Shankweiler, D. P., and Studdert-Kennedy, M. "Perception of the speech code." *Psychological Review,* 74 (1967), 431–461.

13. ARTIFICIAL SPEECH

Coker C., Denes, P. B., and Pinson, E. N. *Speech Synthesis.* Murray Hill, N.J.: Bell Telephone Laboratories, 1963.

David, E. E., Jr., and Pierce, J. R. *Man's World of Sound.* New York: Doubleday, 1958.

Denes, P. B., and Pinson, E. N. *The Speech Chain.* Murray Hill, N.J.: Bell Telephone Laboratories, 1963.

Fant, G. *Acoustical Theory of Speech Production.* The Hague: Mouton, 1960.

Flanagan, J. L. *Speech Analysis, Synthesis, and Perception.* New York: Academic Press, 1965.

Potter, R., Kopp, G., and Green, H. *Visible Speech.* New York: Van Nostrand, 1947. (Reprinted, Dover Press, 1966.)

14. LANGUAGE AND PERCEPTION

Bever, T. G. "The cognitive basis for linguistic structures." In J. R. Hayes (ed.), *Cognition and Language Learning.* New York: Wiley, 1970.

Chomsky, N., and Halle, M. *The Sound Patterns of English.* New York: Harper & Row, 1968.

Savin, H. B., and Bever, T. G. "The nonperceptual reality of the phoneme." *Journal of Verbal Learning and Verbal Behavior,* 9 (1970), 295–302.

15. LANGUAGE AND MEMORY

Fitts, P. M., and Posner, M. I. *Human Performance.* Belmont, Calif.: Brooks/Cole, 1967.

Howe, M. J. A. *Introduction to Human Memory.* New York: Harper & Row, 1970.

Jenkins, J. J. "Language and thought." In J. F. Voss (ed.), *Approaches to Thought.* Columbus, Ohio: Charles E. Merrill, 1969.

Katona, G. *Organizing and Memorizing.* New York: Columbia University Press, 1940.

Weinland, J. D. *How to Improve Your Memory.* New York: Barnes and Noble, 1957.

16. LANGUAGE AND THOUGHT

Brooks, L. R. "The suppression of visualization by reading." *Quarterly Journal of Experimental Psychology,* 19 (1967), 289–299.

Brooks, L. R. "Spatial and verbal components of the act of recall." *Canadian Journal of Psychology,* 22 (1968), 349–368.

Huttenlocher, Janellen. "Constructing spatial images: a strategy in reasoning." *Psychological Review,* 75 (1968), 550–560.

17. LANGUAGE AND PROBABILITY

Attneave, F. *Information Theory in Psychology.* New York: Holt, Rinehart and Winston, 1959.

Cherry, C. *On Human Communication.* Cambridge, Mass.: MIT Press, 1957.

Garner, W. R. *Uncertainty and Structure as Psychological Concepts.* New York: Wiley, 1962.

Miller, G. A., and Chomsky, N. "Finitary models of language users." In R. D. Luce, R. R. Bush, and E. Galanter (eds.), *Handbook of Mathematical Psychology,* vol. 2. New York: Wiley, 1963.

Rubenstein, H., and Aborn, M. "Psycholinguistics." *Annual Review of Psychology,* vol. 11 (1960).

19. COMMUNICATION IN SMALL GROUPS

Bales, R. F. *Personality and Interpersonal Behavior.* New York: Holt, Rinehart and Winston, 1970.

Borgatta, E. F. "The structure of personality characteristics." *Behavioral Sciences,* 9 (1964), 8–17.

Leary, T. *Interpersonal Diagnosis of Personality.* New York: Ronald, 1957.

Mann, R. D., with Gibbard, G. S., and Hartman, J. J. *Interpersonal Styles and Group Development.* New York: Wiley, 1967.

20. MASS COMMUNICATION

Berelson, B., and Janowitz, H. *Reader in Public Opinion and Communication.* 2nd ed. New York: Free Press, 1966.

DeFleur, M. L. *Theories of Mass Communication.* 2nd ed. New York: David McKay, 1970.

McLuhan, M. *Understanding Media: The Extensions of Man.* New York: McGraw-Hill, 1964.

Schramm, W., and Roberts, D. F. *Process and Effects of Mass Communication.* Rev. ed. Urbana, Ill.: University of Illinois Press, 1971.

Wright, C. R. *Mass Communication.* New York: Random House, 1959.

21. NONVERBAL COMMUNICATION

Fast, J. *Body Language.* New York: Evans/Lippincott, 1970.

Feldman, S. S. *Mannerisms of Speech and Gestures in Everyday Life*. New York: International Universities Press, 1959.

Goffman, E. *Behavior in Public Places*. New York: Free Press, 1969.

Goldman-Eisler, Frieda. *Psycholinguistics: Experiments in Spontaneous Speech*. New York: Academic Press, 1968.

Hall, E. T. *The Silent Language*. Garden City, N.Y.: Doubleday, 1959.

Sebeok, T. A., Hayes, A. S., and Bateson, M. C. *Approaches to Semiotics*. The Hague: Mouton, 1964.

22. PERSUASION

Keisler, C. A., Collins, B. E., and Miller, N. *Attitude Change*. New York: Wiley, 1969.

McGuire, W. J. "The nature of attitude and attitude change." In G. Lindzey and E. Aaronson (eds.), *Handbook of Social Psychology*, vol. 3. Reading, Mass.: Addison-Wesley, 1969.

Zimbardo, P. G., and Ebbesen, E. *Influencing Attitudes and Changing Behavior*. Reading, Mass.: Addison-Wesley, 1969.

23. LANGUAGE AND PSYCHOPATHOLOGY

Maher, B. A. *Principles of Psychopathology*. New York: McGraw-Hill, 1966.

Salzinger, K., and Salzinger, S. *Research in Verbal Behavior and Some Neurophysiological Implications*. New York: Academic Press, 1967.

Taylor, W. L. "Cloze procedure: a new tool for measuring readability." *Journalism Quarterly*, 30 (1953), 415–433.

Vetter, H. *Language Behavior and Psychopathology*. New York: Rand McNally, 1969.

24. THE SOCIOLOGY OF LANGUAGE

Fishman, J. A. *The Sociology of Language*. Rowley: Newbury House, 1971.

Fishman, J. A. (ed.). *Advances in the Sociology of Language*. The Hague: Mouton, 1971.

Fishman, J. A., Ferguson, C. A., and Das Gupta, J. (eds.). *Language Problems of Developing Nations*. New York: Wiley, 1968.

Hymes, D., and Gumperz, J. (eds.). *The Ethnography of Communication: Directions in Sociolinguistics*. New York: Holt, Rinehart and Winston, 1971.

Rubin, Joan, and Jernudd, B. (eds.). *Can Language be Planned?* Honolulu: East-West Center, 1971.

25. TRANSLATION AND BILINGUALISM

Haugen, E. *Bilingualism in the Americas.* Publication No. 26, American Dialect Society. Tuscaloosa, Ala.: University of Alabama Press, 1956.

Kolers, P. A. "Reading and talking bilingually." *American Journal of Psychology,* 79 (1966), 357–376.

MacNamara, J. "Problems of bilingualism." *The Journal of Social Issues,* 23, No. 2 (1967).

Weinreich, U. *Languages in Contact.* The Hague: Mouton, 1963.

INDEX